Fighter Pilot

Fighter Pilot

The First American Ace of World War II

WILLIAM R. DUNN

THE UNIVERSITY PRESS OF KENTUCKY

Material in Chapter 5, "The Ace," and the appendix,
"The War Birds," was originally published in different
form in *Air Force Magazine,* April and September 1975,
September 1976, and July 1977. Copyright © The Air
Force Association (1975, 1976, 1977); used by permission.

Copyright © 1982 by The University Press of Kentucky

Scholarly publisher for the Commonwealth,
serving Berea College, Centre College of Kentucky,
Eastern Kentucky University, The Filson Club,
Georgetown College, Kentucky Historical Society,
Kentucky State University, Morehead State University,
Murray State University, Northern Kentucky University,
Transylvania University, University of Kentucky,
University of Louisville, and Western Kentucky University.

Editorial and Sales offices: Lexington, Kentucky 40506

Library of Congress Cataloging in Publication Data

Dunn, William R., 1916–
  Fighter pilot.

  Includes index.
  1. World War, 1939–1945—Aerial operations,
American. 2. Dunn, William R., 1916–
3. World War, 1939–1945—Personal narratives,
American. 4. United States. Army Air Forces—
Biography. 5. Fighter pilots—United States—
Biography. I. Title.
D790.D86   940.54′4973   82-40172
ISBN 0-8131-1465-9   AACR2

**For all fighter pilots, past, present and future
—ours and theirs.**

Here's to the fighter pilot, wherever he may be,
   Aloft in lonely glory,
   At rest in eternity,
Or here, reliving thrills again
Rolling back the years, from now till then.
Here's to the breed apart, to a dying art,
   To the spirit that now binds us;
To the planes and the flak, to the brass and the crap,
   And to battles long behind us.
To the fighter pilot, then, be he friend or foe,
   Let us drink, Gentlemen, and let us shout,
      "Tally Ho!"

Contents

Preface

Say what you will about him: arrogant, cocky, boisterous, and a devil-may-care fool—the fighter pilot has earned his place in the sun. Across the span of nearly seventy years he has given his country some of its proudest moments and most cherished military traditions. But fame is short-lived.

Nearly lost in history's dim past are those magnificent men in their flying machines—the very first fighter pilots—who, in the Great War of 1914–1918, chased the Hun flying circuses, including the Red Baron, from French skies. Almost forgotten are "the few" Royal Air Force fighter pilots who, in the Second World War, stood alone against the might of Hitler's German air armadas during the dark summer of 1940— and, in the words of Sir Winston Churchill, gave England "its finest hour." Gone from the hardstands of Duxford are the P-51s with their checkerboard noses that terrorized the finest fighter squadrons of the Luftwaffe. Also gone from the war-torn skies of Burma and China are the AVGs who, with their shark-jawed P-40s, chewed up the Japs and spit them out again.

Dimly remembered is the 4th Fighter Group that gave Americans some of their few proud moments in the skies over Korea. How fresh in recall are the Air Commandos who valiantly struck the Viet Cong with their aging "Sky Raiders" in the rain- and blood-soaked valley called A-Shau? And how long will be remembered the "Thuds" over Route Pack Six and the flak-filled skies above Hanoi?

So here's a "nickel on the grass" to you, my fighter pilot friends, for your spirit, enthusiasm, sacrifice, and courage—but most of all to your memory. Yours is a dying breed, and when you are gone, the world will be a lesser place.

Even though I'm now an old, shot-up, ex-fighter pilot, I know it's

far   better to   be a has-been than a never-was. I decided to record for
posterity my war story and that of the fighter pilots I knew during the
past several wars and decades. I realize, of course, that the past is for
remembering, not for reliving; but some of you who read this account
may recall similar events and memories of your own.

Prologue: The Early Years

Since I've got to start some place, I'll begin at the very beginning. The Lord said, "Let there be light," and on 16 November 1916 He created me, like you, in His own image. This took place at Minneapolis, Minnesota. My father, Walter, was a doctor of medicine, a physician and surgeon. My mother's name was Ellen. Eighteen months after my birth, my kid brother was born. My immediate family was American born, but our ancestors immigrated to the United States from several European nations. Some came from France, via Canada, in the 1870s. Others came directly from Norway in the 1850s, and from Ireland and Scotland in the 1860s. My most illustrious foreign-born relative—a great grandfather—was a French marquis, the Marquis de Priganier, and a colonel in the French Army during the Franco-Prussian War. The French lost to the Germans, so he left his home province of Alsace-Lorraine to Hun occupation, and came to the New World under the name Gustav Prigan. Other family names in this potpourri of my relatives include Dunn, Taft, Forkrud, Terry, and Ferguson. These related families located in Maine, Minnesota, South Dakota, North Dakota, Montana, and Colorado.

All the male members of our family were soldiers at one time or another, and it seems we all fought against a common enemy, the Germans. My great grandfather, his brother, and his two sons, Lorenzo and Olivier, fought the Germans in the 1870–71 Franco-Prussian War. My father and my uncles fought the Germans in the First World War. My brother, my cousins, and I fought the Germans in the Second World War. Therefore, it is understandable that we refer to our perennial German enemies as Huns, Krauts, Squareheads, Fritzies, Boches, and Heinies, though I suppose all of us family soldiers have been told, at one time or another, to forget and forgive—the war is over. No, we will not forget and forgive the bestiality of the German war machine—the death, the devastation, the murders of innocent people—ever. A new generation of Huns does not suddenly make them "good guys." Their war actions are recorded, generation after generation, in the annals of world history, which should alert all freedom-loving people to the axiom we fighter pilots regarded as absolute truth—"Beware of the Hun in the sun."

During the First World War my father was a first lieutenant medical officer with a horse cavalry regiment. My Uncle John was also an Army doctor. My Uncle Pat was an Army Engineer master sergeant. My Uncle Larry was a captain fighter pilot in the Air Service. All served with the American Expeditionary Forces in France, and their war stories, after they got a little giggle-soup under their belts, left my brother and me spellbound. We were most interested in Uncle Larry's glorious stories of furious air combat with Hun pilots—the twisting and rolling and looping of clashing war birds, fighting man to man, until a deadly burst of machine gun fire sends one of them curving earthward, trailing flames and smoke, to a heroic death. We knew that Uncle Larry had shot down four Huns and was himself shot down twice—he wouldn't BS a couple of little kids, would he? My brother and I decided to become fighter pilots when we grew up.

When I was about seven years old my mother and father were divorced. Why, I don't know. They never told me, I didn't ask. After my mother left our home, my Aunt Bertha, Dad's sister, came to run our household. Her husband and twin-son babies had died several years earlier from scarlet fever. Bertha, or Aunt Bertie as we called her, was really a grand and gracious lady, but to my brother and me she seemed somewhat of a tyrant when she laid down the law to us kids—wash faces, brush teeth, keep clothes clean, pick up our things and make our beds, take out the garbage, do school homework.

She had all sorts of tasks for us, and she had a sharp tongue and a quick, stinging wood paddle that she used very effectively to emphasize her instructions. There was no doubt that my brother and I were in great need of discipline at home, and so Aunt Bertie became the enforcer of our training, which she did with a resounding whack of her paddle on the seats of our pants as the occasion merited. All this resulted in a sort of declaration of war by two mean little kids against Aunt Bertie's authority.

Aunt Bertie was a handsome woman of about thirty-five years, dark haired and dark eyed, large bosomed and wasp-waisted. She had a boy friend named Al who worked for the U.S. Postal Service. My brother and I weren't too keen on Al, nor was he on us. When Al came to visit Bertie in the evening, we were promptly put to bed. Our bedroom was near the top of the stairs that descended to the living room. There was a light switch at the top of these stairs that turned on the stair and living-room lights. Al and Aunt Bertie would sit on the davenport amorously embracing in the darkened living room. We kids would quietly sneak out of our room and listen at the head of the stairs to the soft whisper-ings, rustling, and heavy breathing emanating from the davenport. Then, suddenly, with peals of fiendish laughter, we'd switch on all the lights and run for the safety of our bedroom, where we'd barricade the door with our beds! I'm sure we cut off Al's amorous advances several times at a very crucial point. And yes, I'm sure he hated our guts. As a matter of fact, in later years, when Al and Bertie were married, he still didn't take kindly to us.

Aunt Bertie had an automobile, an old square-bodied Star. She wasn't the world's greatest driver, and there is some doubt if she ever had a valid driver's license. She never could manage to get turn direction straight, especially when she was backing her car out of our driveway. She would post my brother and me on each side of the drive-way to give her back-up directions. Well, there was a big telephone pole at the end of the driveway, a couple of yards to one side. We would give Aunt Bertie good back-up instructions until her car had just about reached the driveway's end, and then would give her a turn that always banged the rear of her car into the telephone pole. Out of the car came an infuriated Aunt Bertie, who, if she could have caught us, would have tanned our hides but good. We got away with guiding her into the tele-phone pole many times. In 1978 I visited the old home near Lake of the Isles Boulevard, and the old, scarred telephone pole was still stand-ing there, some 55 years later.

Oh, we were mean kids. I guess Aunt Bertie eventually married Al just to get away from us. When I reflect on those days, I realize what a wonderful, kind, and generous woman my Aunt Bertie really was and I wonder if I ever apologized to her for all the misery I caused her by my dastardly deeds. If, one day, I ever get to Heaven, I'll bet there will be considerable discussion between Aunt Bertie and Saint Peter as to my eligibility to enter the Pearly Gates.

Aunt Bertie wasn't the recipient of all my brother's and my devilish antics. We had a cousin named Frances, a tall, skinny, awkward, bean pole of a girl, who took ballet lessons. Occasionally there were recitals, which all members of our family who didn't have something better to do or couldn't think of an excuse were invited to attend. My brother and I always managed to get front row seats, where we could easily be seen by the performing Frances, who we said looked like Olive Oyl in the Popeye cartoons or a dancing stork. There we would sit, making faces at poor Frances, pulling our mouths wide from side to side with our fingers, pushing our noses and ears out of shape, and looking cross-eyed at her. We were certainly distracting, to say the least, and these recitals generally ended with a weeping Frances and irate words to us from her mother and father.

My first airplane ride came when I was about twelve years old. We were at our summer cabin when a small county fair was held at the town of Pequot, just north of Nisswa, Minnesota. Some barnstorming guy had an OX-5-powered Travel Air biplane, which he landed on a small grass field near the fairgrounds. For $2 a person he would take two passengers for a ten-minute ride. To heck with the fair; my brother and I headed for the airplane, money in hand, and were soon looking down on the fair-grounds from the Travel Air's open front cockpit. What a wondrous thrill it was to fly high in the sky, circling and swooping above the ant-like people below. Some persons are born to the thrill of flying. There was never any doubt in either of our minds, following this first flight, that we would one day be airplane pilots.

With this goal in mind, we decided to build our own airplane, really a glider. We actually did build one out of bits of wood stringers and laths we swiped from a house under construction, and we covered it with cheesecloth we bought at Woolworth's. For a cockpit seat we found my brother's old highchair in the basement, sawed off the legs, and nailed it to our airframe. Our Dad then began to worry that we really would try to fly the damned thing, so he offered to buy our flying machine for $10—$5 to each of us. No sale.

When we figured we were ready, we and a dozen other neighborhood kids hauled our glider up to a high bank on a railroad track about thirty feet above a small meadow. Since I was bigger and heavier than my brother, it was decided he'd have the honor of being the first to pilot our airplane; anyway, it was his highchair cockpit seat. We all gave a mighty push to get the thing airborne, and it did fly—for about fifty feet—before it fell into a treetop and was wrecked. My brother survived the crash, but darn near hurt himself trying to get down through the tree branches. That evening, when we informed Dad of our most recent flying experience, his face turned white. He gave us $10 not to rebuild our airplane or build a new one.

Our Uncle Larry, the First World War fighter pilot, was now the manager of Wold-Chamberlin airfield, just outside of Minneapolis. He had a Waco 9 biplane with an OX-5 engine, so we began our aviation careers by begging him to take us up for a few flying lessons. I still remember Larry's very first flying instruction to me when I took the Waco's controls. "Loosen your grip on the control stick. Don't try to choke her. Guide her movements by a light finger touch. Handle her gently and she'll fly like a bird." One day I even got a flying lesson from the famous racing and aerobatic pilot, Speed Holman, who was a friend of Uncle Larry's. It was Speed who, when I bothered him too much one day, sent me in search of a can of prop-wash. Flying came easily to me, and by the time I was fourteen I'd soloed the Waco 9.

My mother had remarried by this time to a fellow named Roy Harding. They were living in Dallas, Texas. Roy was a First World War pilot, but now worked for the Texas Oil Company as an aviation representative. He flew a company-owned Stinson Reliant five-passenger monoplane. Roy gave me quite a few hours of stick time in the Stinson when I would visit mother and him in Dallas. We flew from Love Field which, in those days, was an all-grass airfield. I also managed to bum some flying time from Hal Henning and Doc Booth, two local pilots. There was one fellow at Love Field, Cliff Pettit, who had a beautiful Bird biplane with a 100 hp OX-5 engine. I guess I'd have to say that Cliff was my best flying instructor. We spent many hours high in the Texas skies over Dallas in Cliff's blue Bird airplane. It was he who first introduced me to the excitement and thrills of aerobatics. By the time I was fifteen I had logged about a hundred flying hours, had soloed several different types of airplanes, but was one year short of age to obtain a private pilot's license. (I did, of course, have a student pilot's permit to fly.)

In 1932 I went to visit my grandparents, who lived in North Dakota. My grandfather was the Indian agent at the Fort Berthold Indian Reservation in the western part of the state. The Indians on this reservation were of the Gros Ventre (Big Belly) tribe. There were also a few Mandan Indian families. My friends now had peculiar names—Francis Many Ribs, Curly Birdsbill, Jack Little Bear, Ira Running Wolf.

Periodically, at a place called Shell Village, the Indians would hold social dances, which lasted all night long. I was usually invited to attend these affairs, and generally I was the only white person there. Indians of all ages would come from miles around, the very old to young babes in their mothers' arms, to meet, to gossip, to dance, and to eat together. The corrals of Shell Village would be absolutely jammed with their horses by sundown.

Great quantities of prepared foods were brought into the wooden dancehall and arranged by the women on long tables on one side of the floor. Kersene lanterns and lamps provided some illumination to the otherwise dark interior of the building. A huge bass drum was laid flat on its side in the center of the hall floor. At dusk the Indian men drummers and singers took their places around the bass drum and, with the beat of their padded sticks on the deep-noted instrument, the dance began. After a moment the singers, in their high, chanting, falsetto voices, joined in.

At an Indian social dance such as this, the men all sit on one side of the hall and the women on the other side. Two old people—a man and a woman—each carry a cloth-wrapped stick about four or five feet long. The old woman beats the men on the legs with her stick until they get up and dance. The old man does the same to the women. I was never spared by the old woman with the stick because I was white. Dancing with an Indian girl, you put your arm over her shoulders, she puts her arm around your waist, and you both take two steps forward and one backward, side by side, in a circle around the drumming and singing musicians. The old woman with the stick will shout all sorts of things at you, including a few English cuss words, if you don't get up and dance—at which all the other Indians laugh uproariously.

About midnight the dancing stops for an hour or so and the feast begins. I've tasted some queer foods in my time, but this feast beats all, and it's usually a good idea not to ask what you're eating. By 2 a.m. the dancing is going full blast again, and so it continues until the new day dawns. An hour later all the horsemen and wagons can be seen departing in every direction across the grassy plains.

Quite often I used to visit the home of my friend, Francis Many Ribs. He lived in a government-issue wood-frame, three-room house, which sat in a small valley several miles from Shell Village. Behind the house was an old-style buffalo skin tepee. Riding horseback to get to Francis's home, I would follow a trail to the crest of a small hill, where I sat on my horse for several minutes looking down into the valley. Soon I would see Francis's grandparents leave the rear door of the house and go into the tepee. While I was visiting, these two old folks would stay in the tepee, so I never got to meet them. They had lived in the old days, and they didn't trust any white man.

About this time a horse-trader named A.J. Eaton came to the Fort Berthold reservation to hire young men for a wild-horse roundup in the badlands near Medora, North Dakota. He had already hired half a dozen Sioux men at Fort Yates for $15 a month and found (rations and Bull Durham tobacco). Francis Many Ribs and Curly Birdsbill signed on with Eaton and, although I wasn't an Indian, I joined the party for the same pay. My grandfather thought the experience would be good for me, so he loaned me a saddle and other gear. The plan was to gather in the wild horses in a week or so, then trail them down to Sisseton, South Dakota, where Eaton hoped to sell them to farmers for $10 or more a head. In those days—the 1930s—the Dakota badlands were the open range for thousands of wild horses. Today, of course, they are nearly all gone.

We loaded our gear into Eaton's truck and drove to the little town of Medora. From Medora we went south a few miles to Dick Parker's ranch, which was on the Little Missouri River. Eaton made his headquarters there, but we wild-horse wranglers crossed the shallow river bed, then proceeded through a narrow canyon several miles more to the isolated ranch of Bill McCarty. McCarty was "Big Bill," well over six feet tall, raw-boned, tougher than leather, and I'd guess about sixty years old. A real old-time western cowboy and bronc rider, he was our roundup boss.

There were ten of us, including Big Bill, to make the roundup. He briefed us on the badland terrain we would cover, showed us the direction he wanted the various wild-horse bands to be driven, told us where he would point up the collected herd, and where the holding corrals were located. We would probably, he said, make two runs a day until Eaton had enough horses for his drive to South Dakota. A wild-horse roundup, in those days, was one of the most dangerous and exciting, and one of the toughest jobs in the world.

We began our first run at dawn the next morning after we had fanned out to cover a stretch of land five miles wide and ten or so miles long. Everything starts out at a walk. Soon a small band of wild horses is sighted, maybe four or five head. They see you and begin to trot away before you, their long manes flowing and their long tails nearly touching the ground. Pretty soon another bunch of a few head is sighted. They begin to move in the same direction as the first. Now more bands are seen. Their leaders toss their heads in defiance and whinny an alert to the others. The several bands before you have now joined together and are beginning to get excited; they start to canter away from you. You begin a fast trot to keep them in sight so you'll be able to cut off any horses that try to break back past you. Soon there are twenty-five or more wild horses before you, all moving at a lope. You don't want to push them too hard, don't cause them to panic, just keep them going in the right direction.

In another half-hour you begin to see more bands of wild horses pushed ahead of the riders on your flanks. Now these bands are converging on your band, swelling the herd to maybe sixty or seventy head. The wild horses are fast reaching the panic stage; they're about ready to make a run for their freedom. You are riding faster to keep up. The ride becomes rougher as your horse slides down or lunges up a cutbank. Your saddle begins to beat your rear end; the inside of your thighs begin to chafe. At last the wild bunch breaks into a frightened run.

Off and away you go at a gallop, trying to head the leaders, turn back those that attempt to break away, pushing the drags on forward. In your headlong rush you and your horse slide off the edge of a deep wash and fall heavily to the bottom in a shower of sand and rock. You are dumped off hard, the breath knocked out of you, but manage to keep hold of the reins. Your horse is a bit dazed by the fall but seems uninjured. Back into the saddle you go, spurring your mount into a run once again. Down through a narrow canyon you race. Your knee bangs against a protruding rock ledge and hurts like hell. Your horse is gasping for breath and so are you. Go ahead, grab the saddle horn for support, there's no one out here to see. Remember, if you get dumped, it's a long walk back to Big Bill's ranch. The other riders can now be seen, pushing their bands into a herd that must now number a hundred or more head. At this moment you suddenly see, maybe a quarter-mile ahead of the wild horses, Big Bill McCarty picking up the point lead.

It's an odd thing, but when wild horses are being rounded up they will follow a lead horse, even if there's a rider on it. That was Big Bill's job, to take the point and lead the herd through a long valley and into the holding corrals, while we followed on the flanks and brought up the rear. We caught 106 head that first morning, which was outstanding for a bunch of riders who didn't know the country very well.

"Grab some lunch, boys," said Eaton. "Be ready in an hour to make another run." I don't know about the other guys, but I was sore from head to toe, my knee was swollen and bruised, my elbow was skinned and bloody. This was only the first day. We had nearly a week of this work ahead of us, with runs twice each day. Eaton's lunch consisted of fried salt pork, slabs of dry bread, some dried prunes, and weak coffee.

Well, we all survived. One Sioux boy broke his hip in a bad fall. Another was attacked by a wild stallion that bit him in the shoulder. Two of our saddle horses were killed and four were injured. We captured 622 wild horses for A.J. Eaton.

After a couple days' rest, during which time the wild horses were not fed, we began to trail our herd toward Sisseton, South Dakota, some 350 miles distant. Two of us led the point while the others took up flank positions. Eaton brought up the rear with our chuck wagon truck. We moved them very slowly at first, giving the hungry horses a chance to graze and get used to our presence along the way. Within two days the wild ones followed our lead, a good sign that they were becoming trail broken. After we left the open ranges of North Dakota we reached the farm lands of South Dakota, where there were section-line fences to help guard the herd's flanks. At night we'd hold the herd between these fences, which were about 100 feet apart, and set up a guard at each end of a half-mile space. This gave the horses plenty of grazing room during the night. Several nights, when we were all dead beat, we cut some farmer's fence and let the whole herd graze off his growing crops. We were on the move again at dawn, and if the farmer was sore about his crops, we told him to square it away with Eaton.

Our rations went from poor to awful. Almost every morning Eaton would shout out, "Fill your saddlebags with prunes, boys! We're not going to stop for lunch today!" We averaged about twenty miles a day, which means it took us 18 days to trail the herd to Sisseton. Along the route Eaton asked several of us to break a couple of wild horses to the saddle, at $5 per head. These horses, of course, would double in sales value at Sisseton. I rode and broke three of them, one red roan and two bays.

After we arrived at Sisseton, Eaton sold every horse without difficulty to local farmers, and paid us off. Then he asked us to go back to Medora with him and do it all over again—for the same high pay and lousy rations—and would you believe we did it a second time!

That fall we all went back to school, my Indian friends to the reservation school and I to the Van Hook school. In March of 1933 one hell of a blizzard hit northwestern North Dakota. Snow was three feet deep on the level prairie. Wind-whipped drifts piled up to six and seven feet, and the temperature for several days was twenty below zero. A real livestock emergency on the reservation developed because the cattle and horses, which normally grazed on the open range, couldn't get to the grass beneath the heavy snows. Hundreds of head died of starvation or froze to death. Every available man and boy was called out to try to get feed to the animals. Wagons, loaded with hay, and pulled by four- and six-span teams, ventured out on the frozen prairie to find and feed the scattered bunches of livestock. Many of us froze our feet and noses and fingers while searching for and feeding the animals.

After three or four days the storm blew over, followed by a bright sun to warm the earth and melt off the snow during the daylight hours. At night, of course, the temperature would drop to freezing again. Horses are pretty smart and know how to take care of themselves, but cattle are stupid. During the day, when the warming sun shone, the cattle would lie down on the ground to enjoy the sunshine. Then, in the evening, when the temperature began to drop, some of them couldn't get up on their cold-numbed legs. If they lay there through the night they'd freeze and die, so we had to try to get them on their feet. To accomplish this it was necessary to get off your horse near the downed animal, take off your coat, and throw it over the horns and eyes; otherwise it would try to hook you. Next, pull the animal's front legs out in front of it, then go around to its rear end and lift it up by its tail. When the animal was finally standing on its four legs, get back on your horse, ride up close and grab your blindfolding coat off its head. Sometimes, when you grabbed off your coat, the animal would take a quick hook with its horns at your horse, slip, and fall down again. Then you started the whole process all over again to get it up.

In the spring of 1933, Francis, Curly, and I went to work for the

Kendrick Cattle Company in northeastern Wyoming, the ranch head-quarters being about forty miles north of the town of Gillette, near the Montana-Wyoming border. Here, working the spring roundup and branding of calves, we were paid $20 per month and found. I had an additional job of breaking four broncs to the saddle, which paid me $5 a head more.

Late one afternoon, when I was riding a green-broke horse about thirty miles north of the ranch headquarters, he got spooked by some-thing, bucked me off, and, with his tail flying, took off for parts unknown. There I was, way to hell and gone from nowhere, and it was getting late in the day. Nothing else to do but to walk home. I walked until well after dark, then lay down on the ground for some sleep. I didn't dare take my boots off because I knew I'd never get them back on my swollen feet. Next morning I continued my walk, but I was really thirsty. I found a swamply creekbed, scraped the green scum off the stagnant water, and drank my fill. Man, was it ever good! Late that day I made it to the ranch, my feet a mass of blisters, with blood soaking through the leather of my boots. It was nearly a week before my feet were healed. A couple of weeks later we caught the horse again, my saddle still on his back, but my hackamore was lost.

On July 3-5 a big rodeo was to be held at Livingston, Montana, so off the three of us went to try our hand at rodeoing. They offered pretty good money to riders at this three-day affair, which was being put on primarily for the tourists. Winner's prizes were saddles, silver-mounted spurs, boots and hats, but everyone who rode would draw mount-money: $2 for each saddle bronc, $1 for each bareback bronc and bull, and $5 to ride a buffalo! In those days there weren't quite as many rules in rodeo competition as there are today, and our rides then had to be for at least ten seconds instead of the present-day eight seconds.

The first day I drew one saddle bronc, two bareback broncs, and one bull, so I made $5 mount-money. The saddle bronc, a big, husky, long-legged buckskin named "Buckshot," dumped me on my rear end about the fourth jump he made. I rode the two bareback broncs without much difficulty, but the bull slammed me into the side of the chute gate when it was opened and laid me flat in the dirt three jumps farther on. Next day was about the same, except I drew a white saddle bronc named "Little Snow," a mare, but she already had a bad reputation of turning on a bucked-off rider. She also fought the chute, would rear up and fall over backwards. Curly belted me down on her in the chute, while Francis chewed on her ear to keep her mind occupied when I slid into the Association saddle (a standard type saddle for contest bronc riding). I took a long rein, laid my spurs on her shoulders and shouted, "Unchain me!"

The chute gate was yanked open and off we went, Little Snow and I, into the arena before a tremendous crowd. Her first jump was high and straight ahead, landing like a ton of bricks. Then she spun to the left for a couple more jumps, then a quick change of direction to the right with a twisting sunfish. By this time I'd lost a stirrup and presently we parted company. While I was still in the air, Little Snow lashed out at me with her hind legs, kicking me right in the middle of the back. I hit the ground about half conscious, tried to get up, but fell back down. Besides having the wind knocked out of me, being numbed from the kicks, and generally hurting all over, I lost some of my enthusiasm for saddle bronc riding. Although the lower part of my back began to swell from the kick bruises, I had earned another $5 that day.

The last day of the rodeo I stuck to riding just the barebacks, three horses and one bull. But near the end of the show the promoters of the rodeo had promised the audience that wild buffaloes would be ridden, and no one had volunteered to ride one of the damned things. The arena director now told us the buffalo mount-money was increased to $10. Still no takers. Ten dollars was a lot of money in those days, so I said I'd give it a try. We prodded a big bushy-haired bull into the chutes and put a loose-rope around his belly. I slid gingerly onto his wide back, tightened the loose-rope for a good grip, and drew up the flank rope. Now or never, here we go!

Out of the chute he lunged, me tight-legging him all the way. His jumps were hard, but all straight ahead, so I began to spur him. He was easy to ride. I heard the whistle blow, and swung off of him without any trouble. The crowd was on its feet, clapping and yelling. I was suddenly a hero to the dude tourists! That day I made $14, so for the three-day rodeo I earned $24.00—more than a whole month's wages for ranch work.

All this easy money decided Francis, Curley and me to follow the rodeo cowboy trade for the rest of the summer. We rode at Miles City, Billings, Great Falls, and Glendive in Montana; Cody, Sheridan, and

Cheyenne in Wyoming; Pierre and Aberdeen in South Dakota; and ended our season at the Tri-State Rodeo in Omaha, Nebraska. It was a great and wonderful experience for all of us. We won a few and lost a few, we went broke and were hungry, we got hurt and, I think, injured every bone in our bodies. We earned, each of us, probably $300, of which we got paid about half that amount by absconding rodeo promoters. Yes, we learned a lot that summer about people and the real world. That fall I telegraphed my grandfather, collect, for enough money to get the three of us back home in time for school.

In March of 1934, when I was seventeen years old, I told my grandfather that I wanted to join the army and get into the air corps as an enlisted pilot. Fine with him, he said, so he drove me to Fort Abraham Lincoln, near Bismarck, North Dakota, to enlist. Since I was under the legal enlistment age, his signature, as my approving guardian, was required on the forms. He really wasn't my legal guardian, but no one seemed to care one way or the other.

"Oh yes," said the recruiting officer, "you can join the army at Fort Lincoln (a 4th Infantry post) and later be sent to an Army Air Corps field." I showed him my flying log book, which seemed to impress him, but he neglected to tell me the army had many other requirements for acceptance as a pilot. He gave me the impression that I might be accepted, in the near future, as a flying cadet. Oh, how the bastard lied! I ended up in M Company, 3rd Battalion, 4th United States Infantry Regiment—a buck private in the rear rank, a dogface.

M Company was a machine-gun company, with .30-caliber, water-cooled Browning guns mounted on two-wheel carts pulled by mules. So, besides the required infantry training, there were about fifty mules to care for each day—and a mule is mean, stubborn, bites and kicks. On Saturday afternoons, for the fun of it, we used to put an army McClellan saddle on a blindfolded mule, and then try to ride him as he bucked around the stable corral. If he bucked you off, there was a mad scramble to get out of the way of his furious kicking and biting.

Our company first sergeant was named George Strong. He was a Greek whose real last name was unpronounceable, so the army legally changed it to Strong. He couldn't speak English very well, so if you didn't understand his instructions quickly, he would emphasize them with his fists. My platoon corporal was Edvard Viding, a Norwegian who also spoke little English, and had joined the army in order to obtain American citizenship. He was a great hulk of a man who, like Sergeant Strong, enforced discipline behind the stables with his fists. The company commander was First Lieutenant Blue, a gray-haired man in his late forties who had been a lieutenant for twenty-two years. Promotion in the Army at that time was almost nonexistent, especially during the depression years.

My pay as a private was supposed to be $21.00 per month; however, during that period all government employees' pay was reduced by 15 percent, so I actually drew $17.85 per month—less Post Exchange checks, laundry, movie tickets, Old Soldiers' Home deductions. Therefore, in actual cash over the pay table, I usually received about $8.00 per month. Lieutenant Blue, with all his service, only drew $175.00 per month, which gives a pretty good idea of army pay in those days. The city of Bismarck wasn't proud to have an army post nearby, even with the troops spending money in town. Several restaurants in the city displayed window signs that read: "No dogs or soldiers allowed." Such places, occasionally, were busted up by angry troops.

Since I was a good rider, I soon found myself assigned as mounted orderly to Major Burns, the battalion commander. I was issued a big, raw-boned buckskin horse that stood 17½ hands high. His name was "Bean Belly," owing to a lump he had on his stomach. He was a real hammer-head. It took about half a mile to get him into a bone-jarring gallop, his big feet smacking the ground at every step. And it took another half mile, pulling and sawing on the reins, to get him slowed down to a shambling walk. Bean Belly was tireless, and could go on for hours without rest over the North Dakota prairies during army maneuvers.

After several months in the 4th Infantry, I asked for permission to see Lieutenant Blue about my promised air corps transfer. When I finished my discourse, Lieutenant Blue said bluntly, "Private Dunn, you are in the infantry—and that's where you're going to stay." Next morning I went AWOL to the air corps base at March Field, near Riverside, California, where I turned into the 64th Air Service Squadron. Since I had been AWOL for seven days, I was given twenty-one days of KP duty as punishment. Then, when that was finished, I was assigned to a lawn-mowing detail for a couple more months. At that time the pursuit squadrons at March Field were equipped with P-12 biplanes and a few P-26 monoplane aircraft. Of course, I never got close to one of them, but watching them fly made me want all the more to be a military pilot.

One day I was told I was being returned to the infantry. "If all the infantrymen who wanted to be in the air corps left their units AWOL, there wouldn't be any infantry left in the Army," I was informed. So I was assigned to L Company, a rifle outfit of the 3rd U.S. Infantry Regiment at Fort Snelling, Minnesota. At Fort Snelling my father and I went to see the post adjutant to request my release from service because I was under age. "No," said the adjutant, because I hadn't applied for release during the first six months of my enlistment.

I learned, of course, that a recruiting officer or sergeant will promise you anything to get your signature on the dotted line. In 1937, after my discharge from the Army, I went back to school—both day and night classes—for a year and a half, studying industrial design and commercial art. Early in 1939 I went down to Dallas, Texas, with my mother and Roy, her husband, where I went to work for an advertising agency as a commercial artist. Again I managed to get more flying lessons from Roy and Cliff Pettit, increasing my flying hours to a total of about 160.

By mid-1939 the world situation had begun to deteriorate. The Japanese were at war with China, the Russians and Finns were battling each other, and Hitler's German armies were preparing to invade Poland. The Second World War, which would eventually develop into a global conflict of six years' duration, was about to begin.

1. The Ladies from Hades

On September 1, 1939, the German Army invaded Poland. On 3 September 1939 England and France declared war on Germany. On 6 September 1939 I was on a train that crossed the Canadian-United States border enroute to Vancouver, British Columbia. My intention was to volunteer for military service with the Royal Canadian Air Force. Down the narrow aisle in the passenger car came two Canadian officials, a customs and an immigration officer, checking travelers' identification and questioning their purpose for entering Canada. They asked me why I was going to Vancouver and I truthfully told them my purpose. For a moment they glanced at each other, a bit surprised I thought, then one said to the other, "He looks healthy enough to me." Turning to me, they each shook my hand. Said the immigration officer, "Thanks for coming, laddie, and good luck to you." They went on down the aisle checking other passengers.

Next morning in Vancouver, which is a beautiful city, I went to see the adjutant of an RCAF squadron—an Army cooperation unit. I explained that I wanted to join up immediately, showed him my flying log book, and expressed the hope that with a war now on I'd be accepted for military pilot training. Can you imagine my disappointment—with the world about to be consumed in the flames of war—when he told me the RCAF was not accepting American volunteers! Why not, I asked? No authority had been issued, he said, but he thought the Canadian Army was permiting Americans to enlist. Maybe, he suggested, if I joined the army and went overseas I could transfer to the Royal Air Force in Great Britain. I guess I came to Canada too quickly after war was declared; later the RCAF accepted several thousand American volunteers both as aircrew and ground crew personnel. Since I was about broke, I decided my heroic potential might be of some benefit to the Canadian Army after all.

The squadron adjutant told me that the Seaforth Highlanders, at their Burrard Street Armory, were recruiting and that this regiment would be going to England soon as part of the 1st Canadian Division. So it was to be the infantry for me once again—damn it to hell! For some reason I just couldn't manage to get into anyone's air force. My past infantry training was bound to be of some value, of course, but I wanted more than anything to fly. Later I found out the RCAF squadron adjutant had a brother, a lieutenant, in the Seaforths. I'll always wonder if that suggestion of his wasn't given to help fill the ranks of his brother's regiment. All recruiters, including adjutants, are sneaky guys.

So I went to the Seaforth Highlanders' barracks that afternoon to enlist. I was directed to see a Sergeant Major Shipperbottom, a veteran of the First World War, who stared down his nose and over his bushy mustache at me. "Where are you from?" he snapped. I again explained that I was an American volunteer who had come to Canada to help fight their war.

"Can't accept you," the sergeant major said, "but if you go walk around the block, come back in here, and are from someplace in Canada, I'll sign you up."

I walked around the block, returned to the armory, and again stood before Shipperbottom. "Where are you from now?" he asked.

"Moosejaw," I replied—it was the only town name I could think of at the moment.

"Where the hell is Moosejaw?" he questioned.

"How the hell do I know?" I answered, a bit peeved.

"It's in Saskatchewan Province—and don't you ever forget it!" he told me. "Now that we've got that settled you can enlist. Sign here, for the duration."

And so I enlisted for the duration of the war in the Seaforth Highlanders, a Scottish infantry regiment of the 3rd Brigade, 1st Canadian Division. My assignment was to No. 3 Platoon, Headquarters Company, Major Ian Tait commanding. No. 3 Platoon, commanded by Sergeant Major Shipperbotton, was a 3-inch mortar unit with two gun squads. Our platoon sergeant was Archie Proudfoot, another "Old Sweat" from the First World War. Archie knew all the ins and outs of the British and Canadian Army systems and if you followed his lead you would more than likely survive the hazards of war.

Within the next week or so several more Americans turned up to join the Seaforths. One of them, Bill Coss, had previously fought with the Abraham Lincoln Brigade in the Spanish Civil War. Since the regimental officers knew we were American citizens, we were not required to swear allegiance to King George and the British Empire—only to serve faithfully and honorably for the war's duration. At that time it was against United States law for an American citizen to join the armed forces of a belligerent nation. If caught, you could be fined $10,000, or receive a prison sentence of two years, or both. Fortunately for all us volunteer troops, the United States government decided to look the other way when we joined the Canadian forces.

The Seaforth Highlanders of Canada was a sister regiment to the "Imperial Seaforths" of the British Army. Its stag-head cap badge carried the motto, "Cuidich 'N Righ," which means in the Gaelic language, "Serve the King." Its long military history, beginning in the early 1600s, states: "And where the battle raged the loudest you ever did find the Seaforths." It was, without a doubt, one of the finest regiments in the armed forces of the entire British Empire. The kilt was worn by all its troops—therefore the nickname, "The Ladies from Hades."

Now the first time you put on a highland uniform, including the kilt, it feels very different—sort of breezy around the thighs and rear end. Many people have asked me the question, "What does a highlander wear under his kilt?" Well, I'll tell you: shoes. Why? Because a kilt is hot—seven yards of wool material wrapped around your waist, most in the back pleats—which makes you sweat between the legs. If you wore undershorts, the sweat would cause irritation by chafing on long marches. In a gas attack, the gas would first affect sweaty skin areas and incapacitate a number of troops. Many times I have seen a highland unit stood properly at ease, while a sergeant major with a mirror on a long handle checked between their legs for unauthorized undershorts. If caught, the shorts are yanked off then and there, and disciplinary action follows. I might add you've got to learn how to sit down again when wearing a kilt: knees together or crossed; not spread apart, obviously.

There is nothing finer or more stimulating to the military spirit than to view a highland regiment on parade, their kilts swaying to their proud marching pace, rifles at the slope, free arms swinging to the height of the man's shoulder in front, the pipe band playing the rousing tunes of "The Road to the Isles," "The Black Bear Highland Laddie," or "Scotland the Brave."

My past military experience paid off soon and I was promoted to lance corporal. Then, a couple of months later, I was given the rank of sergeant. Now I commanded one mortar section of the platoon, while Archie Proudfoot ran the other section. The 3-inch mortar was a weapon that could be transported by infantry troops in bits and pieces. According to the manual the mortar would never be carried more than 100 yards—BS! We carried the damned thing to hell and back several times. The base plate weighed about 40 pounds, the barrel about 30 pounds, and the bipod about 35 pounds. Mortar shells weighed 10 pounds each, and were carried in three-shell containers of 30 pounds. The average infantryman carried his Lee-Enfield rifle, gas mask and cape, small and big pack, tin hat, and 100 or so rounds of .303 caliber rifle ammunition, in all about 60 pounds. A mortarman carried his regular 60 pounds of infantry equipment, plus a part of the mortar or two shell containers, in all 100 or more pounds. The only ground we could walk across without sinking to our ankles was concrete.

On 11 December 1939 we were alerted for movement to England. On 15 December, at 07:30 hours, we were formed up in the armory for inspection by the District Commanding Officer. A few minutes later the great doors swung open and our pipe band, led by Pipe Major Ed Esson, playing "Scotland the Brave," formed the vanguard of our regiment's march through Vancouver to the railway station. The crowds of cheering people along our route were unbelievable. The Vancouver Sun newspaper reported the event in some detail:

> There was kissing and shouting and tears and brave smiling and long, long waving of hands and hearty back-slaps and shouts of 'Good luck!' and half strangled 'God bless you's' and more kisses and girls weeping and tucking pathetic little notes into uniform pockets to be found later, and an exchanging of souvenir badges and brooches and all the immemorial, sad, tear-dimmed ritual.
>
> And in the midst of it a few civic dignitaries and important personages looked on bewilderedly as their dignity and importance dwindled to nothing in the swelling tide of common emotion.
>
> And when it was all over, the place was empty and the streets around were filled with a thinning crowd of sad-faced men and women, some of whom had not cried before but were crying now.

The crowds near the station broke through our ranks, but we pushed on as best we could. I was now carrying three rifles, my own and the rifles of two guys who were marching along with their arms around their sobbing wives. At the railway station Mrs. Proudfoot asked me to please look after Archie—he wasn't a young soldier any more, she said.

After a five-day train ride across Canada to the port city of Halifax, we left our train and boarded the Royal Mail Line ship "Andes." The "Andes" had been on its maiden voyage to South America when the war started. Diverted to Halifax as a troopship, she still had all her luxurious tourist passenger accommodations. What a delightful way to travel to war: first and second class cabins, a beautiful dining salon, silverware, fine china, ship's stewards, and waiters!

On 22 December, in company with seven other troopships and an escort of British, French, and Canadian naval vessels, we set sail for England. In mid-ocean the Canadian destroyers departed the convoy to return to Halifax. Their place was soon taken by a dozen Royal Navy destroyers. At dawn on 30 December we arrived off the mouth of the River Clyde near Gouroch in Scotland. As our ship passed through the anti-submarine boom at the harbor entrance, we Seaforths gave three loud cheers to the seamen of the escorting warships for seeing us safely across the Atlantic. They, in turn, cheered us. The next day, about noon, we disembarked from the "Andes," boarded a troop train for Glasgow and then on to North Farnborough, England, where we were finally lodged at Delville Barracks near the little town of Cove, not far from the huge military garrison of Aldershot.

About a month later, on 24 January 1940, His Majesty, King George VI, paid our brigade an inspection visit. Our brigade included the Seaforths, the Princess Patricia's Canadian Light Infantry, and the Loyal Edmonton regiment. Archie Proudfoot warned me, "When the king inspects a unit, it's certain to be on its way to the front in a few days." Hell's fire, we weren't even properly trained yet! As King George walked slowly along our ranks on the Cove-Fleet highway, nodding and smiling to each soldier, he stopped short before Archie Proudfoot. Said the king, "Sergeant, how old are you?" When Archie replied, I think he reduced his age by ten or more years.

"I see you are wearing the ribbon of my coronation medal," continued King George.

"No sir," answered Archie, "it's your father's coronation medal."

Archie's name, rank, serial number, and unit were jotted down by one of the king's aides. A few days later Archie was transferred to a replacement training depot as an instructor, by order of King George. We found out later that Archie had joined the Army in 1912, and had served several years in the Royal Navy before that! All added, he was probably fifty plus years of age.

The next week all the officers and NCOs received a personal copy of a letter sent by King George to the General Officer Commanding, 1st Canadian Division. It read:

> Buckingham Palace
>
> On behalf of the people of this country, I extend the warmest welcome to the first contingent of the Canadian Forces to reach these shores.
>
> The British Army will be proud to have as comrades-in-arms the successors of those who came from Canada in the Great War and fought with a heroism that has never been forgotten.
>
> signed: George R.I.

I still have my copy of King George's letter among my war service mementos.

After a period of very rigorous training, I managed to get a five-day leave to London. Being, for all intents and purposes, a military tourist, I took in all the well-known sights. Then one morning I decided to visit the fabulous Westminster Abbey. Not far from the main entrance I came across the grave of the British Unknown Soldier, which was absolutely covered with red paper poppies. One of the poppies lay a bit away from the others, so I picked it up. As I held it in my hand the queer feeling came over me that I should keep it, that it might somehow protect me in battle. I said a little prayer to the Unknown Soldier, asking that God and he, whoever he was, should watch over me and keep me safe from death during the war. Then I put the red poppy carefully in the breast pocket of my tunic.

The commanding officer of the Seaforths was Lt. Colonel J. B. Stevenson, who, unfortunately, had a wall-eye. It was said he would look at one private in the ranks, a second private would snap to attention, and a third private would salute. He was nicknamed, most irreverently, "Swivel-eye." One of the rifle companies had obtained a goose someplace for a mascot, which they had also named "Swivel-eye." The goose, it appears, was being given a bath in the barracks latrine one day at the very same moment that Colonel Stevenson was inspecting the place. As the inspecting party passed through a hallway next to the latrine they heard distinctly the words, "Hold still you swivel-eyed old bastard, or I'll break your bloody neck!" Into the latrine strode the red-faced, angry colonel. There was a sudden quietness among the goose bathers, followed by the colonel's roar, "Get rid of that goddam bird—now—or I'll eat him for my dinner, feathers and all!" The goose was sacrificed to the sergeants' mess that same evening.

Speaking of the sergeants' mess, we held a Vimy Dinner one evening—an annual affair—commemorating the famous battle of the First World War. We wanted roast pork for the dinner; however, since all meat was rationed, we had some difficulty in finding a farmer who would discreetly sell us a live pig. After considerable maneuvering, we finally got the pig into the back of a truck where the medical and mess sergeants were waiting to administer the coup de grace. To be humane, it was decided the medical sergeant would chloroform the pig before the mess sergeant cut its throat. The pig fought back, and although several of us held his kicking legs, we were nearly all gassed before the medic and his chloroform were successful. The mess sergeant began the throat cutting and the pig came alive once again, covering everyone with bloody gore before he finally gave up the ghost.

Back at the mess, the pig's entrails were disposed of by stuffing them down a sewer drain. We didn't realize that English drain pipes were so small, so the entrails caused a jam in the sewer. When workmen came to unclog the pipe they found the entrails, which they believed to be those of a human being. The police were called in and a full-scale investigation began, but all came to a halt when we confessed.

We had our Vimy Dinner, we had our roast pork—but it was almost impossible to eat because every bite smelled of chloroform.

The war in Europe—the "phony war," as it was called—remained dormant all along the Western Front in early 1940. Then, on 9 April 1940, the German Army suddenly invaded Norway. Our Canadian forces were selected to go to Norway, to Narvik, to push the Huns out of that country. We loaded all our gear onto a truck convoy and headed north, but we only got as far as the barren Scottish moors before Norway surrendered. A month after the Norway invasion, on 10 May, the enemy launched a major surprise attack into Holland, Belgium and France. The "phony war" was now a real shooting war.

Then came the Battle of France, the retreat of the Allied armies, and the British Expeditionary Force (BEF) evacuation from the beaches of Dunkirk. For days we were convoyed all over England. Vehicle and unit markings were changed every day or so. The whole effort was, I assume, designed to give enemy spies the idea that there were many more troops in England than there really were.

On 8 June Their Majesties, the King and Queen, paid our brigade a visit—and this time we knew we were going to be sent to France to help stem the tide of the German advance. All sorts of new equipment was made available to us, as well as maps of France. A couple days later, on 11 June, Captain W. G. H. Roaf led our advance party to Brest. Movement of units of the 1st Canadian Division to France was simply a case of too little too late. By 14 June the Germans had entered Paris and by the 16th the enemy had defeated France. A day later Marshal Petain, who had assumed leadership of the French government, requested an armistice. On 22 June, five days later, the war ended in France by the signing of the armistice at Compiègne.

In the meantime, before the Huns could surround our Canadian forces at Brest, an evacuation was ordered. Roads leading into Brest were mined, railway tracks were torn up, and antitank barricades built. Now there was a very tricky way to use 3-inch mortar shells as mines. When the safety cap on the nose fuse is unscrewed, a little cup-shaped striker pops out. This striker releases a small spring in the fuse at the firing pin position. If, at this time, you were to lightly tap the striker the mortar shell would explode. To mine, you would dig a hole in the roadway large enough for the shell, set the shell in the hole nose up, and gently unscrew the safety cap. It was necessary to cover the shell fuse with dirt so it wouldn't be seen by the Kraut troops. Gently, very gently, the loose dirt was packed around the shell case, the touchy nose fuse being lightly dusted over. After mining some forty mortar shells you were covered with sweat and almost a nervous wreck. This system did work, blowing quite a few enemy tanks and armored personnel carriers to bits.

Some of the weapons tactics developed on the spur of the moment were really unbelievable. Soldiers would run up to a German tank, put the muzzle of a 12-gauge shotgun loaded with buckshot against the driver's view slit, and blast the buckshot into the turret. You can imagine the shot ricocheting inside and off the turret walls. "Split this among you, you bastards!" several soldiers shouted as they pulled their shotgun triggers.

Two soliders would tie a cord to an antitank mine, then they would hide themselves on opposite sides of a roadway with the mine on one side and the cord stretched across the road. When an approaching enemy tank was almost between the hidden guys, one of them would pull the mine out into the road beneath the tank's tracks. This trick was best used at night, but could be used in the day if there was a good hiding place along the roadsides.

Mills bombs (hand grenades) just fit into the fuel tank neck of Hun tanks and half-track vehicles. I never saw it, but I was told that some of our troops managed to drop a grenade into these fuel tanks, resulting in a fiery explosion and some scorched Squareheads. Each infantry unit was issued antitank rifles of .55 caliber. This was a useless weapon, since its "armor piercing" shell could hardly penetrate a ration can. Its value did improve slightly when our troops found out the gun worked best when the barrel was jammed into the treads and bogie wheels of an enemy tank.

Things at Brest were in a turmoil; the whole military situation was extremely confused. Since it was not possible to recover all our vehicles, weapons, fuel, and other supplies, the order was given to destroy them. Brand new vehicles were run off the Brest docks to sink in the harbor waters. Everything that would burn was set afire. Fuel supplies exploded with great roars and dense columns of smoke filled the skies above Brest. Someone told me that our brigade alone lost over two hundred vehicles. In two months the Germans had invaded and occupied Norway, attacked all along the Western Front, defeated the Dutch and Belgian forces, driven our BEF to the beaches at Dunkirk, and forced the French to surrender. Maybe we weren't going to "hang our washing on the Siegfried Line" after all.

After the heavy BEF losses at Dunkirk and the Canadian losses at Brest, there was a great reorganization of the armed forces still available for front line service in England. The probability of a German invasion of Great Britain suddenly became very real. Said Sir Winston Churchill, "We shall fight on the beaches, we shall fight on the landing grounds, we shall fight in the fields and in the streets, we shall fight in the hills, we shall never surrender." These certainly were inspiring words—but who the hell was "we"?

Dunkirk had fallen, Calais was surrounded by Germans who had fought the BEF troops in that port's fortress, and the German army was approaching Brest to beat us up—so the 1st Canadian was ordered to get the hell out of there. Most returned to England on Royal Navy troopships, but some of us on Norwegian vessels which, besides troops, carried a goodly number of French "ladies of the evening," brought on board by the sailors.

The Seaforths now became part of a "flying column," ready to move and fight anywhere at one hour's alert notice. Again we were shifted from place to place, sometimes to the east coast where the invasion was expected, sometimes to areas where enemy parachutists might land, and wherever we went we dug trenches, foxholes, and underground bunkers. At one time our platoon provided security guards for a huge, secret communications center that was burrowed beneath a tree-covered hill. This center, built of bomb-proof reinforced concrete, was the nerve center of the entire British Empire. The main entrance to it was through a small door that was completely camouflaged with living grass. Ten feet away the door couldn't be seen at all. Air vents to the center were actually built into tree trunks.

Enemy aircraft began to fly a few bombing sorties over England about mid-July, and we were bombed a couple of times. Our casualties were nil; however, they did kill a cow in a field near our encampment. Within fifteen minutes our platoon troops were out there cutting huge roasts and steaks from the cow's carcass with sharpened bayonets. What a lovely feast we had that evening, thanks to the German Luftwaffe!

In the latter part of July I jumped from a truck (lorry, in England) to the ground, landed on a rock, and broke my right ankle. I was sent off to a field hospital to be patched up with a plaster cast, which I hobbled around with for a bit on crutches. Then, upon release from the hospital, I was assigned to the 3rd Canadian Infantry Holding Unit, near Borden in Hampshire, where I was to remain until fit for active duty.

On 8 August 1940 the Germans launched their mass air attacks on England, and the Battle of Britain began. I think it was about mid-morning of Wednesday, 14 August, that our camp and neighboring Army camps were attacked by German Junkers 88 bombers. The skies that day were overcast and these bombers, two of them, suddenly dropped down out of the clouds above us. They each laid a couple of sticks of four or five high explosive bombs, one of which blew the officers' mess in our camp to hell. Several supply buildings were also hit and began burning. Since an air raid warning was in effect, our troops were safely in bomb shelters when the attack began. In the shelters you could feel the jarring concussion of the nearby exploding bombs and the dust and dirt blew in through the shelter entrance. Unfortunately for one of the Hun aircrews, they made a low second pass over the camp area, were met by antiaircraft machine gun fire from a dozen or so guns, and were shot down. The Ju.88 crashed and burned in an open field not too far from our Borden camp. No one got out of the bomber.

Two days later, on Friday, 16 August, our camp was again attacked by enemy aircraft. This time the attackers were a flight of four Ju.87 Stuka dive bombers. The attack came in the late morning, about 11 o'clock, the Stukas roaring down on us out of a clear blue sky. On their first pass one of their bombs exploded next to an antiaircraft machine gun position. A large bomb splinter cut the gunner's head off, and another fragment wounded the ammunition loader, leaving the position unmanned.

I don't know why to this day, but I ran out of my bomb shelter to the unmanned post, where I set up the Lewis machine gun and readied it to fire. This antiaircraft position was a hole in the ground about five feet deep and maybe five feet wide, the parapet built up with sandbags for added protection to the gun crew. In the center of the pit was a thick wooden post with a swivel pin mounted on the top so the machine gun could be swung about and fired in a field of 360 degrees. The machine gun was a Lewis of the First World War vintage, its ammunition contained in round drums or pans of about forty .303 caliber cartridges each.

The wounded ammo loader had crawled off to a bunker where he could get some medical aid. I glanced down at the gunner's corpse, his severed neck still gushing blood onto the ground. The gunner's head lay a yard or so from the sandbag parapet, the mouth agape, the dead eyes staring at nothing. I don't think any of what I was seeing at the moment registered in my brain.

Now one of the Hun Stukas, flat out, came in a screaming dive toward my gun position, his forward firing machine guns flashing at me. Puffs of dirt, kicked up by his bullets striking near me, showered over me but I wasn't hit. Just as the Stuka began to level out, maybe 50 feet above the ground and at a range of some 200 yards, I sighted the old Lewis gun on the aircraft's prop spinner and fired a burst. I continued firing at the Stuka until it flashed over my head—all this in a few seconds. When the Hun pilot started his pull-up, his engine began trailing smoke and then burst into flames. The engine quit at a couple hundred feet, the nose went down, and the Ju.87 crashed to the ground in a field a half mile from our camp. Later I found out that the two Krauts in the Stuka died in the fiery crash. I reloaded my Lewis machine gun.

A second Stuka was now diving down on our camp, and it looked to me like he intended to lay a bomb right in my hole. I ducked down, flattening myself as best I could against the dirt wall and sandbags. I actually saw the bombs, two of them, fall clear of the Stuka. They hit the ground with a hell of a bang and blast, showering me with clods of dirt, stones and dust—near misses, damned near! As this Stuka pulled out of its dive almost directly over my gun pit, I took a good long deflection shot at it. The aircraft flew right through my bullet stream and I saw some of the bullet strikes on its engine cowling and fuselage. It seemed to falter in the air for a brief moment, then nosed down smoking, leveled out, and crash-landed.

The other two Stukas were now flying away from the battle scene, back to Hunland. I was shaking like a leaf, my breath was coming in little gasps, my legs felt weak, so I sat down on the ground in the bottom of my gun pit. I was still sitting there when the medics came to collect the dead gunner.

I should mention here that my Lewis was not the only gun firing at the enemy aircraft, which always casts a doubt as to who actually shot them down. I know I hit them; others may have, too. Major D. L. Redman, 3rd Canadian Infantry Holding Unit commander, and Captain W. W. Henderson, both of whom witnessed this event, stated that they saw my bullet hits on the Hun aircraft. I didn't realize it at the time, but I had actually participated in the Battle of Britain.

The two Germans in the last Stuka survived the crash-landing and were captured. Next day I took a couple packs of cigarettes to them when I paid them a visit at the hospital. The pilot, a young Feldwebel (Flight Sergeant) named Clausen, had his hands burned a bit. The air gunner—I've forgotten his name—had been wounded in the leg by a

.303 round. Clausen spoke pretty good English, and he didn't seem too sore at me for shooting him down. The other guy, a typical Squarehead bastard, wouldn't even thank me for the cigarettes. We two, Clausen and I, talked about flying for a while. He said he tried to become a fighter pilot, but got stuck in dive bombers. I told him that I wanted to be a pilot too, and how I got stuck in the infantry. Clausen wasn't a bad guy, for a Hun.

The German blitz on London was taking place about this time. During the day we infantry types could watch the contrails of the great air battles taking place high in the skies. Now and then a long plume of smoke would suddenly appear—a falling aircraft. Ours or theirs? At night the search light beams swept the darkened heavens, sometimes pinpointing an enemy aircraft. Then came the bright, popping bursts of antiaircraft gun shells. It was easy for us on the ground to distinguish an enemy bomber at night, without ever seeing it. Their engines had a peculiar low-pitched throb, a sort of unsynchronized beat. Sometimes at night you could see a dull red glow in the sky above London, the reflected flames of thousands of fire bombs dropped on the city by attacking enemy aircraft.

Even with the blitz some of us hardier souls, if we managed to get a pass for a day or so, went to London. There were some guys who wouldn't go near the place during that period. There were numerous air raid alerts, the civil defense sirens screaming a half dozen or more times during the day and night. People streamed to the city's air raid shelters and into the underground stations—thousands of people, young and old. It was an appalling sight, people crunching down, eyes showing fright, some praying, as the bombs, exploding nearby, shook the earth and the shelters. And these places stank of body odor from the multitudes of humanity pressed close together, some people actually living every day in these shelters.

At night, during an air raid, you could actually see sparks fly off the paved streets and building walls as shrapnel from exploded antiaircraft shells fell back to earth. We troops would roll up our greatcoats and hold them over our heads as we went from one pub to another for a whiskey or a pint of ale, or to a fish and chip joint. There was one company sergeant major in the Seaforths who was scared silly by the bombing raids, and I don't think he ever visited London.

One day when Gordon Barr, a platoon friend of mine, and I were walking down a London street, a window opened and a rather pretty lady appeared in it. She shouted to a policeman standing on the corner, "Hey, copper! Come knock me up at eight tomorrow morning!" Gordy and I looked at each other in disbelief. Said Gordy, "I know these English are great for scheduling everything—but that is ridiculous." We found out later she meant for the cop to awaken her at eight. Another time, during a blackout, my date and I were crossing a busy London street. Said I to her, "Be careful or you'll get your fanny full of fender." She slapped me right in the kisser! How was I to know that a "fanny" in England refers to a lady's very private parts? As you see, there are several pronounced differences between the English language and the version we Americans and Canadians speak.

A few months later I was to leave the Seaforth Highlanders of the Canadian Army for other service. I would like to add here that the Seaforths did "their bit for King and Country" in a most gallant and courageous manner in the later battles of the Second World War. Their battle honors included Agira, Sicily, Monte San Marco, Ortona, Hitler Line, Gothic Line, Savio Bridgehead, Italy 1943–1945, Apeldoorn, and Northwest Europe 1945. They suffered heavy casualties during the five years they fought the determined Hun enemy, but they were never defeated. Two of their soldiers, Major C. C. I. Merritt and Private E. A. Smith, won Great Britain's highest decoration for valor, the Victoria Cross. Eight officers won the Distinguished Service Order, and seven officers were awarded the Order of the British Empire. The Military Cross was won by eleven officers. Four enlisted men received the Distinguished Conduct Medal, twenty-one men were awarded the Military Medal, and one received the British Empire Medal. Thirty-five Seaforths were "mentioned in despatches" for gallantry on the battle-field.

Truly they were "The Ladies from Hades," and true to their regimental history: "Where the battle raged the loudest you ever did find the Seaforths."

2. First from the Eyries

In October of 1940 a message was sent from the British Air Ministry to all army and navy units requesting the names of personnel who wished to serve with the Royal Air Force and who had some previous flying experience—at least 500 hours as pilots. These persons, if accepted, were to be immediately transferred to the RAF to make up the heavy pilot losses suffered by Fighter Command during the Battle of Britain. Three of us, all Americans, in the Seaforth Highlanders, qualified more or less and so applied for transfer. We were Corporal Jimmy Crowley, Private Jack Doherty, and myself, Sergeant Dunn.

I don't know about the other two guys, but I was fed up with the infantry and lugging that damned three-inch mortar all over the countryside. Here, now, was the chance I'd been waiting for to get into the air force, to fight the rest of the war sitting on my rear end in a cockpit seat. I really didn't have 500 hours flying time as a pilot—about 160 hours would be a more accurate figure. My pencil may have slipped a bit on the application form with my 160 looking sort of like 560. Anyway, my application was submitted, I passed the medical and mental exams, and on 13 December 1940 I was accepted by the Royal Air Force for flying duties and commissioned a pilot officer (2nd lieutenant).

I had written in the remarks section of my application form that it had been some time since I had last flown—about two years to be exact—and requested a brief refresher flying course. I figured that the RAF would send me off to an Elementary Flying Training School (EFTS) for a couple of months, where I could get back into the swing of things flying a DeHavilland D.H.82 Tiger Moth biplane trainer. Well, I figured wrong. The RAF needed pilots quickly, which was why the 500-hour requirement; they couldn't waste a lot of time on elementary flying refresher courses.

I received Air Ministry orders on 6 February 1941 to report to No. 5
Service Flying Training School (SFTS) at RAF Station Tern Hill, near
Market Drayton in Shropshire, where I would begin my training with
No. 57 Course. After a delightful but devastating "going away party" at
the Seaforth Sergeants' Mess, I proceeded somewhat bleary-eyed to
London, where I purchased my new blue pilot officer's uniform and
other kit items at "Moss Bros." Then, by railway train, I journeyed on
to Tern Hill airfield. (Corporal Crowley's transfer was delayed a couple
of weeks for some reason. Private Doherty failed the medical exams
and, I was told later, was killed in action with the Seaforths during the
Italian Campaign.)

The advanced training aircraft assigned to No. 5 SFTS was the Miles
"Master." The Master was a two-seater, low-wing monoplane, with a
700-hp Rolls Royce Kestrel XXX inline engine, a three-bladed adjust-
able pitch propeller (airscrew, as the English call a prop), a retractable
landing gear (undercarriage), and full landing flaps. With a top speed of
about 225 mph it was a hell of a lot "hotter" and much more advanced
than anything I had ever flown before. Twenty-five Masters, built as
single-seat fighter versions and armed with two .303-caliber machine
guns, were employed as emergency augmentation fighters during the
Battle of Britain; however, these fighter versions were now utilized as
"solo" aircraft at Tern Hill.

Another thing I should mention about our Miles Master aircraft:
they were constructed with a plywood and fabric skin. The wings were
covered with plywood sheeting which, after a rain or period of damp
weather, would actually wrinkle a bit from the wetness. Part of the
pilot's checklist, under such conditions, was to waggle the ailerons so
that the water collected inside that part of the wing could drip out.
Then, as the sun's warmth began to dry the wing surfaces, the wrinkles
in the plywood skin would gradually smooth out. This problem had no
effects on the Master's flying capabilities, but it did cause the pilot to
wonder if perhaps the soggy aircraft might not come unglued in flight.

I needn't have worried so much about the SFTS assignment, because
my instructor, Flying Officer Barker, who at age twenty-two was a
Battle of Britain veteran, soon briefed me into all the intricacies of
handling the big, powerful Master. It was really a delight to fly; very
stable, good for aerobatics and for night and instrument flying. In just
eight hours of dual time Barker had me ready for my first solo. I will
admit that my aerobatics occasionally scared the hell out of both

Barker and me, and most probably the local population of Market Drayton as well.

Flight Lieutenant Lord, the training flight commander, gave me my final check ride, climbed out of his cockpit after I gave him a reasonably bouncy landing, told me to keep my landing approach speed more steady, and said, "Go kill yourself." So, alone in my mighty Master, I poured on the throttle, went bounding once again across the grass airfield and, behind my roaring Kestrel, soared into the bright sky—solo. The flight was uneventful. I flew around for some 45 minutes before I gathered enough courage to land. I guess I wasn't too worried about my flying solo; it was all those other idiot students trying to get into the circuit (traffic pattern) and land at the same time as me. Anyway, I bluffed a couple of student pilots into making "go-arounds" and so landed safely. At last I had conquered the Miles Master.

Hours and more hours were spent on formation flying, aerobatics, cross-country navigation flights, instrument flying, night flying, air combat, and so forth. An odd thing occurred during our night flying training. We had three fellows named Taylor in No. 57 Course, and all three of them crashed and were killed. No one else—just the Taylors. Night flying itself for a solo student was bad enough, but vile English weather, with no visible horizon combined with the blackout of all lights on the ground, made it much worse. It was like being inside a completely darkened room with absolutely nothing, except the cockpit instruments, to provide some sense of balance and orientation. And there was always the chance of smashing into the Wrekin, a very high hill located south of the airfield.

Night flying at Tern Hill really got deadly when far-ranging German aircraft entered the airfield area. The gooseneck flare pots used to mark our landing flare path or runway on the ground were very difficult to see from an altitude of 1,000 feet. When the Huns flew into the area even these flares were doused, leaving the poor, frightened student pilots droning through a pitch-black void. They had to go completely on instruments, black out all aircraft navigation lights, try to remain somewhere in the vicinity of Tern Hill airfield by flying time and distance legs, and hope the enemy aircraft wasn't about to shoot them down. A real nervous twitch could also develop in that darkened sky when you flew unseeing through someone else's slipstream! This ordeal usually continued for the better part of an hour before a green flare fired from ground control signalled the "all clear." Then came a mad scramble to try to locate the airfield again in the night (while the dim flare path was being relit) and get back on the deck, everyone now being short of petrol (gasoline).

I recall a student pilot in our course who landed in a complete panic after a daylight solo flight. It seems he was flying above a cloud deck at about 7,000 feet when he saw a twin-engine aircraft in the distance. Curiosity got him, so he flew toward the unknown aircraft and found, to his dismay, that it was a German Messerschmitt 110! With the bejesus scared out of him, our student flew straight and level with the enemy fighter flying alongside. The German pilot could see that the Miles Master was an unarmed training aircraft by its yellow painted underbelly and underwings. He waved to our student pilot, as if to say "See you later when you learn to fly," banked away and disappeared into the thick clouds. Not all RAF student pilots were as lucky as this one. Not all enemy airmen were as gallant as this Me.110 pilot. I've often wondered who he was and what happened to him. I hope he survived the war, if only as a reward for this one honorable act.

There was another American in No. 57 Course, a lanky, dark-haired fellow named Bill Sharp. He had one hell of a time getting to England. First off, his ship was torpedoed in mid-Atlantic by a German submarine. While his ship was sinking, Bill decided that it was going to be damned cold in an open lifeboat, so he went back into the ship and got some coats, sweaters and blankets to keep himself warm. When he climbed into one of the last lifeboats, all his warm collection was taken from him and given to other unthinking, freezing survivors. So poor Bill shivered and froze and cussed.

Several times in the next couple of days they saw planes searching for them, but couldn't attract their attention. For food, Bill had several packages of chewing gum, which he divided among the lifeboat's passengers. Finally, when at last they were spotted and a Canadian corvette arrived to pick them up, Bill, the last to leave the lifeboat, slipped and fell into the sea between the corvette and lifeboat hulls where he was nearly beaten to death by the pounding waves. At last he was pulled on board, dried out, and eventually reached England's shores. "The straw that broke the camel's back," said Bill, "was when the corvette captain asked me if I'd like to join the Royal Navy!"

Bill Sharp was undoubtedly the world's worst navigator. Off he'd go on a cross-country flight of about two hours duration, and that's the last you'd see or hear of him. Many hours later he'd phone Tern Hill from some outlandish place where he'd finally landed. I actually saw written in one of Bill's navigation logs, "Turned port 10° over red cow." His instructor once asked him if had a watch to help him navigate by time, speed, and distance. "Yes," replied Bill, "but it doesn't work."

When Bill Sharp graduated from No. 57 Course (don't ask me how he did it) he was posted to, of all things, the Merchant Service Fighter Unit (MSFU). This unit provided Hawker Hurricane fighter aircraft and pilots for Catapult Armed Merchant (CAM) ships. The idea was, when a CAM ship was about to be attacked at sea by a German long-range bomber, the Hurricane and its pilot were catapulted into the air to chase the Hun off or shoot him down. If this action took place close to land, 150 miles or so distant, the MSFU pilot could land his aircraft safely at some airfield after completing his mission. That's the good part of this operation; now for the bad part.

If the action took place far out at sea, the Hurricane pilot, after running off or downing the enemy aircraft, was to either ditch his aircraft in the sea a short distance in front of his ship, or to bail out and hope and pray the Navy guys he had protected would pick him up. Sometimes, if there were also enemy U-boats lurking beneath the waves, the CAM ships did not make any effort to pick up the pilot drifting helplessly in his Mae West or dinghy. He was expendable. Anyway, Bill Sharp of the RAF, by an unexplained quirk of fate, went down to the sea in ships once again. I never did hear anything more about Bill.

During the two months I spent at Tern Hill enemy bombers attacked the station only once. This attack occurred about 9 o'clock one dark, moonless night—the bomber's sky. Sirens blared out their wavering notes of warning, and a couple minutes later the bombs began to fall. There was a lot of racket, to say the least, with the shrill shriek of the bombs and the heavy explosions combined with the rapid banging of our anti-aircraft gunfire. However, it was all over in ten minutes and, would you believe it, no one on the station was killed or wounded. Most people who were hurt were injured in their mad scramble to get into the bomb shelters and slit trenches—skinned knees and shins and stubbed toes.

One bomb in particular hit on the concrete ramp in front of a hangar, bounced through the open hangar doors, and then careened out through the glass skylight in the roof before exploding. No damage except for broken glass. Most all the other bombs struck on the grass airfield, exploding harmlessly and causing small craters, which were soon patched up.

When the German aircraft broke off their attack and headed for home we could hear, in the distance, other aircraft engine sounds and machine gun and automatic cannon fire. Next morning when I went down to the flight line, I saw two black-painted Bristol Beaufighters parked on the ramp. An airman was painting two small white swastikas on the nose of one of the night fighters, a Beaufighter named "Destroyer" by its aircrew. The airman told me that these two aircraft had gone into action for the first time the previous night and that the Destroyer's aircrew had shot down two of the Ju.88s that had bombed Tern Hill. Good show! That ought to teach the damned Squareheads to stay home.

The SFTS courses at Tern Hill were, as would be expected, very much accelerated due to the urgent need for fighter pilots. As an example, the day started with flying training from 7 a.m. until noon (weather permitting), and then ground school throughout the afternoon until about 6:30 p.m. This schedule went on and on seven days a week. Sometimes the program was altered with ground school in the morning and flying in the afternoon. If we were to do some night flying, our day flying schedule was reduced so that between the two flying periods we did not exceed a total of five flying hours. It usually worked out to three hours of day and two hours of night flying, plus ground school, which made a long day of it.

During periods of bad weather, when the airfield was muddy, a lot of mud from our flying boots would collect in the bottom of the cockpit. When we were sent up to do some aerobatics or simulated dogfighting, all that dirt would come raining down into our faces and damned nearly blind us when we turned the aircraft on its back or did a loop. Therefore, a part of the flight of the last guy to fly the aircraft each day was to open the cockpit hood (canopy), roll the aircraft on its back, push forward on the control column (stick), and get all this trash to blow out of the cockpit.

Although smoking in an aircraft was prohibited, there were usually a few cigarette butts and chewing gum wrappers mixed in with the dirt. One thing that could really get your undivided attention was to be smoking in the cockpit and suddenly discover that the fire ash had fallen off your cigarette! Where the hell did it go? Down near the petrol cocks and fuel pump? There were always gasoline fumes in the cockpit that could torch from a spark. You prayed a fire wouldn't start, and you immediately swore off smoking in the cockpit once again. Bloody dangerous and stupid thing to do. So, open the hood, roll on your back, and hope the hot ashes would fall out of the cockpit.

In the Royal Air Force the pilot training system was that the highest rated one-third of each SFTS class were commissioned as pilot officers, and the remaining two-thirds became sergeant pilots. Now this didn't necessarily mean, in the long run, that the selected officers were always better pilots than the sergeants. It is worth remembering that two-thirds of the fighter pilots who fought and won the Battle of Britain were sergeants.

We had one sergeant pilot instructor in No. 57 Course, a fellow named Smythe, who was absolutely amazing when it came to flying skill. He was a big, husky guy—looked sort of like a boxer—and he sported a "gladiator nose." Now a gladiator nose, in those days, was a mark of distinction for a fighter pilot. The last of the RAF biplane fighters to see service in France and Norway during the early months of the war were the Gloster Gladiators. The cockpit of the Glad was rather small, with the gunsight mounted just a few inches in front of the pilot's face. Whenever a Glad accidently nosed over on landing— whop!—the pilot smacked his face into the gunsight, thereby bashing in the bridge of his nose. This peculiar type of facial injury became known throughout the RAF as the "gladiator nose."

Anyway, this sergeant pilot was one of the best pilots I've ever known. Prior to the war, he and two other seargeant pilots did air show aerobatics in their Gladiators with the wing tips tied together by about 10 or 15 feet of rope. Not only that, I've personally seen him tape a piece of white school chalk to the wing tip of his Miles Master and then, flying upside down in the number two position of a formation, chalk out the red center of the roundel fuselage insignia on his leader's aircraft. He was utterly fearless, and when you flew with him you'd better be, or at least act, fearless too. Some months later Sergeant Pilot Smythe received a direct commision as a flight lieutenant (captain), and he ended the war with the rank of wing commander (lieutenant colonel). As a sergeant he was awarded the Distinguished Flying Medal (DFM) for his bravery in action in France with the Advanced Air Striking Force (AASF). Later, as an officer pilot and squadron and wing leader, he received the Distinguished Service Order (DSO) and the Distinguished Flying Cross (DFC).

Generally SFTS student pilots were given the rank of leading aircraftsmen (LAC) and they wore a small white cloth tab in the front of their uniform caps. However, those who were to be commissioned later as pilot officers also wore a white cloth band around the left sleeve. Sergeant pilots could be promoted to flight sergeants, then to warrant officers, and, if selected by their squadron leaders, commissioned as officer pilots. In many RAF squadrons experienced sergeant pilots acted as section and flight leaders, leading inexperienced officer pilots into battle. The RAF considered combat experience and pilot skill above rank, especially during air operations, and rightly so.

Many of the RAF's well known fighter aces were sergeant and warrant officer pilots before they received commissions. Flight Lieutenant George F. "Screwball" Beurling, DSO, DFC, DFM, the famous Canadian ace with thirty-three victories, is probably the best known. Poor George was killed in a flying accident near Rome, Italy, on 20 May 1948, while enroute to serve with the Israeli Air Force. Frank H. R. Carey, DFC and two Bars, AFC, DFM, was another ex-sergeant pilot, with twenty-eight confirmed victories, who eventually became a group captain (colonel). He was a Battle of Britain ace. Later, serving in the Burma Campaign, he increased his score to forty plus; however, all those official records were lost. Frank gave me some very valuable instructions and words of advice, as will soon be noted. Another ex-sergeant pilot was James H. "Ginger" Lacey, DFM and Bar, who became a squadron leader (major). Ginger shot down twenty-eight enemy aircraft. One of them, an enemy bomber, he shot down over Buckingham Palace in full view of the King and Queen. He is, however, best known as the RAF's leading Battle of Britain ace.

So the days passed into weeks and months at Tern Hill, with all of us student pilots studying and flying like mad. We learned all the nuts and bolts about our aircraft airframes and engines, armament, Morse code, radio-telephone communications, airmanship, navigation, plus a host of other things. And most important, we learned to handle our aircraft in any position or situation without busting our rear ends. Of course, like other student classes, we had our fair share of prangs (crashes). There were several engine failures followed by belly landings. Cadet officer pilot Frank Pargeter forgot to put the undercarriage down on his Master when landing and went skidding across the airfield and into a pond on the far side. There was a warning horn in the cockpit that blew when the throttle was retarded and the landing gear was not locked down. A drenched Frank stated, when extracted from the wreckage, "The damned horn was making such a noise I couldn't hear the radio warning from the control tower operator."

At that time (1940-41) there was a very real shortage of food in England, so each class of student pilots was required by the chief flying instructor (CFI) to dig, plant and cultivate a vegetable garden during the spring and summer months. We in No. 57 Course began our garden on a grass plot just outside the hangar crew room in early April of 1941. Thereafter, if the weather got too bad for flying, we all became gardeners.

The flying training course was tough, to say the least; however, we did get a bit of relaxation now and again. Across from the station main gate was the Stormy Petrel, a pub of some repute in that region. There, on occasion, we student pilots knocked back our fair share of ale, beer, whiskey, and gin and bitters. Yes, there were some aching heads and bleary eyes the next day, but we managed to survive such hangovers, even though we sometimes felt like death warmed up. A sure cure for a bad hangover, which all airmen soon discovered, was to get in the cockpit, put on the oxygen mask, and sop up pure oxygen for about five minutes or so.

Perhaps it was a good thing that our pay wasn't too much, so we couldn't afford to drink at the Stormy Petrel too often. My monthly pay as a pilot officer was about 18 English pounds (roughly $85 U.S.), and out of that I had to pay 4 pounds 5 shillings income tax, which left me with 13 pounds 15 shillings (about $65 U.S.) to pay my mess bills, batman, laundry, etc. When people asked me why I joined the RAF long before the United States entered the war, my reply was: "For the high pay, what else." Of course, in those days, our pay went a lot farther than it would today.

We students could have bought drinks at the mess bar for less cost, but there we were always under the watchful eyes of our instructors and other senior officers who continually frowned upon us and our youthful antics. Another thing, we were not allowed to exceed a 5-pound bar bill each month. If we did exceed that amount, we had to explain the reason to the CFI, who always took a dim view of the affair no matter how good was our explanation. So, the Stormy Petrel became the student pilots' hangout at RAF Station Tern Hill.

In the middle of April 1941 I was called to Flight Lieutenant Lord's office and told that my SFTS training was over; I was to be assigned directly to a fighter squadron. Now this was a most unusual occurrence, since I still needed to attend an Operational Training Unit (OTU) course. I had entered No. 57 Course a couple weeks after it had begun, and here I was leaving the course several weeks before it was to graduate, with only 56 hours of Miles Master flying time. I asked, "What about my OTU training and getting checked out in a Hurricane fighter?" Lord said that my fighter squadron people would get me checked out, that there was no OTU vacancy for me at that time, and that I had been rated by the SFTS as an "above average" pilot. The last bit—the above average rating—was good to know, but I certainly wasn't overly enthusiastic at being sent directly to an operational unit with so little flying time and no OTU training at all. I could only assume that somebody at Air Ministry knew what the hell was going on (which, of course, was a gross error on my part).

My posting was to No. 71 "Eagle" Squadron, then based at Martlesham Heath airfield, near Ipswich, Suffolk, on England's east coast. This particular squadron was composed of Americans who had joined the RAF as volunteer fighter pilots. Several of them had served in other RAF units prior to the formation of No. 71 Squadron, and a couple of them had fought in the Battle of Britain.

It seems that an influential American who lived in England, Charles Sweeny, got the idea of forming all the American volunteer pilots into one unit—an American Eagle Squadron—something similar to the Lafayette Escadrille of American flyers who served in the French Air Force during the 1914–1918 World War. His idea was approved by Air Ministry, with No. 71 Eagle Squadron being organized in September 1940.

The transferring of American pilots from their original units to the newly formed Eagle Squadron didn't go over so well with everybody. Many of the fellows were quite happy where they were, and not at all pleased to be suddenly stuck into an inexperienced, untried squadron. However, the Air Ministry decided such an organization would provide good propaganda for the American press and public consumption, so the decree went out. And that's how the first American Eagle Squadron, No. 71, was born. Charles Sweeny, if I remember correctly, was made an honorary RAF group captain for his efforts. No. 71 Squadron first trained at Kirton-in-Lindsey airfield, in Lincolnshire, for several months, and then moved to Martlesham Heath airfield where, in April of 1941, the unit became operational.

I arrived at Martlesham in the afternoon of a bright, sunny, warm spring day. After reporting to the squadron adjutant, Flying Officer F. H. Tann, and to Squadron Leader W. E. G. Bill Taylor (an ex-U.S. Navy officer), commanding officer of No. 71 Squadron, I strode over to the unit's dispersal hut to meet some of the other guys. Also, I wanted to get my first close look at a Hawker Hurricane fighter aircraft.

I'm not sure why, but I felt that my reception was somewhat cool. Maybe it was because I'd been an enlisted infantryman in the Canadian Army who had crawled from the muddy trenches into their blue heaven. Maybe it was because I was just a "new boy" in the squadron. Maybe they had read too much propaganda about their unit and thought they were already war heroes. Well, I could tell them all something of war, on the ground, at least. I'd been shot at before, I'd already shot down two German Stukas during the Battle of Britain, and I knew that most of these characters had never heard a shot fired in anger.

I did finally strike up a friendly conversation with two guys, Uncle Sam Mauriello and Red Tobin. Sam Mauriello got the nickname "Uncle Sam" because he was the oldest fellow in the squadron—about 30 years of age I'd guess. I found out later that his brother was the famous boxer, Tammy Mauriello. Eugene Q. Tobin, "Red" for short, was one member of a famous trio of American pilots who fought for England during the Battle of Britain. It seems that Red Tobin, Vernon C. "Shorty" Keough (4 feet 10 inches, the shortest pilot in the RAF), and Andrew B. Mamedoff—"The Mad Russian"—originally volunteered to serve as pilots with the Finnish Air Force in that nation's fight against the invading Russians. That flap, however, petered out before they got into it. So they went to France to join the French Air Force, presumably having to first enlist in the French Foreign Legion. When France fell before the German armies in the spring of 1940, the three of them escaped to England where they joined the RAF, serving with No. 609 Fighter Squadron during the Battle of Britain. Shorty Keough had been killed in action on 15 February 1941, but Tobin and "The Mad Russian," Andy Mamedoff, were still in the squadron.

That same evening Squadron Leader Taylor called me to his office, telling me that the squadron was too busy on operations (Channel convoy patrols) to train me and that he'd managed to get a place for me in the Hurricane OTU at Debden airfield. So, next morning, off I went to Debden.

My instructor at the OTU was Flight Lieutenant Frank Carey, the ex-sergeant pilot and fighter ace I've previously mentioned. We did a couple of "circuits and bumps" in a Miles Master just after dawn my first day at the OTU, then I read the pilot's notes on how to fly the Hurricane about lunch time. Following lunch, Carey gave me a blindfold cockpit check (to see if I knew where all the knobs were), and by mid-afternoon I was ready to taxi out onto the airfield to solo the Hurricane fighter. Patting me on the shoulder, Carey said, "Take her up for an hour. Get plenty of altitude before you attempt anything drastic. Try not to bust the aircraft or your butt. We need you both. Good luck."

Gingerly I opened the throttle, causing the big 1,030-horsepower Rolls-Royce Merlin II engine to roar. Releasing the brakes we—my Hurricane Mark I and I—surged forward, the tail plane lifting immediately, and off we went racing across the wide grassy expanse of Debden airfield. In a very few seconds we rose from the ground and began our climb out of air traffic. I selected the undercarriage "up," adjusted the propeller pitch, slightly reduced the throttle boost setting, and trimmed the Hurricane.

Like most pilots checking out in a new aircraft, I made a long, gradual climb out from the airfield before closing the hood and starting a gentle turn to port (left). At about 5,000 feet I set her up for normal cruising, then began to feel out her maneuvering capabilities. I rocked her wings with the ailerons and tested her elevator and rudder control. Her response was quick and light and I could feel her great power— much greater than the Miles Master. I slowed her up a couple of times so I could get the feel of her with landing gear and flaps down, also what trim she'd need on landing.

Then I climbed on up to about 10,000 feet where I put her through several fast, shallow dives and some fairly steep turns. Getting up a bit more nerve, I decided to try a low-speed stall. Slowing her up, I held her nose high while I watched the airspeed fall off. As we neared the stalling speed she began to shudder, then we fell off sharply on the starboard (right) wing, the nose went down, and we began the first turn of a tailspin, which, surprisingly, was not too violent. Throttled back, neutralized controls, and with opposite rudder, she quickly recovered in a steep dive, losing in all about 2,000 feet or so. No big thing.

She was very nice to handle in the air. She didn't appear to have any bad habits at all. After a couple more low-speed stalls and spins, I did several high-speed stalls. These last were, of course, a bit more violent, but still not too bad. I could see this aircraft and I were going to get on real well together. She was a real fighter; I felt fully at ease flying her. This Hurricane Mk I, according to the pilot's notes, had a top speed of 328 mph at 17,500 feet.

My hour of solo flying up, I rolled the Hurricane over on her back and did a split-S which, as I watched the airspeed indicator, just exceeded 300 mph in our fast dive. I entered the airfield circuit amid a batch of other student pilots, set up my approach, and made a landing I thought wasn't too bad for my first Hurricane flight. Carey met me when I taxied in to the aircraft parking ramp. When I shut the engine off he called to me, "Well, at least you didn't kill yourself. Not too bad for a beginner." When I climbed out of the cockpit, the airman fitter (erk, crew chief) patted his Hurricane affectionately on the side and said to me, "I've seen aircraft bounce on landing before, sir, but this is the first time I've ever seen one bounce to circuit height." Between these two guys my small bubble of egoism was properly popped.

Next morning I made another Hurricane familiarization flight, then that afternoon Carey and I flew in formation out to the English Channel for some "splash" practice. "Splash" is nothing more than an introduction to firing the Hurricane's eight .303-caliber machine guns into the water. Later on in the OTU course student fighter pilots fired at towed aerial drogue targets to learn something of deflection shooting. While Carey circled above watching me, I made several shallow dives aiming my reflector gunsight at the whitecaps on the waves. When Carey thought my runs in to the target looked OK, he directed me by R/T (radio-telephone) to begin firing passes. I turned the gun firing button on the control column to "fire," and when I was lined up with my selected whitecap, pressed the trigger. The aircraft shuddered as each gun belched fire; in the cockpit it sounded like a sudden blast of escaping steam. My bullets, happily, hit where they were aimed, sending up little geysers of spray. I had always been a good shot with a rifle, pistol and shotgun—why not with machine guns as well. I made four or five more firing passes before my guns were empty (total ammo load permitted 14 seconds of continuous fire), then we headed back home to Debden. Cordite fumes were fairly strong in my cockpit—a kind of stimulating odor, I thought.

After four days at the Debden OTU, and with only 7 hours and 40 minutes flying time in the Hurricane, I was suddenly posted back to No. 71 Eagle Squadron at Martlesham Heath. Why I wasn't permitted to complete the six-week course, no one at the OTU knew. I had only fired "splash" twice, had never fired at a drogue target, and actually I'd only had a little over an hour of simulated dogfighting in the Hurricane. So, all in all, my total RAF flying time when I went operational was about 64 hours.

Frank Carey came to see me as I was checking out of the Officers' Mess. "I'm sorry, Bill," he said. "We both know you need a hell of a lot more Hurricane time before you'll be ready for combat. That's a crazy outfit you're being assigned to. They all lack proper training. I called George Brown, he's an English flight commander in 71 Squadron, and asked him to take you under his wing for a bit. George is a well experienced fighter pilot. He'll show you the ropes. One word about gunnery before you go. Don't waste ammo on long range firing. If an enemy kite fills your whole windscreen, the range is right and the deflection is nil. Give him a good squirt and you've got him. Take care, Bill, and don't get your ass shot off by some bloody Hun bastard. Keep your eyes open and your head on a swivel. Good luck to you, Yank."

3. Baptism to Air Battle

Back at Martlesham Heath, Flight Lieutenant George Brown took me under his wing—and some wing it proved to be. We spent at least five hours in the air the first day doing formation flying, aerobatics, simulated attacks on bombers, and simulated fighter-to-fighter dogfighting. George was a very tough instructor. He was a stickler for perfection, and nothing less than perfection suited him. He was a strict, hard man who demanded every ounce of effort from the pilots of his flight. In summary, he knew his business as a fighter pilot, and he expected us to damned well know ours. I can truthfully say that I thought George was a bit rough on me in the beginning, but now, when I look back on those days, I sure as hell am glad he was. I survived the war, and I'm certain that George's strong guidance was one of the primary reasons. Too bad every new boy in a fighter squadron didn't get a George Brown for his flight commander. I might add that George, too, survived the war.

No. 71 "Eagle" Squadron was then equipped with the Hawker Hurricane Mk IIA fighter. This aircraft had a 1,280 hp, two-stage supercharged, Rolls-Royce Merlin XX engine, which produced a top speed of 340 mph at 22,000 feet and a service ceiling of 32,000 feet. Like the Mark I model, the Mark IIA was armed with eight .303-caliber Browning machine guns capable of 14 seconds of continuous fire. Since its flying characteristics were pretty much the same as the Mark I version, I had no big problem checking out in the Hurricane IIA.

Our combat aircraft were camouflage-painted green and brown on the upper surfaces, with a pale sky-blue on the undersides. No. 71 Squadron's identification code letters—XR—were painted on the fuselage side in light gray, just in front of the RAF roundel insignia. A single letter was painted just aft of the roundel, indicating to which flight—A or B—the aircraft belonged. For example, my Hurricane was code lettered XR-D, meaning the aircraft was assigned to No. 71 Squadron's A Flight according to an alphabetical designation; Hurricane XR-T belonged to 71 Squadron, B Flight.

Our propeller spinners were painted white, indicating that our unit belonged to No. 11 Group. Around the rear part of the fuselage, just in front of the tail plane, was a broad white-painted band, which meant that our squadron and group were assigned to Fighter Command. Fighter Command was formed by a number of groups, each group being responsible for the air defense of its geographically assigned area of Great Britain. No. 11 Group's area was the eastern coastal region, including the city of London.

Each RAF fighter squadron was authorized sixteen aircraft, with generally a couple of spares, and eighteen to twenty pilots. In the organization of No. 71 Squadron, our ground crews were all English. The squadron intelligence officer, the "spy," was Flying Officer J. Roland Robinson (a Member of Parliament, later Lord Martonmere), and both flight commanders, Flight Lieutenants George Brown, DFC, and R. C. "Wilkie" Wilkinson, DFM and Bar, were also British. So was Tann, the adjutant. Squadron Leader Bill Taylor, Flight Lieutenant A. S. "Doc" Osborne, our medic, and the other squadron pilots were Americans.

My first roommate in the officers' quarters at Martlesham was Pilot Officer H. S. Fenlaw. Fenlaw married a lovely English girl, but shortly thereafter was shot down and killed in action. My next roommate was an eighteen-year-old boy named Thomas P. McGerty. Tommy was a happy-go-lucky kid, and we soon became close buddies. Not wanting to worry his parents in California by telling them he was an RAF fighter pilot, Tommy told them he was a Link instrument trainer instructor. He had a cute little blonde English girl friend whom he loved very much. To me alone he would reveal all his innermost secret hopes and dreams of the future for the two of them when the war was over. Tommy asked my advice many times—should they marry now or later? I suggested they wait; she couldn't have been more than sixteen or seventeen years old.

The station commander at Martlesham was an elderly First World War pilot, Wing Commander Vivian Ian Parker, DFC, AFC, who, because of his somewhat odd first name, we nicknamed Lovely Parker. Although he was much older than the rest of us, he took an active part in nearly everything we pilots did, especially in our frequent mess beatups.

One night in particular, when we were enjoying a really rowdy party, old Lovely, bent out of shape with giggle soup, lay on top of an upright piano near the bar door, and when anyone entered the room he poured beer on their heads. After awhile, in fun, several of our guys grabbed Parker off the piano, pushed him to the floor, rolled him up in the large anteroom rug, and sat on him. We had a little slender fellow in the squadron named Oscar Coen; periodically Oscar would crawl down into the rolled rug and give Lovely a bottle of beer to keep him quiet. When it got late, everyone buzzed off to bed and Lovely Parker was completely forgotten, snoozing away in his rug.

Early next morning several airmen mess attendants came into the anteroom to clean up the shambles we'd created the night before. Seeing the rolled-up rug, one of them gave it a swift kick to start it unrolling. A grunt and several muffled swear words were heard before the amazed airmen released the well hung-over station commander from his prison.

Lovely Parker had one bad habit that always got him into trouble. When he got a bit in his cups, he delighted in knocking out all the mess light bulbs with pool balls. This cost him several pounds and a reprimand when word of his escapades occasionally reached No. 11 Group Headquarters. Other than that, he was a first-rate station commander, always making certain his troops, both airmen and officers, got the very best of base services. Wing Commander Parker was no longer on flying status, but I know his heart flew with each one of us. He saw us off on squadron missions, wishing us "good luck and good hunting," and he was always there on the tarmac waiting for us when we returned.

One night in early May we were bombed by a lone Ju.88. The enemy bomber came in fast and low, dropping a stick of half a dozen HE (high explosive) bombs before it pulled up into the darkness and headed for its home base in occupied France. Luckily no one was injured, but the station parachute shop was destroyed, and our squadron's single Harvard (AT-6) aircraft was blown to bits. A couple of days after this incident George Brown told Squadron Leader Taylor that he considered me now operational. For the next several weeks I would fly as George's number two wingman on combat sorties. So the day had finally arrived; I was now combat ready.

I won't try to tell you that I wasn't scared, because I was. These guys were playing for keeps in this war. One mistake and you were dead for a hell of a long time. There was a poster in our pilot's ready room that outlined the Ten Commandments for Fighter Pilots. These commandments were designed to keep a guy from getting his hide punched full of bullet holes, and I made a special effort to memorize every one of them.

TEN COMMANDMENTS FOR FIGHTER PILOTS

1. Never fly straight and level for more than 30 seconds in the combat area.

2. Always keep a sharp look-out for enemy fighters. Keep your finger out and your head on a swivel. Watch for the enemy in the sun.

3. Height gives you the initiative. Don't waste it.

4. Always turn and face the attacking enemy.

5. Make your decisions promptly. It is better to act quickly, even though your tactics are not the best.

6. When diving to attack, always leave a portion of your formation above to act as top cover.

7. Wait until you see the whites of your enemy's eyes. Fire short bursts of one or two seconds, and only when your gunsight is definitely "on" the target.

8. While shooting, think of nothing else. Brace the whole of your body, have both hands on the control stick, concentrate on your gunsight and the target.

9. Go in quickly—punch hard—get out!

10. Initiative, aggression, air discipline, and team work are words that mean something in air fighting.

Several other members of the Eagle Squadron got "nervous in the service" and chickened out. In such cases the RAF quietly removed them from the squadron, released them from British service, and sent them back to the United States without any disciplinary action. Their service records were simply marked "returned home." And you'd be surprised to know how many of these characters, once they got safely home, shot a terrific line about what bloody great heroes they were. One of them even expounded his glorious "war experiences" in a ghost-written book and got it published! Well, I guess it takes all kinds. I did feel sorry for some of them, especially those who were really good guys, but just hadn't the intestinal fortitude to do a fighter pilot's job.

My first operational missions weren't much to talk about, just ship convoy patrols. When a British convoy sailing in the English Channel passed through our assigned sector, between Clacton and Great Yarmouth, we were directed to maintain a fighter cover of two aircraft over it. Convoy patrols were monotonous—just boring a hole in the sky over and around the ships for a couple of hours two or three times a day.

Once in a while our sector controller would call us on the R/T: "Parson Blue Section. Heads up. Two bogies approaching from the northeast, seven miles. Vector 055, Angels 8, Buster!" (This message, translated, meant that two unknown aircraft were approaching our convoy position, seven miles distant. We were to fly a course of 055 degrees at 8,000 feet at a fast speed to intercept the bogies.) The sector controller obtained this information from his Radio Direction Finder electronic scanner, which was the original version of search radar. This intercept action caused a little excitement while it lasted; however, the bogies usually turned out to be some of our own aircraft—or a large flock of birds picked up on the RDF screens.

In several instances the bogies did turn out to be enemy aircraft bent on attacking the ship convoy. One day a Ju.88 came swooping in on our convoy, flying just below a layer of low clouds and scud. This time there was no radar warning; the enemy bomber was too low to be detected on the RDF screen. George and I knew the convoy was being bombed only when we saw white geysers of water in the sea made by exploding bombs. George notified sector control of the attack; then he told me to stay above the cloud layer, which was only about 100 feet thick, while he began chasing the Hun beneath the clouds.

George took a squirt at the Ju.88, which caused the German pilot to climb away from him up through the cloud for protection—and there I was waiting. I fired at the enemy kite and down through the cloud he went, where George was waiting to squirt him again. This up and down through the cloud layer happened several times as we chased the Hun back toward the French coast. About this same time our controller directed us to break off the attack. Ten enemy fighters were in the area and trying to make an intercept on us. When last seen, the Ju.88 was limping home on two smoking engines, so we were credited with damaging this enemy aircraft. The whole episode, though it lasted only about ten minutes, was most exciting for me. The Ju.88 was a fairly fast aircraft. I'm sure if we had been flying the faster Spitfires we would have caught it quickly and shot it down.

These convoy patrols could really get dangerous. The ships' anti-aircraft gunners fired warning shots at you if you got too close to their vessels, even when they knew you were friendly aircraft. If the ships were attacked, they fired at everything that flew. Therefore, it was a good idea to always patrol at about 2,000 feet and circle at a distance of half a mile from the ships. During bad weather we sometimes had to circle lower and closer, which, when the gunners had quick trigger fingers, could get a bit sticky.

In addition to the convoy patrols, our squadron stood alert readiness from dawn to dusk daily, usually with two sections of two fighter aircraft each. During the hours of darkness we were released, while the night fighter squadrons assumed the readiness status. In England, especially during the spring and summer months, our duty day was long—from 4:30 A.M. to about 11 P.M. With the seasonal change to shorter fall and winter days, the night fighter guys got the long-duty nights.

Upon radar detection of approaching bogies or bandits, depending upon the number of suspected enemy aircraft, our sections would be scrambled to make the intercept. RAF Fighter Command operations directives allowed two minutes to get a section of two fighters off the ground, three minutes for a flight of six aircraft, and seven minutes for a full squadron of twelve aircraft. This time allowance began upon receipt of the telephoned scramble order and terminated the moment the airborne fighter leader checked in with his sector controller.

Our fighters were parked in concrete and sand-bagged dispersal bays around the edge of the airfield. Upon receipt of a scramble order and the blaring sound of the Klaxon horn, a mad rush of pilots to their aircraft ensued. The airmen fitters kept their assigned aircrafts' engines warmed up all the time the squadron was on alert readiness, and, when they heard the Klaxon, they immediately started up the engines. When the pilots arrived—usually out of breath after running from the dispersal hut to the dispersal bays—they climbed into their cockpits, hurriedly strapped on their parachutes and Sutton harness, pulled on their flying helmets, and poured the coal to their engines. A red Verey cartridge flare, fired from the control tower, arched into the sky to warn all other aircraft in the vicinity of the airfield to stay clear, that a scramble was in progress.

In those days our airfields were all grass covered—no runways—so the scrambled fighters came blasting straight ahead out of their dispersal bays. Things could get pretty hairy at that moment, especially when it was a flight or squadron scramble with everyone taking off in various directions. A scramble takeoff sometimes looked like organized confusion, and I guess that's really what it was, but we did get into the air quickly when every second counted. The excitement of the moment reached its absolute peak when you launched out of your bay and went blasting at full throttle across the grass and there, roaring almost head-on toward you, came some other sod who was being scrambled from the opposite side of the airfield. Some near misses and some prangs did occur, but not as often as you would think.

Many times on a scramble you didn't bother to hook up your parachute or Sutton harness until you were airborne. During the first part of the war we were issued some parachutes that caused several unnecessary and tragic deaths to our guys. These parachutes were detachable from the parachute harness. Consequently, the fighter pilots would wear their harness when on alert, leaving the parachute pack in the cockpit seat. When a scramble occurred, the pilot would rush to his aircraft, jump in the cockpit, and sometimes forget to snap his parachute pack to the harness. Some of these pilots were shot down and bailed out without their parachutes.

My first use of a parachute came early one bright morning when I took off in a repaired Hurricane for an air test flight. At about 8,000 feet the engine suddenly began to surge, the coolant temperature went up to the peg, and just before the engine seized, it began to burn. There was only one reasonable thing to do—get the hell out of that burning bird, and quickly. I rapidly undid my Sutton harness, squawking "May Day" over the R/T a couple of times before I pulled the radio plug and oxygen hose connection. Rolling the elevator trim full forward, I pushed back the hood, and rolled the Hurricane over on her back. As soon as we were upside down, I released the back pressure on the control column, which popped me out of the cockpit when the aircraft's nose snapped upward. With a sudden blast of slipstream I was carried clear of the fuselage, missing the tail plane by just inches. (Many bailing out fighter pilots are seriously injured or killed when their bodies strike either the stabilizer or vertical fin.)

For a moment I fell through the silent sky, the earth below me spinning crazily. Then I pulled the ripcord D-ring and my chute streamed and blossomed open over my head. At that moment I realized I'd done everything to get out of the burning kite exactly right without thinking—the result of my excellent RAF training at SFTS. I was somewhat panicked at first, but now the worst was over and I was only slightly singed. Swaying gently beneath my slowly descending, beautiful parachute calmed my nerves considerably.

When I reached the ground in a farmer's pasture I hit harder than I thought I would, the billowing chute dragging me some twenty yards before I could spill and collapse the thing. The burning Hurricane and my open chute had been seen by the troops at Martlesham Heath. Within a few minutes the meat wagon (ambulance), Doc Osborne, and his medics arrived on the scene.

"Are you hurt?" Doc asked.

"Don't think so," said I, gingerly moving my arms and legs.

"Well, you'll hurt later. Here, drink this," and Doc poured out half a water glass of whiskey for me. With that, he and his medics sat down beside me on the grass and we proceeded to kill Doc's jug then and there. I wasn't feeling any pain at all when we finally arrived back at the airfield in the meat wagon.

My first fight with enemy fighters occurred on an evening in late May, 1941. We got a squadron scramble and, after climbing to about 12,000 feet, were vectored out across the Channel toward the French coast. Here we ran into a squadron of German Messerschmitt Me.109Es patrolling their side of the Channel coast. We were some 3,000 or 4,000 feet above the Huns when Bill Taylor ordered us to attack. Being a new boy, I was totally unprepared, confused, frightened, and in near panic. One moment our squadron was flying in formation; the next moment they were all diving down to mix it up with the Krauts, leaving me sitting alone above the milling gaggle of fighting aircraft.

I remember that I cursed myself for holding back, even if it was just momentarily; then I too dived down into the melee. A 109 crossed my gunsight and I fired a long burst at it, without results. Range too far. Remember what Carey told you—short range, fill the windscreen, then fire! Now a stream of tracer bullets went whizzing past my cockpit hood—little glowing white-hot balls of fire—but I took no hits. I yanked the control column hard over to the left and back, and, hitting a high-speed stall, went into a snapping spin.

By the time I'd recovered, well below the flight, I was all alone a couple of thousand feet above the channel waters. To be very frank, I'd had the bejesus scared out of me. My knees were actually shaking with fright. My grip on the control column was so tight that my fingers began to feel numb. The only thing I could think of to do was to get the hell out of there, fast, and safely home in one piece. I believe at that moment, for just that moment, I turned yellow, really yellow, a coward.

Flying back to the airfield I told myself I'd had enough of this air combat; I'd get a transfer back to the infantry somehow. Yes, I'd gladly carry that damned 3-inch mortar again from here to hell and back. Inwardly ashamed, I landed safely at Martlesham, the ignoble hero returned. I felt terrible inside, sort of sick to my stomach. Never in all my life had I experienced the anguish of such fear. I was thoroughly disgusted with myself. Maybe it would be best for the Royal Air Force to post me "returned home."

Actually, the fight between the two squadrons lasted for only a few minutes—it had gotten too dark. No one was shot down on either side, not even damaged, so it really wasn't much of a fight at all. After the brief fight Uncle Sam Mauriello, joining up with the squadron to fly home, noticed they were going in the wrong direction. A quick glance through the darkening evening sky toward his wingman revealed that the other guy was flying an aircraft with a big black and white cross painted on the fuselage side, an Me.109! A startled glance to the other side confirmed to Sam that he was flying right in the middle of the German squadron. The Krauts must have seen the RAF roundel insignia on Sam's Hurricane at about the same moment, because everyone suddenly broke formation and scattered all over the sky. Uncle Sam did a split-S (roll on your back and pull the control stick back, dive down and pull out in the opposite direction) and headed for home, flat out, with six or seven Huns after him. After a brief chase they turned back toward France, probably short of gas. Sam's face was sort of green when he got back to Martlesham and told his story of the incident.

Well, my face was sort of green, too, after my poor showing in my first air combat. Nobody, however, seemed to have noticed my "strategic withdrawal" from the fight, for which I was very thankful. Following our debriefings by Robbie Robinson, the intelligence type, I went quietly to my quarters, lay face down on my bed still fully clothed, and silently sobbed myself to sleep. I just couldn't believe myself to be a coward. I'd been in action against the enemy before. I'd been shot at many times, and bombed several times as well. Why should this terrible fear of air combat suddenly come upon me now?

After a fitful night, my dreams filled with shot-down aircraft—all on fire and burning furiously and I, the pilot, couldn't get out—I awoke at dawn, my entire body covered by a cold sweat. Sitting on the edge of my bed, my aching head cupped in my shaking hands, I began anew to silently curse myself as a gutless bastard. "You can't quit," I told myself. "You've got to get hold of yourself. If these other guys can do it, so can you. Those goddam Squareheads aren't any better trained than you are, and they're probably just as scared, too. You are not going to quit, you stupid, yellow son of a bitch!" And I hit myself hard in the jaw—not just once, but several times until it really hurt.

I was not scheduled to go on readiness until noon that day. After a cold shower and a bit of breakfast, I walked out on the airfield to the squadron dispersal hut. There I checked the Form 400 on my Hurricane, telling the maintenance officer I was going to take her up for a flight of an hour or so. The day was beautiful and sunny, with a high, clear blue sky.

After takeoff I climbed and climbed and climbed toward the heavens, leveling out at about 25,000 feet. There I flew in a great wide circle, being able to look down from my height on a large part of eastern England, the whole width of the Channel, and the distant French coast. And there I gave myself a furious tongue-lashing. I talked to myself and I talked to God. Yes, I really prayed for Him to give me the mental and physical strength I needed to face my ordeal with courage. At that moment, in the high untrespassed sanctity of space, I believe I really did put out my hand and touch the face of God. A great calmness seemed to descend upon me; I could feel a powerful strength surge through my body. And from that moment I knew my prayers had been answered. I was a new man, a man reborn.

I laughed aloud at my past fears of combat flying. The wings of my Hurricane began to feel like they were a part of my body, gracefully flashing and wheeling through the bright sky. The Merlin engine began to throb in unison with the quickened blood that pounded through my veins. The absolute thrill of flying settled firmly upon my whole being, and I became one with my aircraft.

Gently I turned my Hurricane over on her back and began my descent in a long series of slow rolls, entered the airfield circuit, and made a wizard landing—not even one small bounce, a grease job. I was free—completely free—of my fears. Now I could proudly hold up my head and look any SOB right in the eye. I knew I had the guts, once again, to stand up against anything. Bring on those Hun bastards! Have no fear, Dunn is here!

Throughout the month of June our squadron continued combat operations by providing convoy patrols, alert readiness fighters for the home defense of England, participation in fighter sweeps against the German Air Force in France and Belgium, escort fighters for our bomber forces, and air strikes against targets of opportunity in enemy-occupied territory.

Some squadron personnel changes occurred during that same month. Bill Taylor, our squadron leader, resigned his RAF commission and returned to the United States Navy. I don't know the exact reason for this, but I was told that some of our fair-haired boys thought Taylor was too tough on them, too severe in his ideas of discipline. As a squadron leader he properly, in my opinion, maintained his senior position and didn't mix socially with the squadron junior officers. The old military adage, "Familiarity breeds contempt," is true, and Taylor knew it to be so. Anyway, somebody must have bent the ear of the AOC (Air Officer Commanding No. 11 Group). So Bill Taylor was told he was too old at thirty-six years of age to lead a fighter squadron and he was offered a job in Training Command. If he refused the job, the AOC said he would accept Taylor's resignation of his commission. Taylor said, "the hell with it," and was replaced by an Englishman, Squadron Leader Henry de Clifford Anthony Woodhouse, whom we called "Paddy."

Personally, I liked Bill Taylor as our squadron leader and got on well with him. I thought he did a hell of a fine job organizing a bunch of odds and sods like us into a fairly good fighter squadron, especially since ninety percent of our people had absolutely no basic military discipline or military flight training. This incident was the first I knew that we had a clique of any sort in the squadron—"the fair-haired boys," as we began to call them. Once I became aware of this clique, I could easily observe that they used political influence to gain promotions in rank and the news media to gain publicity for their "heroic" war endeavors. Later, the more appropriate term "brown-nosers" defined their activities. If you didn't belong to their clique, you were cut out of the pattern and pushed into the background. I would soon encounter these "boys" myself.

Jimmy Crowley, the ex-Seaforth corporal, whom I'd left at Tern Hill, joined the squadron. With Jimmy came Michael G. McPharlin—"Wee Mike," as we called him—who became a very good friend of mine. Ken Taylor was killed in a flying accident. Bill Hall, Bill Geiger, and Jack Fessler were shot down and captured. Fenlaw and Virgil Olson were killed in action. Several others lost their stomach for the war and were "returned home." About mid-June I graduated from George Brown's protecting wing and was made a section leader—the leader of a two-aircraft element. Tommy McGerty became my wingman. In the latter part of June our squadron moved from Martlesham Heath airfield to North Weald airfield, near Epping in Essex.

Early one morning we got a squadron scramble against a gaggle of Hun bombers, Ju.88s and He.111s, coming across the Channel. At about 20,000 feet we met a couple of squadrons of escorting Me.109s over the Thames Estuary. We were still climbing eastward, into the bright sun, when two 109s came streaking down past our formation, their guns blazing at us. Now this was an old Hun trick, a bait for some eager guy to break formation and go after them. We'd all been warned not to give chase to these first two 109s. If you did break, there were two more Squareheads right on your backside, boxing you in between them.

One of our squadron pilots, a Polish-American named Mike Kolendorski, unluckily took the bait this day. As the first two 109s flashed past, Mike whipped his Hurricane around in a fast turn to get on their tails. The second pair of diving 109s were on Mike's tail in a moment, both firing their cannons and machine guns. A warning was shouted by someone over the R/T, but it came too late. Mike's Hurricane was hit, and I assume Mike was killed in the cockpit because he made no attempt to bail out. I watched Mike's Hurricane, spinning down on its back, until it crashed into the estuary thousands of feet below us. Mistakes like that in combat result, as in this instance, in a sudden and useless death. It was all over in less time than it takes to write about it.

The German bomber formation, now coming under attack by a half-dozen RAF Hurricane and Spitfire squadrons, turned tail and headed flat out for home. Their Me.109 escort, short of gas, followed in their wake. Our squadron, still climbing below the battle, never got into action that day, except for Mike.

Some of those squadron scrambles really gave a guy a bad case of the brown-ring twitch. When the initial scramble order was received you might, as an example, be told by the controller that there were fifteen plus bandits at 8,000 feet—which weren't too bad odds when you were intercepting with a full squadron. However, after you were airborne the controller would come on the R/T with more tactical information concerning the incoming enemy force: "and twenty plus at 10,000 feet, forty plus at 15,000 feet, and thirty plus at 20,000 feet." Great, now there were over a hundred enemy aircraft reported in the raiding force, and you are climbing out to attack them with all twelve of your squadron fighters! The odds were eight plus to one!

One instance I'll never forget was when the enemy formation totalled 360 plus aircraft—bombers and fighters—and we had 10 RAF intercepting squadrons scrambled. The end result of that great air battle, which was furiously fought just off the east coast of Kent, cost the Germans 185 aircraft shot down within thirty minutes. RAF losses were about 40 fighters, but well over half of our pilots were safely recovered by parachutes and air/sea rescue launches. Only three Hun bomber aircraft managed to cross the English coast near Ramsgate, and they jettisoned their bombs in open fields. All the remaining Krauts turned tail before our fighter onslaught, flying "balls out" back to France. I took a squirt at a couple of bombers, a Ju.88 and a Do.17, during this fiasco, but only managed to knock some chips off the first one and send the second home with smoking engines.

My first big day came on 2 July 1941 when our squadron formed part of the fighter escort for twelve Blenheim bombers on Circus 29 (the code name for a daylight bomber raid) to bomb the Lille electric power station in occuped France. Just before reaching Lille we were attacked by two enemy squadrons of Me.109Es and 109Fs. Their attacks continued during the bombers' run to the target and for about thirty minutes after, until the French coast was crossed near Gravelines. Since we were flying Hurricanes we formed the close escort for the Blenheims. High cover escort was provided by the faster Spitfires of our fighter wing.

I was flying the Red 2 position, with Squadron Leader Paddy Woodhouse leading, when I saw an Me.109E diving through the bomber formation at about 6,000 feet, squirting at the Blenheims as he dove. The 109 pilot made his break to port, right in front of me, maybe 75 or 100 yards away. I jammed the throttle wide open and, attacking the Me.109 from the port quarter, fired one burst of four seconds and three bursts of two seconds each. At about 50 yards range (the Hun kite filled my whole windscreen) I could see my machine gun bullets striking all over the German's fuselage and wingroot. Then he began to smoke. I continued my attack down to 3,500 feet, again firing at point-blank range. Now the 109 began burning furiously, dived straight down to the ground, where it crashed with a hell of an explosion near a crossroad. Scrub one Squarehead!

People have, on occasion, asked me what it felt like, inside me, to shoot down and kill an enemy pilot. To be truthful, I was elated— elated that I'd shot the bastard down before he could shoot me down. Of course I was very pleased with my first victory—that's what I was hired to do—and, happily, this victory was confirmed by Pete Proven- zano and Bob Mannix, two other Eagle Squadron pilots.

I should mention here that the RAF was very careful concerning victory claims, which they classified as "confirmed destroyed," "uncon- firmed," and "probable." To get a confirmed victory the enemy aircraft had to be seen to crash, or to blow up or break up in the air, or to be forced to descend and be captured, or the pilot had to be seen to bail out—and this confirmation required the action to be witnessed by pilots other than the one who claimed the victory. An unconfirmed victory indicated that an enemy aircraft was claimed to be shot down, but only the pilot who shot it down witnessed the action. A probable victory occurred when an enemy aircraft was presumably shot down, but no one actually saw it crash, so its destruction was considered uncertain. There was also a "damaged" category, which simply meant that the Hun had some holes punched in his aircraft, but was not shot down.

Confirmed victories were hard to come by in the RAF, since every- one in a dogfight was either shooting at some poor sod or trying to keep his own rear end from being shot off. RAF Fighter Command

Headquarters was the final authority for approving all victory claims, based on written and witnessed combat reports. I don't believe many victory claims were willfully misrepresented or exaggerated by RAF fighter pilots. Of course, we had 16mm gun cameras installed in our fighters which automatically operated when the guns were fired. They helped to confirm some victories, providing they were serviceable and the deflection firing angle wasn't too great.

The German system for approving victory claims, so I have been told by German fighter pilots, was considerably different from that of the RAF. As an example, a Hun fighter pilot—who didn't need a witness—could make a confirmed, an unconfirmed, a probable, and a damaged claim, and be credited with a victory for each. Enemy aces attained high scores because they, being considered the best shots in their staffels (squadrons), did most of the shooting, while other less experienced staffel pilots covered the ace's tail. This system made some very high-scoring enemy aces, but was hard on their wingmen who, trying to defend their leaders, got shot down.

It's not my intent to dispute the validity of their victory claims; however, one Luftwaffe ace claimed thirteen victories during one engagement. Now, let's be reasonable; their guns didn't carry any more ammunition than ours, so at that rate he expended one second of ammo per victory, which is hard to believe. Several others claimed seventeen and eighteen victories in a single day. One German ace, following an engagement over the English Channel, claimed he had shot down three Spitfires; upon landing at his home base it was noted that his guns had not been fired and that all his ammunition was still in the aircraft. According to Luftwaffe records, 94 German aces shot down a total of 13,997 Allied aircraft. Some hundred German pilots claimed a hundred to a hundred fifty victories each, fifteen of them over two hundred, and two of them over three hundred victories. With the enemy scoring like that, how in the hell did we win? Most of the top Allied aces scored about forty times.

Following my first confirmed victory I ran head-on into our squadron's "fair-haired boys" clique. Gussy Daymond, a pilot from California, and I had both gotten kills on Circus 29—the very first victories for the Eagle Squadron. My victory, according to the official combat report, occurred at 12:35 hours and Gussy's occurred at 12:40 hours, clearly giving me the credit of being the first Eagle Squadron pilot to shoot down an enemy aircraft. However, since I was not a member of the clique, my claim was played down in favor of Gussy's. I have never believed that Gussy had anything to do with this, although he was one of the clique. It didn't really make a hell of a lot of difference at that time, but it did make a difference in my later military career. (A number of years afterward, when military aviation historians were reviewing Eagle Squadron combat records, the Historical Branch of the RAF at Air Ministry did confirm—and the combat reports are still on file today—that I was, without a doubt, the first Eagle Squadron pilot to shoot down an enemy aircraft.)

Four days later, on 6 July, while flying in the fighter escort for six Stirling bombers on Circus 35 to bomb the Lille steel factories, I saw a Hurricane from No. 306 (Polish) Squadron beating up an Me.109E that refused to go down. The Polish pilot, flying about 250 yards behind the 109, was pouring a steady stream of machine gun bullets at his target and I could see he was getting hits on the German kite. Since I was closer and slightly above the 109, I thought I'd give my Polish comrade some help. Turning onto the Kraut's tail, I fired two good bursts into it from a range of less than 50 yards. Heavy black smoke began to pour from the enemy fighter, which then dived straight toward the ground, crashing in a ball of flame. This action took place at about 12,000 feet over Merville, France, at 14:30 hours.

The German fighters kept up their attacks on our formation until we reached the French coast on our way back to England. None of the big four-engine Stirling bombers were lost, but a couple of Spitfires and several Hurricanes were shot down. The Huns lost eight Me.109Es and 109Fs, plus a half-dozen or so damaged in the fighting. This was the first time I'd ever escorted Stirlings, so I flew up alongside of one to look it over. The tail gunner in his turret gave me a friendly wave. At this time I noticed he was wearing an army steel helmet over his leather flying helmet. With all the flak that was fired at the bombers, I think I would have sat on the tin hat if I had been that gunner.

The Polish Hurricane from 306 Squadron kept following me all the way back to our airfield at North Weald, where he too landed. At our intelligence debriefing I met the Polish pilot, Leon H. Jaugsch, a real nice young fellow who had fought against the German enemy since the day they had attacked Poland. Leon told me that he had almost, by accident, shot me down when I suddenly got between the Me.109 and his Hurricane. The armorers noted that Leon had fired over 1,200 rounds at the 109, and I had fired some 400 rounds, all of which must have made the Hun kite look like a sieve. We then prepared our combat reports together, giving them to Robbie, the squadron spy.

Next day Leon and I were each credited with half a victory by Fighter Command. There was some speculation, but I don't know to this day how true it was, that the German pilot was Reichmarschall Hermann Göring's nephew. Major Adolph Galland, the famous enemy ace who was leading the Hun fighter formation at that time, later said it was about that date, time, and place that the nephew's Me.109E was shot down. That, of course, is no real confirmation that Leon and I shot him down, but it is possible we did. (Leon H. Jaugsch now lives in Los Alamitos, California, and after forty years we still correspond with each other.)

On the morning of 21 July, on Circus 54, again close escort for Stirling bombers attacking the Lille steel factories, I was leading White Section. Enemy 88mm flak guns had been banging away at us continuously ever since we'd crossed the French coast, some of the ugly black bursts coming close enough for us to hear the crack of the exploding shells. Most of the shells, however, burst behind and slightly below our Circus formation, causing little or no damage. Over the target area the flak increased in accuracy and intensity, which was an indication that enemy fighters were not yet in position to attack us. Late scramble, no doubt.

Shortly after the Stirlings had dropped their bombs and we were leaving the Lille target area in a shambles of bomb bursts, shock waves, billowing dust, smoke and debris, I spotted two Me.109Fs climbing up fast behind our formation to attack the bombers from below. The time was about 08:35 hours and we were flying at 16,000 feet.

I pulled my Hurricane around in a steep turn with White 2, Tommy McGerty, flying just off my starboard wing. One Squarehead saw us coming to attack, took violent evasive action, and breaking away went into a fast, steep dive. We couldn't hope to catch him with our slower Hurricanes. We fared well enough against the Me.109Es, but the newer 109Fs were just too fast for us. Spitfires would have gotten him.

The second Kraut took no evasive action other than a shallow climbing turn. I attacked him from the port beam at 50 or 60 yards, firing two bursts from my eight machine guns into him. The 109's rudder and port elevator were completely shot off, and its starboard elevator was ripped to shreds by my blast of bullets. At first the Hun went into a gentle dive, which soon steepened until the 109 was falling fast on its back. The pilot jettisoned his hood, bailing out at a very high speed, his chute undoubtedly giving him a hell of a jerk when it popped open. At least the lucky SOB got out of his busted kite. I didn't actually see the Me.109 go in, but there could be no doubt that, pilotless, it did hit the deck some 14,000 feet below—another confirmed kill. My gun-camera filmed the whole episode.

In the space of the few seconds this action took, Tommy McGerty lost me, or I lost him, one or the other. This losing each other in a hostile sky could prove very dangerous for both of us, since, as a fighter section or team, we provided mutual defensive protection for each other. I'd find out what happened to Tommy when I got back to North Weald. More than likely he didn't or couldn't stay with me during several of my more violent maneuvers after the 109. That is how a lot of wingmen are lost and shot down in combat—the result of not sticking close to their leaders during a fight.

I should mention here that I was never able to black myself out in a violent maneuver; gray out once in a while, but never black out. And I have done some maneuvers that actually bent the wings of my fighter. Later some RAF doctors put me through a series of tests to determine why. Their decision was that my physical build, stocky, and a certain tightening of my stomach and chest muscles when I did some violent maneuver, contributed to my not blacking out.

Speaking about violent maneuvers, one time I got this Fokker on my tail—the Fokker was flying a Messerschmitt 109—and I couldn't get rid of him. We were both turning as tight as we could, pulling streamers off our wingtips. He couldn't get his deflection shot at me, nor could I get a shot at him, so around and around we went. I decided we couldn't keep this up forever. A vertical reversement would give him a squirt at me, so, to put an end to this fiasco, I yanked the stick back hard and kicked bottom rudder. I haven't the slightest idea of what happened next, except it was bloody violent. My Hurricane's hood ripped off, banging me on the head and taking my flying helmet, goggles, and oxygen mask with it. All the fabric on the left side of the fuselage tore loose, streaming out behind my aircraft. My face was cut up, and my left eye was swelling shut and filled with blood. Yes, I lost the Fokker

in the 109 off my tail; the Hun pilot probably figured I'd kill myself
without his help. By the grace of God, I made it safely back to England,
where Doc Osborne sewed me back together again.

In late July we got some good news. No. 71 "Eagle" Squadron was
to be equipped with Spitfires! We flew our old faithful and reliable
Hurricanes to Kenley airfield, where we picked up the Spitfire Mk IIAs
of another squadron that was getting the newest Spitfire MkVBs. That
was a day to be long remembered. None of us had ever flown a Spitfire,
but what the hell—read the pilots' notes (Air Publication 1565B), get
into the cockpit for a short familiarization check of the knobs and
switches, and then go. I wish you could have seen our squadron take
off! It was an unbelievable gaggle, with our Spits all over the sky.

The Spitfire was much cleaner, lighter, and touchier on its controls
than the Hurricane, so everyone was over-controlling for the first few
minutes. The Spit's Rolls-Royce Merlin XII 1,175 hp engine, using 100-
octane fuel, combined with its Rotol constant speed propeller, gave the
Spitfire II an airspeed of 370 mph at 17,000 feet, and a service ceiling
of 33,000 feet. Like our Hurricanes, the Spit IIs were armed with eight
.303 Browning machine guns, 300 rounds per gun.

Through his frantic and commendable endeavors, S/Ldr Paddy
Woodhouse finally got all of us roughly together in the same piece of
sky and headed back to North Weald in formation, if you can call a
batch of just-checked-out guys all flying in the same general direction
a formation. After circling the airfield at North Weald a couple of times
to really get the feel of my new Spitfire, I glided gently down to the
deck and set her down as lightly as a butterfly with sore feet.

4. For the King's Shilling

August proved to be a month of contrasting events—some good, some bad, some in between. To begin with the bad events, elderly Air Chief Marshal Sir Hugh "Boom" Trenchard, the father of the Royal Air Force and its first Chief of Staff, paid an inspection visit to No. 71 "Eagle" Squadron at North Weald, "To meet our very first American allies," he said. Well, we had a terrier-mix dog, our squadron mascot, named "Pipsqueak," who didn't approve of all the pomp and ceremony of this inspection nor of the inspecting officer. Commented Sir Hugh when he returned to the safety of Air Ministry's Adastral House, "That damned dog of the Americans ran up to me when I was taking the salute during their march past and bit me on the leg!" Pipsqueak was never awed by rank. Thank goodness the inspecting officer that day wasn't King George VI. Once, when the station commander was visiting our squadron dispersal hut, Pipsqueak urinated on the leg of the chair in which the group captain was seated.

Shortly after this a Hollywood movie called *Eagle Squadron* was to be previewed in London. The whole squadron was released from alert readiness and all the pilots directed to attend this first showing at a little theater near the Strand Palace Hotel. We were given two rows of reserved seats up front, the rest of the seats being filled with senior British military officers and some high-ranking civil service types. The movie was bloody awful, the plot was all BS; to be frank, it stank to high heaven.

In the theater darkness I noticed several Eagle Squadron pilots slouch down in their seats, and then, to escape notice, ducked low as they scooted up the aisle and out of the theater. In this manner I too departed the place. Entering the Strand Palace Hotel bar, I was amazed to find nearly all our guys bending an elbow there. I understand that when the film ended and the lights came on, not a single Eagle

Squadron pilot was in the theater. The film producer was a bit pissed off, uttering several unkind words about us.

Then one evening over a couple of drinks in the mess bar, I happened to mention that I didn't think the London balloon barrage was too successful a deterrent against Hun bombers. Someone else had a different opinion, which they stoutly defended by betting me a fiver (5-pound note) I couldn't fly through the balloons. This challenge, of course, was accepted—which in turn caused a flurry of side bets—all of this to be kept secret from our squadron leader, the wing commander, and the station commander.

The next morning I took off on the pretence of a flight test, circling some distance to the south of London and coming back in toward the city from the east over the Thames Estuary. The day was bright and sunny. All the balloons were up at varying altitudes. Some were between 2,000 and 7,000 feet, some were even higher, and somewhere between these heights and the deck were the steel cables that could, upon collision, tear an aircraft's wings off. Some even had explosive charges attached at intervals along the cable lengths. It was going to be a tricky attempt, and probably a bit stupid as well.

My plan was simple. I'd thought it all out logically. The Balloon Corps people had the whole London area well covered, including the River Thames. But they'd neglected one important area, the railway tracks that passed through the entire city. Since trains were continually passing over the tracks, they couldn't very well attach balloon cables between the rails. So down I dove, leveling out on the deck at the Thames mouth, and then at about twenty or thirty feet flying directly above the railway tracks along the river's side. I flew in this manner across the whole city of London—east to west—no sweat.

My action, however, caused the expected panic with the Balloon Corps people. They got my squadron identification markings as I flew past their sites, and soon their telephone conversation with North Weald's station headquarters grew hot and heavy. Who was that crazy SOB? What the hell did he think he was doing? Take disciplinary action against him the moment he lands, unless he kills himself first. Even the AOCs of 11 Group and Fighter Command got into the act.

Upon landing I was met by three irate, grim-faced types—our squadron leader, wing commander, and station commander—each of whom, at the same time, began tearing wide strips off me. Why did I do it, they roared in chorus at me? I told them why. I was placed on CB (confined to barracks) for a week, and the balloon people were ordered by Air Ministry to adjust their balloon dispersal to close this previously unrecognized gap in London's air defenses.

Wee Mike McPharlin, who had studied at a German university before the war and who could speak German fairly well, always seemed to collect a cloud of Me.109s when we were on a fighter sweep or bomber circus over France. We knew, of course, that the Krauts were listening to our radio conversations, and every once in awhile some English-speaking Squarehead would say a few naughty words to us on our R/T frequency—mostly concerning the legitimacy of our births. Wee Mike couldn't contain himself and would come right back at them in their own language with a steady flow of equally derogatory remarks, followed by an invitation to "get off their fat asses and come up and fight." I'd be willing to bet that every Hun squadron in occupied Western Europe knew of Wee Mike by name and reputation.

Well, the Squareheads did get off their fat asses several times, goaded by Wee Mike's challenges, engaging us in force. And a couple of times a half dozen of them found Wee Mike's kite in the melee, with Mike shouting over the R/T in English to us, "OK, you guys, I got them up! Now get them off my rear end before they punch it full of holes!" So we'd go to Mike's rescue. More than once three or four Huns, buzzing after him like mad hornets, chased Mike all the way back to England. They did manage, occasionally, to put a few holes in Mike's Spitfire. Mike, in turn, shot down a couple of their Me.109s and damaged several others. It was really funny to hear Wee Mike and the Germans, all on the same frequency, jabbering away at each other. (Later in the war, after Wee Mike McPharlin had transferred from the RAF to the U.S. Army Air Force, he was killed in action in France on 6 June 1944.)

Sometimes the German controllers would come up on our R/T frequencies and, in English, try to give us bum fixes and vectors for steering a course home when we were flying in very bad weather and required navigational assistance from our ground stations. They'd try to vector us out to sea where, they hoped, we'd run out of gas and go into the drink. English ground controllers got to know me pretty well by a little poem I'd say over the R/T when they'd ask me for a short transmission so they could get a fix on my aircraft. It went like this:

> Her has gone, she has went,
> Her has left I all alone.
> Must me never come to she?
> Must her always come to I?
> It can never was.

That verse screwed up the Hun controllers who, knowing I'd discovered their little game, would cuss me out. British controllers always came back to me with a coded reply, so we both immediately recognized each other.

One afternoon an elderly, distinguished officer arrived in a posh, chauffeur-driven Rolls-Royce automobile at North Weald's main gate. Since this officer wore the uniform of an air commodore (brigadier general), the sergeant of the guard turned out the full guard at "present arms," then notified the orderly officer and station commander of the presence on the base of this very senior officer. The usual panic reigned among the admin types when the air commodore strode into station headquarters. Heels clicked and salutes were exchanged, with the air commodore being invited into our group captain's office for a spot of tea.

"What can I do for you, sir?" asked our groupy sweetly.

"I'm assigned here," replied the elderly officer. "Here are my posting orders."

"Oh Christ," thought our groupy, "I've been fired! What did I do to deserve this?"

Groupy took the orders, read them, then his face turned white, then red, then he began to laugh. It seems the orders posted this old boy to the station as an assistant administration officer with the rank of pilot officer (second lieutenant). He came straight out of "civvy street"—a very wealthy man who wished to do his bit for king and country—so he had no idea of uniforms or rank insignias.

According to the story we were told later, when he received his direct commission he went to an exclusive London military tailor to obtain his uniforms. The tailor asked him what rank should be sewn on the cuff of the tunic sleeves, to which the old gentleman replied, "Just one stripe will be sufficient." The tailor, assuming from his customer's age and distinguished bearing that he most certainly was a senior officer, sewed on the single, broad stripe of an air commodore. The old boy was also provided with a senior officer's gold-emblazoned hat.

The air commodore was soon put straight, being busted on the spot to the lowly rank of P/O Admin by his highly amused group captain boss, who very gently explained the facts of military life to the embarrassed ex-air commodore. However, be that as it may, this old gentleman was the only junior officer I ever knew who had a chauffeur-driven Rolls-Royce at his beck and call. And, at fairly regular intervals, he would loan us fighter pilots both chauffeur and car to drive us to and from our favorite pub in town, where we usually had a riotous evening.

Sometimes, after a hard day of operational flying, when we were all dead tired, we'd hit the sack early for a good night's sleep before we were called to readiness again next dawn at 4:30 or 5 a.m. At other times, especially if the weather was bad or we got a squadron release from duty for twelve hours or so, a boisterous party would erupt in the officer's mess that you wouldn't believe. Someone would get on the blower (telephone) to a London contact—North Weald airfield was just a few miles outside the city—and pretty soon Noel Coward, the famous actor and playwright, would show up with a gaggle of gorgeous show-girls. Oh, war is hell! Noel Coward would play the piano and sing many of his hit show songs, while we all vied for the attention of the lovely girls ("Popsies" in RAF terms). Later, when our guests had departed the mess, the real rough-house fun and games began in earnest.

We had a large wheel in the mess bar, sort of like a wheel of fortune, and on it were printed the names of about every kind of alcoholic drink one could imagine. We would get a pint-sized mug and the first player in the game would spin the wheel. Wherever the pointer stopped on the wheel, that was the first drink poured into the mug—say, as an example, Scotch whiskey. The first player took a sip, passing the mug to the second player who spun the wheel, which might stop on rum. He added the rum, sipped this concoction, and passed the mug to a third player, who might put in a shot of gin. As you can well imagine, the mixture in the mug began to taste bloody awful as each player spun the wheel, added another shot of booze of some sort, and took his sip.

About this time some wise guy who had the mug in his possession would suddenly feel the urge to go to the latrine. He wouldn't leave the mug with us at the bar—he didn't trust us. There were howls of protest and loud calls to measure the depth of the mug's contents before he left the bar—all to no avail, and so he took the mug with him. When he returned every eye was on the depth of giggle soup in the mug. Did he or didn't he, was the question? And, of course, the next player had a real problem. Did he trust the wise guy not to have added anything while he was in the latrine? Should he courageously take his sip? Oh well, after several passings of the mug's depth-charge mixture among the several players, no one really gave a damn one way or another.

If any of the fighter squadrons based at North Weald had some new boys who had recently gone operational (combat ready), our party really blossomed into a perfect fiasco. Two or three of us would grab a new boy, pin his arms so he couldn't struggle, then pull off his shoes and socks and roll up his trouser legs. While we were so engaged, a couple of other guys got an empty fire bucket, climbed into the ante-room fireplace, and scraped black soot into the bucket. The soot was then mixed with water, making a thick gooey mess. Into the bucket went the new boy's bare feet, and then, with several of us holding him upside down on our shoulders, we made him walk across the white anteroom ceiling. After this he wrote his name and the date beside his black footprints.

If there were several new boys being indoctrinated into our hallowed ranks as full-fledged fighter pilots, the walls and ceiling of the anteroom and mess bar were literally covered with big black footprints going up one wall, across the ceiling, and down the opposite wall. Sometimes a strict station commander would tear a strip off all of us and dock our pay for a new paint job of the mess interior, especially if the station was visited frequently by Air Ministry staff weenies. Other station commanders weren't so chintzy, joining in with our peculiar form of fun and games. One I remember always wanted us to hold the new boys upside down to do a dance of footprints around the anteroom chandelier.

A New Zealand night fighter pilot friend of mine, Guy Corbett, was vectored one dark night to intercept an unidentified bomber, which the sector controller declared to be "hostile." Guy found the bomber in all that darkness by spotting the exhaust flame from its engines, gave it a good squirt, and sent it down blazing to crash a couple of miles from our airfield. About an hour or so later, when Guy had finished his night patrol and landed, he came rushing into the mess bar excitedly telling us all about his victory.

Before he'd gotten half through his story, he noticed several hard-eyed, strange aircrew types bellied up to the bar. They were wearing flying suits and glared at him with some degree of hostility. Yes, it was the crew of the bomber Guy had shot down. They were British, their bomber was a four-engine Stirling, and, to say the least, they were all as mad as hornets. Luckily, they'd all parachuted safely, were picked up by Home Guard troops, and brought to our airfield mess.

Since the bomber crew was in our mess and somewhat outnumbered, the whole affair was satisfactorily settled when Guy offered his profound apology and bought drinks for the crew for several hours. In the wee hours of the morning, with the bomber types feeling no pain and having all the makings of a huge hangover, we poured them into a lorry and sent them safely home. We all wrote the incident off as an occupational hazard.

Those of us fighter pilots who were on dawn readiness that morning, after downing several cups of hot black coffee, were most thankful to sit quietly in our Spitfire cockpits for a bit sucking in pure oxygen to quickly sober us up.

On 9 August at 11:30 hours, while providing fighter escort for our bombers on Circus 68 to attack targets in occupied France, I was leading White Section of A Flight. When we were about 15 or 20 miles into France my Spit's engine started to surge. Then it quit. I was left a mile and a half behind the rest of the formation, gliding down at 120 mph and planning to belly land in a field just west of Mardyck. I fully expected to be captured by the Squareheads, to spend the rest of the war in a POW camp.

At 4,500 feet, just above a scattered cloud deck, I saw an Me.109E some 2,000 feet above me and coming after me fast. The Kraut pilot tried to shoot me down from his higher position, but he missed. I pulled my gliding Spit's nose up sharply and fired my guns from 100 yards range, hitting the 109 squarely in the cockpit hood as it passed by me, a lucky shot. Practically on a stall, I half rolled and, following the Hun in his dive, fired three more bursts at him from a range of about 300 yards. Luckily, my engine started up again after the half roll, but it was running very rough without much power.

We both went down through the clouds, then just as we broke clear, a second Me.109, flying under the clouds, flew between the first 109 and my Spitfire. Firing at this second enemy aircraft from 75 yards, I shot some pieces off its starboard wing. This 109 had already been shot up by someone else, since I observed that it was trailing white glycol with black smoke pouring from its engine. The second 109 went down on its back, but I did not see it crash.

I continued to follow the first 109 down to about 900 feet, from where I saw it smash into the ground and explode in a fiery sheet of flame. With my engine giving me at least enough power to stay airborne, I decided that this wasn't going to be the day the Huns captured me. So I headed westward toward Gravelines at about 800 feet.

Since I was flying so low and could only get about 130 mph out of my slowly failing engine, I made a good target for the German antiaircraft gunners. They fired everything they had at me, including the kitchen sink, but didn't hit me. They did come close enough several times for me to actually hear their shells explode and rock my Spitfire, which, to say the least, scared the hell out of me. After taking a couple of quick squirts at their flak positions, I passed safely over Gravelines on the French coast at 600 feet.

Gradually losing altitude to 200 feet above the Channel waters, I began squawking "May Day!" Soon I was joined by two Spitfires of No. 403 (Canadian) Fighter Squadron. They escorted me to Manston airfield, on the English Channel coast of Kent, where I landed without further incident and had my Spit's engine repaired. Then, in the late evening, I flew back to North Weald, where I filled out my Form F Combat Report for Robbie.

Several days later our whole wing of three squadrons headed across the Channel on a fighter sweep, just looking for trouble. We soon found all the trouble we wanted in mid-channel, since a like number of German Me.109E and 109F squadrons were headed our way on, I assume, the same sort of mission. We closed at about 22,000 feet, with fighters twisting and turning in air-to-air combat for at least ten minutes. The blue sky, perfectly clear before the dogfight began, was soon criss-crossed with white vapor trails and tracer bullet streaks. In less than a minute several aircraft were falling, some shot down in flames, some emitting whitish glycol or black oily smoke.

Let me tell you it was some fight, with more than sixty fighters all milling around at full bore, all squirting cannon shells and machine gun bullets at each other. I had my Spit's throttle firewalled and, with both hands on the spade grip of the control column, yanked her around in high-speed tight turns, dives, stall turns, half rolls, split-S and anything else I could do with her to keep from getting my rear end shot off or from ramming some other sod. I got off a quick squirt once in awhile at a 109, but the action was so fast and furious that there wasn't time to get on a Hun's tail and stay there long enough to get in a good shot. About the time I fired a few rounds at a Kraut, one or two of them were firing at me.

Hauling my Spit around in a tight turn to port, some Squarehead let me have it good—bang!—right in the upper fuel tank, which was located just forward of the cockpit and windscreen. I caught a momentary glimpse of his yellow-nosed Me.109F as he dove past me—one of the "Abbeville Kids," as we'd nicknamed the enemy pilots of Jagdgeschwader 26. Flames burst out from under my Spit's engine cowling, gasoline fumes filled my cockpit, the whole works was about to explode in my face within the next few seconds. There was nothing to do but get the hell out of her before she blew.

The next thing I remember I was falling through the sky, still in the middle of the dogfight with aircraft whizzing by in all directions, with bullets flying every which way. "Don't pull your parachute ripcord yet," I told myself. "Wait until you've fallen clear of this mess." So I waited until several seconds and a couple thousand feet had gone by, then I pulled the chute's D-ring. And once again I saw that lovely canopy blossom open above me with a jerk I didn't mind at all.

I had gotten some of the flame when I bailed out. My tunic sleeves were singed and my left trouser leg still smoked a bit, but other than that I was OK. Luckily for me I always flew with my silk-lined leather gloves on. If I hadn't, my hands could have been burned so badly that I wouldn't have been able to pull the parachute ripcord. My goggles and oxygen mask certainly saved my face from being burned. The last I saw of my flaming Spitfire was when she exploded in the air, her bits and pieces showering down into the Channel and disappearing beneath the dark waters.

I could see I was going to get a dunking in the Channel, which, I'd been told, was damned cold in any season of the year. From my rate and angle of descent, I expected I'd land in the drink about six or seven miles from the Dover coast. Landing in water is a hell of a lot different from landing on the ground. You've got to get clear of the chute just before you go into the water, otherwise, if there is any sort of breeze, the billowed chute will drag you under the water and you can very easily drown. You must also be prepared to immediately inflate your Mae West the moment your feet touch the water and you release your parachute harness. If the Mae West is inflated too soon, while you've still got the tight chute harness on, the air-filled life vest will just about crush your chest—at least it will be difficult to breathe.

After you're in the water the next thing is to inflate your dinghy, know how to get into the damned tricky thing—and, of most importance, be absolutely certain which direction to start paddling for home. There are a couple of other gadgets to help the rescue people find and pick you up: a yellow dye sea marker, a signalling mirror, and a whistle to blow when a boat comes near your position. Other than all these life-saving bits and pieces of equipment, you're going to get doused in icy salt water, swallow at least a couple mouthfuls of the brackish stuff, gag on it and throw up, lose a perfectly good pair of leather flying boots, shiver and freeze in your soaked clothes, and have a terrible urge to urinate.

If you do your splash-down drill right and survive these several inconveniences, the second problem confronting you becomes very clear. Will the air/sea rescue people find you—ours, not theirs—before you get swamped by huge waves and go down to Davey Jones' locker, thirst to death in a couple of days if you aren't picked up, drift out to sea or into a coastal mine field, or just plain freeze to death? Any guy in a like situation who thought he was an atheist was a bloody idiot. I, at that particular moment, had a short but sincere conversation with God, with Saint Peter, with any saint in Heaven I could think of who would listen to my immediate problems and provide a reasonable solution to me in this dire situation.

The water was coming up fast now—I could actually hear the rolling and splashing of the gray, white-capped waves. Turning the quick release on my parachute harness, I waited until I thought my feet were about to touch the water, then pushed the release. I'd say that I misjudged my height by at least twenty or thirty feet. Falling clear of the chute harness, I plunged into the drink, where I must have gone down about ten feet below the waves. Struggling to the surface, I got hit square in the face by a big wave, swallowed my fair share of the English

Channel salt water, gagged, vomited, pulled the cords to inflate my Mae West, and lay there gasping for breath and bobbing up and down with the swells for a couple of minutes.

Yes, I lost my best leather flying boots, which were hard to come by in those days. Then I pulled the dinghy to me, inflating it with its CO_2 bottle. My first couple of attempts to get into the damned thing were most unsuccessful, since as soon as I put my weight on one side the dinghy flipped over upside down on top of me. When I finally got the knack of it and clambered in, amid a torrent of cuss words, the goddamn dinghy was full of water. Using my flying helmet, I bailed out some of the water; however, every time I shifted my position the dinghy would flood again. I soon gave that up as a bad job, deciding my rear end would just have to get water-logged.

A couple of minutes later a yellow-nosed Me.109 flew low over me— I suppose it was the son of a bitch who had shot me down. He waggled his wings at me, I thumbed my nose at him. Another few minutes and two Spitfires circled me before heading back to England. I could see by the aircraft markings that one of them was piloted by my buddy, Tommy McGerty. The other kite was Uncle Sam's. With any luck they had passed my position by R/T and radar fix to the air/sea rescue guys, which was a somewhat cheerful turn of events. Now it was a case of hurry up and wait.

I messed around with the packet of yellow sea marker dye for a bit, managing to get my soaked uniform covered with the damned stuff. The dye spread on the water pretty well, but I noticed it began to turn my blue uniform a ghastly pea green in splotches. I tried to blow the whistle to see if it worked. My mouth was so salty and dry that I couldn't even get a toot out of it. I never did find the signal mirror. I'd be willing to bet that some airman plonk back at North Weald was using it as a shaving mirror. I couldn't find the paddle either, so I figured I'd better start using my hands as oars.

Now came that sudden urge to do the first and last thing an airman does on earth—urinate. Being somewhat of a gentleman, I tried to unbutton my trousers fly and get on my knees so I could urinate over the side of the dinghy. Not bloody likely! During this intricate maneuver the damned dinghy capsized, dumping me into the drink once again. While I was struggling to get back on board, I decided to hell with it, being a gentleman that is, so I added a bit more liquid to the English Channel waters. There I sat in the middle of the drink, soaked to the skin, freezing cold, miserable, beginning to get seasick, but alive.

In about forty minutes I heard the sound of a boat's motor coming toward me. My first impulse was to stand up and wave like mad, "Here I am! Come and get me!" Experience, however, had taught me that a rubber dinghy was a very unstable device, so I just sat there trying to blow the stupid whistle. Another moment and a rescue launch came alongside me. At that particular time I didn't really give a damn if it was ours or theirs.

Happily, the launch was one of ours. Some husky "swabby" reached out with a boat hook, pulled my dinghy against the launch hull, and, with the help of a couple more sailors, dragged me on board the launch. When I staggered to my feet, someone wrapped a heavy blanket around my shoulders, then a medic asked me if I was all right—not wounded, burned, or busted up. "No big problem," said I as I slumped down on a bench, totally exhausted.

About that time the medic put a tin cup in my hand, telling me to drink its dark contents which, at first, I thought was coffee. The first swallow darn nearly gagged me—wow! It was blackstrap Navy rum, about 150 proof I'd guess. I could feel its warmth flow all the way to my toes, a sort of glowing sensation. Well, you can't waste such good stuff, so down the hatch it went. Man oh man, it sure as hell was powerful. I'd be willing to bet that tin cup held at least a half pint.

As soon as I began to take note of my surroundings, I noticed there were three other RAF pilots on board, as well as two Huns, all of them wrapped in blankets and sipping cups of rum. How bloody jolly. The Krauts couldn't speak any English and we RAF types couldn't speak German; however, we all toasted each other's good luck to be picked up, and then drank a second toast to the Royal Navy for providing the grog. The day wasn't a complete loss, after all.

On the way back to England I got another cup of rum, which I slowly sipped for the better part of an hour. I could really feel it taking hold, taking the freezing cold shivers out of my bones. By the time we reached the Dover docks we pilots were in fine spirits, including the Squareheads, who joined right in with our rum-inspired festivities. On the dock we bade a fond farewell to the two Germans as they were hustled off by military police to interrogation and then to a POW camp for the duration. Poor bastards. They weren't such bad guys after all and about our same age. The six of us pilots could really have turned one on that evening, if the stiff-necked MP officer had let our two Hun buddies join us at a local pub to celebrate our miraculous escape from the briny deep.

The next morning, suffering from a terrible Royal Navy rum hangover, shoeless, unshaven, dressed in my splotched green and blue uniform, I was picked up at Hawkinge airfield and flown back to North Weald by Tommy McGerty in our squadron's "Maggie" (Miles "Magister"). Tommy, with some truth, said I looked like I'd been shot at and hit—several times. I hit the sack until about noon when S/Ldr Paddy Woodhouse came into my room in the mess and gave me a three-day pass for rest and recuperation. It was the first pass I'd had in four months. I certainly could use it.

By tea time that same afternoon I was ship-shape and, in my best and only other uniform, headed for London. After checking in at the Overseas Club for a room, I strode down through the lobby where I intercepted a pretty little blonde lady about twenty years old. Her name was Wendy. She worked as a receptionist for the service club. We hit it right off together, and after an enjoyable dinner followed by a delightful variety show at the London Palladium, we went to her Kensington flat. In this situation I had no need for my Overseas Club room at all, so I picked up my kit next morning and brought it to Wendy's place.

Our relationship worked out very well. We walked and talked together in St. James Park, we lunched at a quaint little French restaurant just off Piccadilly, we went to the tea dance at the Dorchester. That evening Wendy insisted on preparing our dinner at her apartment—she was a marvelous cook, managing somehow to produce a delicious steak. Everything was rationed then, especially meat. Later, when we were in each other's embrace, we quietly spoke of our futures while we watched through an open window the bright beams of London searchlights scanning the night skies for enemy bombers. Occasionally we could hear the unsynchronized throb of Hun bomber engines, hear the bursts of our antiaircraft shells flung high into the heavens, hear the distant explosions of sticks of bombs falling in the London dock area.

Wendy was a wonderful, sweet girl. She certainly was good to and for me. She kept me out of the London pubs, watched to see that I didn't foolishly spend too much money, and she never asked for anything from me. She managed to get off work for the short period of my leave just to be with me. And before I knew it, my three days were up, so back to the war I must go. Our parting wasn't so easy. I had learned to like Wendy a lot. As a most thoughtful and unexpected gift for me, she pressed into my hand a small medallion of silver, the Church War Cross. On it were engraved the words "Christ died for thee." Before kissing me goodby at the railway station, Wendy said, "Always keep this with you. It will bring you safely back to me." There were tears in her eyes. My own eyes were sort of misty, too.

I had nothing to give Wendy in return, not a damned thing. There was a big lump in my throat; I was very much touched by her farewell gift. But, wanting to appear in her eyes as a devil-may-care fighter pilot, I gallantly gave her a light slap on her behind, saying, "Be good, old girl, and don't worry about me. I'll be back." We smiled at each other for just a moment, each of us knowing what the past three days together had meant to us, we fondly kissed, and then she was gone.

Yes, dear Wendy, I will come back to you just as soon as I can manage it. Your little silver cross will always be with me, I promise. It looks like a long war. I'll need all the help I can get to stay in one piece. (I still have Wendy's silver cross.) Back to North Weald airfield and the goddamn war went I; however, I wasn't so bloody enthusiastic about it this time. I could feel something in my heart that was strangely different. My guess was that Wendy had found a place there.

During my brief absence from the squadron two more of our guys, Bill Driver and Jack Weir, had bought the farm, been killed. They were replaced by a couple of new boys just out of OTU, one of whom was Carroll W. "Red" McColpin. (Red, whose military career began in the RAF, became an ace, a USAAF fighter group commander during the last years of the Second World War, and later, in the USAF, a major general commanding the 4th Air Force.)

5. The Ace

It was still pitch dark on the morning of 27 August 1941 when the bat-woman (yes, I said woman, a WAAF type) knocked on my quarters door, entered the room uninvited, and turned on that bloody bright light. "Four o'clock, sir," she cheerfully informed me. "You've got to be at dispersal in an hour. Come on now, sir, hop to it." Then she shoved a cup of boiling hot tea under my nose. How the hell could she be so cheerful at such an ungodly hour as four in the morning. I think she took a perverted delight in waking me up. I opened one eye to look at her. She was short and dumpy, just what you'd expect the RAF to pick for this duty.

"OK, OK, I'm awake," I responded sleepily. "What's the weather like?"

She said the sky was brilliantly clear with twinkling stars (bloody poetic), dawn would soon be upon us, and it looked like the day would be lovely and sunny. Hell's fire, I mused, why couldn't it be raining and socked in with fog so our squadron could stand down, or be released, and I could sleep in for a few more hours. Not today, kid. Get your can out of the sack if you want any breakfast. I could hear the WAAF going down the corridor knocking up the other pilots. How about that "knocking up" bit. In England it means waking someone up.

I struggled out of bed, took a semi-cold shower, dressed in my old flying uniform, and went to the mess dining room for a bit of breakfast. Some of the other guys were already there—Tommy McGerty, Uncle Sam Mauriello, Jimmy Crowley, Gussy Daymond, and Pete Provenzano. Several others straggled in during the next few minutes. I was sort of surprised to see so many of the squadron pilots being routed out; usually only four or six of us were required to be on readiness at this time of the morning. So I wondered out loud what was going on. Uncle

Sam told me we were going on another circus this morning, the whole squadron, and that's all he knew about it.

Our breakfast was nicely served to us by more WAAFs. It consisted of two sausages (90 percent bread filler and 10 percent meat mix), a damned fried tomato which I grew to hate with a purple passion, toast, jam, and some sort of brackish liquid the English mistakenly called coffee. No sense in complaining—the stock answer was: "Don't you know there's a war on?" Yes, we knew there was a war on. Maybe, we occasionally suggested, the Germans had a better mess; maybe we ought to transfer to the Luftwaffe. By the way, we were rationed one egg per month; everyone, even the admin types, got up for breakfast on that morning.

In ten minutes breakfast was finished and six of us piled out of the mess and into F/Lt George Brown's little canvas-covered truck for our ride to the dispersal hut on the far side of North Weald airfield. The others caught a ride with S/Ldr Paddy Woodhouse, who had been issued a staff car. At dispersal we were assigned to our flight and section positions. I was assigned Blue 3. My aircraft was a Spitfire Mk IIA, code letters XR-D, serial number P7308. I usually flew aircraft XR-D or XR-T. Both were good kites, but XR-D had just a bit more zip, I thought. Just as we went out to the dispersal bays to get our aircraft ready, lugging our parachutes and flying helmets, I heard the operations corporal calling No. 11 Group to report No. 71 "Eagle" Squadron's readiness status.

The fitter (crew chief) had already run up my Spit's engine. He told me she checked out OK. I stepped up on the port wingroot and straightened out the Sutton harness to suit me, put my chute in the cockpit seat, and climbed in. After checking the petrol gauges, I selected most of the switches to the "on" position, except for the master switch. Then I unscrewed the Ki-Gas pump, but left it closed. Next I set up the throttle, mixture, and propeller pitch for quick starting. I plugged in the radio cord and oxygen tube, and placed my flying helmet over the gunsight.

Then I checked the maps in the map case, and reaching up above the windscreen, I adjusted the rear-vision mirror. The engine coolant temperature was normal, about 85°. Hydraulic and oxygen pressures were good. After this I climbed out of the narrow cockpit and did a "walk-around" inspection of the aircraft. All OK, ready to go. I patted my XR-D affectionately on her brown and green camouflaged fuselage. By this time the sky was fairly light with the coming dawn. I signed the Maintenance Form 700 for the fitter and walked back to the dispersal hut.

Now there was nothing to do but wait. Damn, I hated that waiting! I put on my Mae West, and then, like the other pilots, settled down in a chair to catch a few more minutes of shut-eye. I must have dozed off, because when the ops phone rang I really came alive—we all did. The squadron leader was called to the blower for a briefing on the circus by some 11 Group staff weenie. Following a few minutes of muffled conversation, Paddy hung up the phone, picked up his hurriedly scribbled notes, and walked over to the briefing blackboard.

"OK, boys," he began, "the operation is on—Circus 86. The wing will escort nine Blenheims to bomb the steel plant at Lille. We will fly top cover. The other two squadrons of the wing will provide close escort. Intelligence says we can expect enemy fighter reaction—a couple of squadrons at least, probably the Abbeville Kids—so keep your eyes open. And, damn it, if you see a Hun, give your call sign and his clock and altitude position. If you just call out "Bandits," you'll give everyone in the circus a dose of the brown-ring twitch. Start engines time will be at 06:00 hours—in ten minutes. We'll pick up the bomber formation over North Foreland. You new boys stick with your section leaders if we get into a flap. Any questions? No? OK, let's go!" Paddy's briefing was short and sweet and to the point.

Out the dispersal hut door we go to our waiting aircraft, the old adrenaline starting to pump. Just as I'm ready to climb into my Spit, the ops corporal runs out of the hut to Paddy's aircraft, telling him something. Paddy waves his arms to all of us—meaning the operation has been delayed for some reason or other. So we all troop back to dispersal to wait some more. Now what the hell's going on? When you're primed and cocked and ready to go, it grates on your nerves to have the mission delayed, especially when you aren't told why. It's usually the fault of the bomber guys. Those truck-drivers never can get anything straight. That's why they got stuck in bombers in the first place. Takes a whole crew of them in a single aircraft to figure out who is doing what to whom. Just goes to show you the much higher mentality of a fighter pilot, who must be his own pilot, navigator, gunner, and, at times, bomb aimer.

Woodhouse came back from the phone—delayed until 07:00— another hour to sit around and sweat it out. Damn, damn, damn! I tried to snooze again, but Pipsqueak jumped onto my lap and decided to wash my face with his tongue. Then he looked at me with those big brown eyes of his. I knew what he wanted. I dug in my pocket for a piece of hard candy, which he took with a "thank you" wag of his tail. Off my lap he went to his private corner of the room, where, with a lot of crunching and munching, he chewed up the candy.

The time was now 08:15 hours. I am flying with my squadron at 18,000 feet near the French city of Lille. Our position in the forma- tion, top cover, is to protect the nine Blenheim bombers from surprise top and rear attacks by enemy fighters. We had crossed the French coast near Cape Gris Nez at 15,000 feet, and then climbed to 18,000 on our course to Saint Omer and on toward the steel plant target at Lille. Our entire formation, nine bombers and thirty-six fighters, comprised Circus 86.

Far below me, through the scattered clouds, I see the bright flashes of German 88-mm antiaircraft guns firing at us from the seemingly peaceful green fields. The brownish-black shell bursts come quite close to us at times, though usually a little behind and below our formation. I can easily see the course we have flown by glancing behind my Spit- fire at the long avenue of slowly diminishing dark smoke puffs. From the moment we had crossed the French coast the Huns had fired at us constantly.

Our squadron leader had ordered us to fly in a wide "vic" battle formation, to keep changing height, and to weave back and forth above the Blenheims. His voice came to me clearly through my R/T earphones as he delivered his orders to the section leaders.

"Parson leader here. Parson White Section keep together. Don't straggle White Two. Blue Section, you're too far out. Close up that gap."

I look over at the right side of the formation, A Flight's side, to see if White Two had received the instruction and is getting back into position. He has. It's like asking for it to straggle. One seldom sees what happens to stragglers. They just disappear. They're easy prey for enemy fighters to bounce and shoot down. As ordered, our Blue Section altered course to close the gap in our top cover formation.

Again Paddy's crisp voice comes to me over the R/T: "Parson Squad- ron, heads up! Red flak. Watch out for 109s."

Behind us I see several red antiaircraft smoke puffs. Not dangerous looking stuff, but it means that enemy fighters are up and being vectored towards us by a combination of these red visual markers and radio communications. The brownish-black flak is still being fired at us, and intermingled with these dark bursts are the bright red puffs. Every time I see these red bursts I get a kind of tingling sensation running up and down my spine. I know that within the next ten minutes my life may end. It just doesn't seem possible that in this bright, beautiful, sun-filled summer sky there are men waiting to kill me—or for me to kill them. I wonder if the Hun pilots have these same feelings. I suppose they do.

I reach up to the instrument panel and switch on my reflector gun-sight. Its circle and dot glow a faint orange color on the glass plate before my eyes. I double check the gunsight's span setting (32 feet) and the range setting (250 yards). Then I check the fuel contents gauge. Yes, plenty of petrol. Enough for another hour, even at high boost. Next I set my compass ring on the reciprocal of my present course heading—the return direction to England. This latter simple precaution eliminates the initial orientation problem after the confusion of an air battle. Last, I turn the gun button on the control column to "fire." I am now ready to fight.

I continue weaving across the back of the formation, watching to the rear and above, peering out of my aircraft's hood, first to one side and then the other. Far below me I see the aircraft of the two close escort squadrons surrounding the nine bombers. Their Spitfires look small and black and deadly.

"Hello Parson Leader. Blue One here. Three 109s, seven o'clock high!" My head snaps around toward the left rear and I search the sky until I see three little light-colored specks—enemy aircraft—flying about 4,000 feet above us. They are flying the same course as we are. Although they are some distance behind us, they are evidently waiting to jump some straggler.

Now, suddenly, startling, like a whip crack, white streaks shoot past my starboard wing. I yank the control column hard to the left and back as I jam the throttle full open, whirling around in a steep climbing turn. I switch my R/T transmitter to "send" and, while trying to control my inward excitement, say in a slow, even voice, "Parson Squadron. Blue Three. Snappers, six o'clock high!" My job as top weaver is done. I've warned my squadron and the other Circus 86 aircraft. Maybe a bit late for the first attacking enemy fighters—but I've alerted them against those Me.109s that follow.

Below me there is no longer a formation of our eleven top cover fighter aircraft. The individual sections of my squadron have split away, breaking up the wide "vic." They're all mixed up in groups of twos, threes and fours. Each little group is twisting and turning as the air battle's individual combats develop. The attacking Huns have come straight down on us, hoping to break through the escort and get to the bombers. It was the leader of the first section of four 109s that had taken a quick squirt at me as he dove past.

Over on the right side of the formation I see a long trail of white smoke. One of our Spitfires is in a fast, steep dive with glycol streaming out behind it. He has been hit in the radiator or engine coolant system and is making for the French coast and home with his damaged aircraft. Hope he makes it before his engine seizes. Getting shot up in the first few seconds of an attack sometimes happens; somebody must be unlucky and get clobbered first.

Another section of four Huns comes hurtling down to join in the scrap. The bluish-white bellies of their aircraft flash in the morning sun. I can clearly see the black crosses, bordered with white, painted on their stubby, square-tipped wings. All the Messerschmitts' noses are painted a bright yellow. We know this German unit—we've met in battle before—as the "Abbeville Kids." Most of the Hun kites are Me.109Es, with a few of the newer type Me.109Fs.

A Spitfire from A Flight—Flight Lieutenant George Brown, I think—climbs up to engage the four newcomers. I watch his eight machine guns send a long burst of .303s into the belly of the third 109. The enemy aircraft's fuselage is blown in half just in front of the tail section. Then the port wing explodes and rips off as the ammunition tray for the 20-mm cannon in it is hit. Another second and the Messerschmitt's hood jettisons off. Out comes the enemy pilot from his cockpit. I momentarily watch his body falling through the air until his parachute snaps open far below the fight. How he was able to get out of that 109 alive, I'll never know. The lucky SOB.

On the far side of the scrap there is a large flash—just a flash and that's all. Someone has been blown to bits. I can't tell whether it was a Spitfire or a 109. Fragments, all that remains of the aircraft and its pilot, rain down from the sky.

The fight is now about twenty or thirty seconds old. Things happen very fast in air combat. To the onlookers, or rather the uplookers, our fights last for only a few minutes, but to us, the fighter pilots, they sometimes seem an eternity.

So far in this engagement I have only been attacked by the first enemy section. I look around for a 109 that will give me a good target. In the previous months I had shot down four enemy aircraft. Now I needed one more victory to earn the coveted title of fighter ace. Just above the scrap I see two Me.109Fs that are evidently waiting for a shot-up Spitfire or Blenheim to drop out of the fight and try to get home. Then they'll dive down and finish it off—easy meat.

I climb fast behind and above the two Huns. I'm about 1,500 feet above them now, and I have the sun at my back. I give my engine full throttle and dive on the rearmost enemy aircraft. The German leader of the two sees me coming and quickly half-rolls onto his back, diving away from me. The second 109, my target, does a climbing turn to the left. I close the range to about 150 yards, line the Hun up in my gun-sight, then I press the gun-firing button. My aircraft shudders as I hear the sharp chatter of its eight machine guns. Acrid fumes of burned gun-powder fill my cockpit and sting my nostrils. I like this odor. It seems to stiffen my spine, tighten my muscles, make my blood race. It makes my scalp tingle, and I want to laugh.

I see the grayish-white tracer streaks from my guns converge on the Messerschmitt's tail section. The elevators and rudder disintegrate under the impact of the explosive DeWild bullets. Pieces fly off the enemy's fuselage. The range is now down to 50 yards. Black liquid—engine oil—spatters my windscreen and a dense, brownish colored smoke is flung back at me. My enemy is finished. Splash one, but good! I've got my fifth victory!

I lift my gloved thumb from the gun button and do a steep climbing turn, first to the right and then left, as I watch the German fall to the French fields below. His aircraft is burning furiously now. It doesn't leave a long fiery trail behind it. This one looks like the blue-white flame of a blowtorch. It seems odd that the Hun pilot didn't really try to get away from me. I guess he must have been a new boy. Well, what the hell, they all count.

The sections of my squadron are fighting at about 11,000 or 12,000 feet now. I am a couple thousand feet above them. I see the buildings

and tall chimneys of the steel plant, the Blenheims' target, far below
and on the outskirts of Lille. Sticks of bombs are now falling. Soon I
can see the shock waves caused by their heavy explosions in the target
area. All nine Blenheims are still with us, surrounded by the defending
fighters of our close escort. Now, to get them safely home again.

From what I can see, the scrap below is breaking up into a number
of running dogfights. Our Spitfires use a lot of petrol in a battle such as
this one. The fuel left in our tanks will get us back to England, but it
isn't enough to allow us to stay over enemy territory and fight much
longer. Maybe another ten minutes or so.

My port wing jerks and skids my Spitfire to the right. Now there
are several long rips in the metal skin and a jagged hole near its tip. I
look back quickly and see my attacker coming at me from the left rear
quarter, slightly higher, and closing fast. I think he is the leader of the
pair I had first attacked.

There are perhaps three seconds left between life and death for me.
The German's tracers, glowing like little balls of fire, flash past my
cockpit. I yank back the throttle, give my prop full fine pitch, jam the
flaps down, and violently skid my aircraft out of his gunsight. He is
now closing too fast. I have greatly decreased my speed by changing
prop pitch and by dumping flaps—luckily the flaps didn't blow off. He
overshoots me, skimming not more than ten feet above my head.

The bluish-white belly of the 109F fills my windscreen. I can even
see oil streaks and rivets on the underside of its fuselage, and above that
the black cross insignia, unit markings, and a red rooster painted on the
side of the cockpit. The Hun pilot is looking directly down at me. His
expression tells me that he fully realizes (Gott in Himmel!) the mistake
he has just made.

I fire. I can't miss. My guns chatter for no more than three or four
seconds. I see the bullets smashing into the Hun aircraft's belly. Pieces
fly off the 109. Then a wisp of gray smoke streams back from its
engine, and then the whole aircraft is suddenly engulfed in a sheet of
white-hot flame. It rolls over slowly onto its back and starts down at a
high rate of speed. The tail section breaks off. I last see it, tumbling as
it falls, far below me. Splash two! My face is wet with nervous sweat.
I can hear myself gasping in my oxygen mask.

I see another 109 flying level some 500 feet below me and crossing
my path from left to right—heading for home, I assume. The Hun pilot

has now seen me. He starts taking violent evasive action as I make a diving turn toward his tail. I close to 75 yards. He suddenly pulls up into a steep climb. I fire a short burst into his back. He flicks over into a right turn and flies straight across my gunsight. No more than thirty yards separate our two aircraft. I fire again. He begins to smoke.

At this moment, in my rear-vision mirror, I see four Me.109s climbing up to intercept me. This is getting too hot for me. I jam the throttle through the gate, jerk the control column back into my stomach, and climb up and over them. The nearest one takes a squirt at my fast-moving Spitfire. His deflection is bad, luckily. The 20-mm cannon shells and machine gun bullets streak past me and then veer off my tail.

I roll my Spit onto its back, pull on the stick, and the reversed horizon comes up to meet me. I hear explosions and a banging like hail on my aircraft's fuselage. My port wing is hit again. I see splashing holes and rents send pieces flying off. A ball of fire flashes through the cockpit, smashing into my instrument panel. My right foot takes a heavy blow, bounces off the rudder pedal, and is numb. Two sharp blows bang into my right leg. My head snaps forward and my vision bursts in a blinding white flash. Then comes a soft, deep darkness. I can just faintly hear bits of broken glass and metal strike the cockpit floor.

Fear grips me with strong arms. It is finally happening to me, the one who wasn't going to die in this war. The one who had planned so many things to do when the war ended. The one who had seen so many aircraft shot down, but had always told himself, "It won't be you—you'll live through." I am being shot down and killed!

My neck and the back of my head ache horribly. My arms and legs seem to be floating lightly on air, yet I can feel their weight against my body. My hand on the control column becomes leaden. I want to let go of it, but I haven't the strength to loosen my fingers. It doesn't make any difference anyway. In a few seconds it will all be over. There will be a grinding crash, an explosion, and then nothing. I shall be smashed into fragments of bone and burned flesh.

Visions of my family and friends, those I'd loved in life, appear before my mind's eye. I can see them all smiling tenderly at me. I hear familiar voices murmuring softly, caressingly. They seem to give me a sense of being watched over and comforted during the passage of these last fleeting moments.

My swaying head strikes the side of the cockpit hood. It jars my vision. The deep darkness that covers my eyes lightens little by little. Dimly I see my instrument panel, broken and shattered.

I raise my head and look through the windscreen toward the swirling fields of earth charging madly upward to enfold me. Suddenly I become conscious of my two hands tugging back on the control column. The nose of my Spitfire is slowly lifting. The land below me stops whirling as earth and sky return to their rightful places. The horizon reappears. My brain tells me that I live! I laugh without sound. I still own life!

Strength has returned to my body. My pulse is beating violently. My skin feels cold and clammy, yet I know that I am perspiring profusely. I shiver. My brief interlude with death has ended.

I am again in level flight at 1,200 feet. I look behind and above me for attacking enemy aircraft. There are none. I am alone in this hostile sky, near the little town of Ambleteuse, and about five miles from the French coast. I point my Spit's nose toward England as I inspect its and my own damage.

There are large holes and rips in the port wing, though the aileron controls seem right enough. A shaft of light penetrates the left side of my cockpit. It must be the hole made by the 20-mm cannon shell that struck my instrument panel. Bits of broken glass from the smashed instruments and twisted scraps of metal lie scattered on the cockpit floor.

I look at my right flying boot. The whole toe of the boot is shot off and covered with blood. My top rudder pedal is also blood-spattered and bent out of shape. My right trouser leg, just below the knee, is drenched with blood and is dripping on the cockpit floor. My head and neck pain me terribly—but I am afraid to inspect myself further. I can feel a wet stickiness in my hair, seeping from under my leather flying helmet onto my neck and cheek. I turn on full oxygen and breathe deeply. I must not pass out now!

Ahead of me the waters of the English Channel gleam. My Spitfire's engine is running rough, surging. I have enough petrol to get me home. I gently weave, as assurance against further enemy attacks. The flight across the channel seems endless, until in the far distance I see Dover's white cliffs reaching out to greet me. My engine is losing power. I am now down to 800 feet. I switch on the R/T and squawk "May Day." In no more than a minute or so two Spitfires join me. The leader waggles his wings and directs me to follow him. The other Spit drops into a position behind me to protect my tail.

My escort leads me across the coastal cliffs to the little grass airfield at Hawkinge, near the town of Folkestone. I change the fuel mixture to "rich," set the propeller to "fine" pitch, select the undercarriage "down," and, as I turn to final approach, drop the flaps. One of the escorting Spitfire pilots signals that my landing gear is down. I have no indicator lights in the cockpit. Everything is smashed. I follow my escort's descent and air speed until the grass surface of the airfield is rushing under my wings. Gently I close the throttle, feel a slight sinking motion, then my wheels are rolling smoothly across the green turf.

I'm home! I'm safe! A feeling of complete relief from the last hour's extreme tension envelopes me. Thank you, dear God, thank you.

I see an ambulance parked at the edge of the airfield, so I taxi over to it and stop my aircraft's engine. A medical orderly points toward a fuel bowser and several other fighter aircraft parked near a dispersal hut, telling me that I must go over there to refuel and rearm. I tell him that I'm wounded and to help me get out of my kite. He looks at my bloody face and helmet, then at the bloody mess in the cockpit, vomits, and promptly slides off the wing.

A medical officer now arrives, quickly takes in the situation, and has me out of the cockpit and lying on the grass in the shade of my Spitfire's wing in a minute. I feel very weak now. My fingers close on the cool, crisp blades of grass. It's good to be back on earth again. Someone puts a lighted cigarette between my lips.

I hear cloth ripping—my trouser leg—two machine gun bullet holes in the right calf. My flying boot is cut off. The front of my right foot has been blown off by a 20-mm cannon shell. The medics carefully remove my leather helmet, just creased across the back of my head by a machine gun bullet. Lucky! Bloody lucky!

Two medical airmen help me onto a stretcher and carry me to the waiting ambulance. The Doc gives me an injection in my arm and says he's sending me to the Royal Victoria Hospital in Folkestone. So long XR-D. You were a good kite. Hope they can patch us both up.

As the ambulance starts to drive me away an intelligence officer scrambles in and sits down on the opposite stretcher. He asks my home station and squadron number. He'll let them know where I am. Then, briefly, I dictate my combat report as he writes in a little notebook. I have done my job today; now he must do his. He must inform No. 11 Group and Fighter Command Headquarters that today, 27 August 1941, we have fought and destroyed enemy aircraft, and that most of our aircraft and aircrews have returned safely, one way or another, from these combat operations.

The injection in my arm begins to take effect and I—the Ace—pass out.

6. Holiday at the Seaside

I awoke sometime in the late afternoon of the next day, 28 August, still groggy from the pain-killing shot the doctor at the airfield had given me and the other medications they gave me in the hospital operating room. I didn't seem to hurt any place, just felt lousy and tired out. The hospital room appeared to be very white and clean, with bright sunlight streaming through two tall windows. There was one bed next to mine. It was empty. In the sunlit corner of the room was another bed, and in it was a young fellow about twenty-two years old, reading a magazine. In the darkest corner of the room was a fourth bed, occupied by a patient who seemed to be completely swathed in bandages. Even his head and face were bandaged, with two little openings for his eyes and a small slit for his nose. His breathing was very loud and harsh, almost like he was gasping for each breath of life.

Well, I thought, I'd better have a look at my right leg and see if it's still there. The way it was shot up, those medics might have decided to cut the damned thing off. I moved my left leg first and saw the bedsheet move, then the right leg and it moved too. Well hell, at least I was still in one piece. Then I propped myself up on my elbows to get a better look at my surroundings.

"Good afternoon," says the young guy politely. "My name is Tomlinson. I'm RAF. How do you feel?"

"I feel like hell. Glad to know you. I'm Bill Dunn, 71 Squadron. Where am I?"

"You're in the Royal Victoria Hospital at Folkestone," Tomlinson tells me. "They brought you in here yesterday evening from the chopping block (operating room). Got shot up, eh? I got mine from a parachute jump. Jumped pretty low. The chute opened just before I hit the deck. Yanked my back out of joint. Broke a leg when I landed hard. Been here a week. The poor fellow over in the corner is Captain Stevens, an Army ordnance bloke. Got all burned up in an accidental gunpowder explosion a couple of days ago. He's unconscious most of the time. When he does wake up, he starts moaning and the nurse gives him a shot to quiet him and put him back to sleep. Can you smell him? It's his burned flesh—cooked to a crisp, he was. Smells sort of sickly sweet, doesn't it. Poor sod has bought it, I think."

About that time the door opened and in popped a white-starched, prim little nurse. "So you're finally awake," she says. "I'll get the doctor to have a look at you," and out she darts. Five minutes later she's back in the wake of a white-coated doctor. I should mention here that the Royal Victoria Hospital was a civilian establishment, but did take in emergency military patients.

The doc asked the same question: "How do you feel?" Then he continued, "You may not realize it, but you are a pretty lucky fellow to still be alive. You got a cannon shell through the right foot, which blew off the front of your foot, but we've managed to save the rest of it. Two machine gun bullets went through the calf of your right leg. One of them knocked a splinter off your shinbone. But your greatest luck was a machine gun bullet that hit you in the back of the head and then glanced off your skull. Cut the scalp for about three inches. Damned lucky it caught you a glancing blow. Just had to clean up the wound and sew you up. Your right leg, however, from the knee down, is in a plaster cast and we'll leave it like that until the wounds are well on the way to healing—probably about six weeks. It's a new method of treating gunshot wounds. Lets them stew in their own juices, so to speak. Very effective treatment."

I thanked the doc for putting me back together. "Has my squadron been notified that I'm in the hospital?" I asked. The doc said he thought so, but he wasn't sure because that action was the responsibility of the RAF station commander at Hawkinge airfield, where I landed after yesterday's fiasco. "How long will I be here?" was my next question. He said probably a week, and then I'd be sent to the RAF hospital at Torquay. Torquay, he told me, was, in peacetime, a seaside resort town in the southwest of England, not far from Plymouth. The RAF had taken over a large hotel there and converted it into a convalescent hospital. A real nice place, he assured me. I'd probably have to spend about three months there before I'd be serviceable for flying duties again. Doc said he'd look in on me again tomorrow, then he and the nurse left the room.

During the remainder of the afternoon Tommy Tomlinson and I got fairly well acquainted. Seems that before the war he was an actor, both stage and movies. He was a handsome guy and had a little mustache, sort of like Errol Flynn's. Poor Captain Stevens just lay there gasping and moaning softly, but I think he was listening to our talk. It seemed sometimes that he was about to say something, then he'd groan and try to shift his position in his bed a little bit.

About five o'clock there was a sudden shrieking roar, like a railway train rushing by, followed by a terrific explosion!

"What the hell was that?" I yelled, and damned near jumped out of bed. "Are the sons of bitches bombing the hospital?"

"No," said Tomlinson. "That was a German long-range artillery shell. They fire the shells from their big guns on the French coast near Calais and the bloody things land hereabouts. Haven't done much damage so far. They usually burst in the open fields between here and Dover. Sometimes, if you're looking in the right place, you can actually see the shells hit the ground at a fairly flat trajectory, bounce back up into the air, and then explode. They're annoying, but you'll get used to them in a couple of days. They fire about ten or fifteen rounds every day just to let us know that they're still over there, the bastards."

Ah, into the room comes a hospital orderly with a tray of food, which he gives to Tomlinson. Suddenly I'm as hungry as a bear. My tray will be next, I figure. Out goes the orderly—and I wait and wait and wait. Nothing.

"How do you call the nurse, Tommy? I want something to eat, too. I'm starved. I haven't eaten since yesterday morning." He pushed a little button on an electric cord. Pretty soon the same crisp little nurse poked her head in the door. "Yes," she smiled sweetly, "what do you want?"

"Where's my dinner?" I demanded. "The orderly brought Tomlinson's food but not mine, and I'm hungry too!"

Then, astonishingly, she explained to me that I had arrived at the hospital without a ration card, and since it was a civilian hospital they could only obtain food for those patients who had ration cards. Sorry about that. Maybe my squadron, when they learned where I was, would send me a card. In the meantime, she continued, she'd see if she could scrounge up something for me to eat. It was absolutely unbelievable to me.

"Damn it to hell!" I exploded. "You mean I can't get fed without a bloody ration card? I could damn well starve to death before our squadron admin officer pulls his finger out and sends a card here. I came over here to help you British fight a war, I get my rear end shot off and dumped in this place, some Kraut SOB now shoots a cannon at me each day to blow the rest of my can off, and to top it all off you're going to starve me to death! Don't you people know that I'm an ally of yours? I'll bet if I'd got shot down in Hunland the Squareheads would at least feed me as a POW. I'm going to get the hell out of here right now! Where are my clothes?"

Just at that moment Captain Stevens rolled over slightly in his bed, looked at me through the dark eye-holes of his bandaged face, and said in a muffled, quiet voice, "Nurse, please let Pilot Officer Dunn use my ration card. I'm not hungry."

Silence. I didn't know what to say except, "Thank you, Captain, but I can't do that." Then the nurse touched me lightly on the arm and whispered that Stevens couldn't eat anything. The bandages covered a face that was nearly all blown away. He was fed intravenously. "Yes, Captain," said the nurse, "that's a good thought, and I thank your generosity." Away she went, and in about fifteen minutes I had a tray of food before me—a hard roll, two slices of beef so thin I swear I could have read a newspaper through them, a spoonful of carrots, and a cup of boiling hot tea that was strong enough to curl your hair. I thanked the captain again for his kindness and apologized for my earlier rudeness. I looked at Tomlinson, but he was staring at something through the window. I looked at the little nurse. She smiled slightly at me and I could just see the misty tears gathering in the corners of her blue eyes. It was awfully hard to swallow Stevens's food.

Lights-out came at about 9 p.m. Next morning when Tomlinson and I awoke, we saw that Captain Stevens's bed was empty. He had died during the night and the orderlies had quietly removed his corpse from our room. I continued to use his ration card until I left the Royal Victoria Hospital for Torquay. Rest quietly, gallant Captain Stevens, with God in Heaven.

Two or three days later our squadron intelligence officer, J. Roland Robinson, came to visit me. He needed more information for my combat report; Air Ministry wanted some specific details, he said. Did I observe any special markings on the Me.109s I had shot down? "Yes," I recalled. "One had a red rooster painted on the side of the cockpit. I mentioned that in my initial combat report."

"Ah ha," says Robbie, "that's what we wanted to know for sure. Our intelligence people have learned that a famous German ace—he had some fifty victories—was shot down that same day and at about that same time and place by a Spitfire. This German pilot's personal insignia was a red rooster. No. 402 Squadron's Canadian pilots reported seeing your fight, and they confirm that both enemy pilots bailed out of their aircraft." Robbie told me that the German ace was a Major Gerhardt Weick or Weiss, I don't remember which now.

The two victories were positively confirmed, he said. My air victory score now totalled six and one-half enemy aircraft confirmed destroyed, so I had finally become an ace fighter pilot, the first Eagle Squadron ace and the first American ace of the Second World War. How about that! My Uncle Larry and my stepfather, Roy, both of whom were fighter pilots in the First World War, would be proud of me when they heard the news. It was a damned good thing I didn't know who the enemy pilot in that red rooster 109 was at the time. If I had known, I'd have gotten a real bad case of the brown-ring twitch. Sometimes it pays to be ignorant. I was glad to hear that both the Kraut ace and the "new boy" got out of their aircraft and parachuted to safety. Sort of eased my conscience, I guess, to know that I didn't bump them off.

Near the end of my second week in the Royal Victoria Hospital the Doc told me that I was now well enough to be transferred to the RAF hospital at Torquay. I had been up and about for several days, hobbling around on crutches, with which I had learned to navigate fairly well. It's a funny thing, but my wounds never really did hurt much after the first day. I was rested up, and all the nervous tensions of combat operations had slowly disappeared from my mind and my body. Wendy came down from London to visit me for a few hours, which made me very happy to be alive that day.

I felt completely relaxed, knowing that for another couple of months at least I wouldn't have to fly any combat missions. Even the daily explosions of the German long-range artillery shells didn't bother me too much. Now I could think about tromorrow and know that tomorrow night I'd still be alive—not shot down, burning, crashing, and killed. The fearful dreams—nightmares, really—left me and I began to sleep peacefully through each night. To be frank, I was almost glad that I had gotten shot up. I wonder if other fighter pilots sometimes felt that way?

So the morning arrived for me to depart for Torquay. An orderly brought my uniform, which had been thoughtfully cleaned, pressed, and repaired by someone on the hospital staff. (I suspect it was the same little starched nurse who looked out for Tomlinson and me so faithfully. She was really a dear.) Tomlinson had to remain in the Royal Victoria Hospital; his back injury wouldn't permit him to travel yet.

Off I went about 10 a.m., first in a wheelchair, then in an ambulance, to the railway station in Folkestone. An orderly assisted me into the waiting train and seated me in a carriage compartment next to a window.

"Have a good journey, sir," says he as he picks up my crutches and starts out the door.

"Hey! Where are you going with my crutches?" I shout at him. Once more I got an astonishing explanation. The crutches, I was told, were hospital property and could not go with me! The RAF hospital would issue me another pair when I got to Torquay.

"But I need them for the trip," I protested. "Suppose I've got to go to the WC (English for toilet) or something? I can't walk without them, damn it." The orderly was sorry, he understood my problem, but he took my crutches anyway.

Not long after that two elderly ladies entered the compartment and began to make a motherly fuss over me, the poor wounded hero. The train finally pulled out of the station with a shrill whistle, and I was on my way, immobilized, to Torquay. Soon a pleasant conversation was going and the ladies served up cups of hot tea from a big thermos, along with some delicious sweetcakes; my cup was filled and refilled several times.

After an hour or so of this I began to feel the urge to use the toilet, which was in the far end of the railway coach; the urge became more critical as we traveled over the clicking rails. "No, no more tea for me, thank you." My bladder was swelling fast. I began to wonder if we'd ever get to Torquay. The kind ladies tell me we'll arrive in another thirty or forty minutes. Can I hold out? I grit my teeth; try to think of other things. No use, it won't work, I'm about to burst. I can't ask one of the ladies to help me to the can. Nothing to do but grin and bear it. I am in utter misery by now.

Finally the train pulled into the Torquay railway station and I peered frantically out the window for a medical orderly who was supposed to meet me. At last I spotted an RAF sergeant with a Red Cross armband. I opened the window and yelled for him to come quickly—it's an emergency! As he entered the compartment I told him to get me to the WC double-quick. Being a good smart sergeant, he immediately understood the situation. And let me tell you that I just barely made it; if the zipper on my pants had jammed at that moment, I'd have been a drowned duck. Oh, what a wonderful relief!

Following this near catastrophe, the sergeant gave me a set of elbow crutches and off the train we went to a waiting staff car. After driving maybe a couple of miles, we arrived at the grand portals of a very large resort hotel—the RAF Convalescent Hospital—my home for the next several months.

This hospital was unusual in several ways. It was managed like a hotel, with a reception desk, bellboys, large private and semiprivate rooms, spacious dining rooms with liveried waiters, a music salon, a movie theater, a swimming pool, game rooms, and a fully stocked and operating bar lounge. The hotel, or hospital, grounds were beautifully landscaped, and off a large terrace was a huge formal garden filled with multicolored flowers, trimmed hedges, and stately shade trees.

I was assigned to share a room with a little English flight lieutenant, John Barrow, who had a broken back. Johnny was returning from a bombing mission over Germany one dark night in his Wellington bomber (usually called a "Wimpy") when the aircraft hydraulic system got shot out by flak. The crew managed to get the undercarriage down for landing, but hadn't enough hydraulic pressure left to operate the flaps and brakes. Johnny landed the Wimpy pretty hot. It rolled off the end of the runway, with its nose section stopping just over the concertina barbed wire that was strung around the airfield perimeter. Johnny didn't know the wire was below the cockpit hatch—it was too dark to see it—and so he dropped through the hatch, landing right in the middle of the wire coils. The wire entangled his feet and legs, upended him, and he fell heavily to the ground, breaking his back. He had been at Torquay for several months. When I first met him he was in a cast from his hips to his neck, sort of like an armored breastplate worn by knights of olden days. I'll bet that cast weighed fifty pounds at least. He could walk once he was helped out of bed or a chair by an orderly, by me, or by some other kind soul. He was a happy, friendly little fellow and a fine roommate.

There were lots of other guys in the hospital, mostly Battle of Britain types. Quite a few were amputees, mostly legs; some had broken pelvic bones from high-speed parachute jumps; others suffered from gunshot and flak wounds; a number had broken arms, legs, and necks; but the worst cases were the poor guys who were burned. Some of the latter had hardly any faces left—noses, ears, hair, eyelids, lips, all burned off—and hands that had been burned to crisps and looked more like claws.

Fire in the air or after a crash is the most fearsome thing to the airman. If you get shot down in flames the fire is like a white-hot blow torch around the cockpit, and when you open or jettison the hood to bail out, the terrible flames are sucked in, and in those few seconds burn the airman horribly. To crash and burn, to be injured or unconscious or trapped in the burning wreckage of an aircraft, is terrible to contemplate. I once knew a guy who crashed in a Hurricane fighter, had his legs jammed in the cockpit and couldn't get out, when the aircraft burst into flames. He crashed in a heavily wooded area where the crash trucks just couldn't get to him. We could see him burning in the cockpit and hear his pitiful cries, but there was no way we could get through the flames to help him. A senior officer (name purposely omitted) did the only humane thing possible under the circumstances: he shot and killed the burning pilot. Before his death this Hurricane pilot weighed nearly 200 pounds. When the fire finally burned out, what was left of his smoking corpse weighed less than forty pounds.

There were two wonderful doctors at this hospital—one was a Scot, Dr. Archibald McIndoe, and the other a New Zealander, whose name I don't remember now—who worked with the burned guys. I am certain a host of RAF airmen remember these doctors and thank them for their lives and reconstructed faces, hands, and bodies. By skin grafts and other surgical means, they actually rebuilt burned-off noses, eyelids, lips, and ears, repaired burned hands, and even grafted hair back on their patients' burned heads. They were real artists, so to speak, who remade men.

After I had been at Torquay a couple of days, Johnny and an Australian pilot decided to show me the local sights. We left the hospital on a bright, sunny afternoon and boarded a city bus for the brief ride downtown. The Aussie, who was a night fighter pilot, had been badly burned in a crash. His face still looked rather bad, with the burned skin stretched tightly over his cheek bones, his ears gone, his nose partly gone, and his eyelids and eyebrows burned away. His face looked more like a skull. His hands had also been badly burned, so he wore white silk flying glove liners to keep the painful skin grafts covered. Johnny and I were used to his appearance and I guess we never really thought about his terrible disfigurement.

After we got on the bus and began our pleasant afternoon outing, a woman passenger said to another woman loud enough for the Aussie to hear: "How awful and inhuman he looks. They should not allow him to be out among other people." The Aussie stiffened at this cruel, unthinking remark, telling Johnny and me that he was going back to the hospital. I blew my stack at the damned woman and told her several things about her questionable birth, the stupid old bitch! We got off the bus at the next stop, walked back to the hospital, and our Aussie friend went directly to the seclusion of his room without a word. If his burned eyes could have done so, I know he would have wept. Never again, at least while I was at Torquay, did he leave the confines of the hospital. I hope the doctors finally got him rebuilt so he could face the ungrateful bastards of this world.

The hospital bar, which was open each day from about 11:30 a.m. to 1 p.m. and 5 p.m. to 11 p.m., was a great morale-builder. When someone was to be discharged from the hospital, or was going on a good long sick leave, there was always a big bust the night before. There were also welcoming parties when "fresh meat" arrived at the hospital, providing, of course, they weren't in too bad a shape to withstand the rigors of our hospitality. Another American, Reade Tilley, whom we nicknamed "Clark Gable" because he sort of resembled the actor, arrived at Torquay with back and leg injuries sustained in a bailout. He received the appropriate welcome and indoctrination through one of our busts. Later, in 1942, Reade became an ace while fighting in the air battles over Malta.

There was usually a party of some sort in progress or planned to celebrate just about anything one could think of. We kept a checklist of days to celebrate—not in order by the calendar, just a long list. The next event on this list was celebrated, no matter what the date might be. If someone entered the bar at the height of one of our busts and asked what it was all about, he might be informed that we were celebrating Saint George's victory over the dragon, Peary's discovery of the North Pole, or the invention of the steam shovel—anything. We just celebrated these events in the order indicated on our bust list, and when we had finally established 365 daily celebrations, we began to divide the days in half, establishing one celebration at noon and another in the evening. Eventually we reached our goal—730 parties per year, which was just about all we could handle. I even had one bust approved and entered on the list—the Battle of New Orleans—that some of my British colleagues weren't too sure about.

One noontime, when we were celebrating the discovery of Haley's Comet, we got a little bent out of shape and consequently missed our lunch. Of course, when the bar closed at 1 p.m., we were starved. A couple of guys got a cab, went to a seafood shop where they bought several buckets of boiled lobsters, and brought them up to Johnny's and my room for a feast. Johnny, by this time, had passed out and was lying on his bed, snoring softly.

We found the lobsters rather difficult to get out of their shells, and we didn't have anything to crack the shells. One of our brighter boys unbuttoned Johnny's shirt, laid the lobster on Johnny's thick chest cast, then took off his shoe and gave the lobster a mighty whack. It worked, so Johnny's cast became our anvil. No, the cast didn't break, luckily, but you can imagine the fishy smell of the lobster juice that ran down inside it.

The broken shells and other trash were tossed into the wastebasket. After a bit the wastebasket was full and someone decided to empty it out the window. About this same time a titled lady was officially visiting the hospital, escorted by our gallant hospital commander. Standing below our second-story window and viewing the delightful formal gardens from the terrace, they were suddenly showered with bits and pieces of defunct lobsters!

The hospital commander arrived with a thunderous roar in our peaceful midst, pieces of lobster clinging to his hair, his handlebar mustache, and his uniform. The roaring continued unabated for a very long time. Our names were taken by the orderly officer, and we were all confined to quarters until further notice. Johnny's odorous condition was immediately noted. He was hauled off by a squad of orderlies, his stinky cast sawed off, his body cleansed, and a new cast put on him, through all of which he continued to snore softly in a gentle drunken stupor. We weren't in an acceptable condition to apologize to the titled lady, and it might not have been wise anyway; I understand she really flamed after the "lobsters from heaven" incident.

Another somewhat unusual thing about this hospital was a bevy of young ladies who attended most of our more genteel social functions. We had tea dances and dinner dances, and it was quite a normal thing to see guys on crutches, or all bandaged or casted up, trying to dance with these girls. They didn't do too badly either, for a bunch of shot-up cripples. To an outsider our dances may have appeared somewhat bizarre, but we all enjoyed such functions. And sometimes, if you were a good guy and not in too bad a shape, you might be encouraged to escort one of these young ladies home. Then, if you had really lucked out, you might not get back to the hospital until dawn or even later the next day.

I knew one guy, Timmy, who had broken his leg in a parachute jump, who took such a young lady home to her second-floor apartment. About dawn there came a heavy knock on the door. "Who is it?" she calls sweetly.

"It's your husband, home from North Africa," answers a powerful, deep voice.

"My god!" exclaims the lady.

"Adios," says Timmy, as he bails out the window partly dressed, with the rest of his clothes tucked under his arm. He landed with a crash in the bushes twelve feet below and broke his leg cast all to hell. Somehow he managed to get himself fairly well dressed, and, using his crutches, hobbled back to the safety of the hospital where his damages were soon repaired.

Several days later Timmy and I saw this same young lady again, on the arm of the biggest, meanest looking captain in the whole British Army. That's about as close to being shot down in flames as Timmy ever came. I experienced no problems of this nature since, during my sojourn at Torquay, Wendy came down from London twice to visit me.

Each evening in our hospital, about 6 p.m., a loud speaker system would blare forth: "Drunks' bus leaving in five minutes!" This meant that a regularly scheduled bus was leaving for downtown Torquay and would deposit its passengers at various local pubs, hotel bars, or cinemas of their choosing. At closing time, about 11 p.m., the bus would stop at the same locations, collect all the odds and sods, and drive them back to the hospital.

One time Johnny, Timmy, and I decided to go to a downtown pub for the evening. We had an Aussie friend (not the burned guy) who had crashed and broken his pelvis in a couple of places. He wore a cast from his waist that extended down each leg, and he navigated with elbow crutches. He wanted to go with us, but since he couldn't bend in the middle to sit down on a bus seat, we put him in the rear baggage compartment where he could lean, standing upright, against the side of the bus. So off we merrily went to town.

When we arrived at the hotel pub of our choice, we all streamed out of the bus, almost forgetting our Aussie friend, who was yelling at the top of his voice, "Get me out of here, you bastards!" We trundled him into the bar and securely propped him up in a corner where he could lean, with some degree of safety, against both the wall and the bar counter. By closing time he was resting comfortably, with his lower half standing straight up in its cast and his upper half flat on the bar, both sections being full of gin and bitters.

After great exertions, we reloaded him into the bus baggage compartment and headed for home. He was so quiet back there that we completely forgot him. The next morning the garage manager called the hospital orderly officer for an ambulance to come to the bus depot and pick up our Aussie friend, who, he said, was mumbling something about causing serious injury to a couple of Englishmen and an American.

All was not fun and games at the Torquay hospital. The burned guys were constantly undergoing excruciatingly painful skin grafts. The doctors stripped pieces of hide off their rear ends and thighs, and then transplanted this skin to horribly scarred faces. The skin of their burned fingers was grafted together, like a frog's webbed feet, until it covered the raw flesh; later, when the hands were fairly well covered with new skin, the fingers were cut apart. A terrible ordeal, to say the least.

The amputees were being trained to use their artificial limbs, and occasionally, especially those with legs gone, would slip and fall. Someone would immediately rush to help the patient up and would be told, amid a torrent of swear words, to "Leave me alone! I'll learn to use this goddamn thing if it kills me!" Those with broken bones, or who had been shot up, periodically exercised their injured bodies, and I've seen their faces, paled by pain, covered with a cold sweat.

Finally, after a month or so, the cast was cut off my right leg, giving me my first look at the damage done. The whole thing had healed well, stewing in its own juices, as the doc had told me. The two machine gun bullet holes left reddish scars, each about the size of a quarter, except for the place where one of them had exited against my shin bone. I gingerly felt the bone splinter, which protruded a bit, but which was growing back slightly out of place. My head wound, of course, had long since healed into a ridged scar.

My right foot, however, didn't look so good. The cannon shell had blown off three of my toes and shattered most of the bones on the top of my foot and the arch. My big toe was OK, but the one next to it was sort of shriveled and drawn up. Since the connecting bones in the foot were shot away, the toe didn't join on to anything; it just flapped loose. The doc said that it should have been amputated at the Royal Victoria Hospital, and that if it bothered me he'd cut it off. Not bloody likely. To hell with that! The only time my wounds hurt was when they cut the cast off; the saw cut slightly into my ankle flesh.

I hobbled around bandaged up for a few more days, until they made a steel and leather plate for my foot. This thing fitted inside my shoe and was designed to give me added support when I walked. After several more weeks of getting used to the foot plate, a shoe, and a cane, I was told that I would be discharged from the hospital. A month's sick leave was granted to me in the United States by Air Ministry, and, following the leave, I would be assigned for six months as a flying instructor some place. Posting orders would be sent to me, via the British Embassy in Washington, D.C., when my future assignment was confirmed. Of course, that evening we all roundly celebrated Dunn's return to active service.

The next morning, supporting an aching head and with somewhat foggy vision, I departed from the RAF Convalescent Hospital by railway for London and a visit to my squadron, which was still located at RAF Station North Weald, before going on leave. As the train pulled out of the Torquay station fond farewells were shouted to me by my late comrades-in-arms: "You poor bastard, returning to active service. How bloody awful! Get another piece shot off your rear end soon and hurry back, Bill! This is the place to fight a war—booze and babes, not bullets! Send us a CARE parcel from the States! Don't forget to write— if you know how to write!"

What a motley crew they were, standing there on the station plat- form, all casts and bandages and burns and bullet holes—my good and true friends. "So long, you crazy bunch of characters. Keep a light in the window for me. Take care of yourselves. Be seeing you around."

7. In the Eye of the Storm

I arrived back at North Weald airfield and the squadron about noon the next day, after a pleasant overnight visit with Wendy at her London flat. My squadron buddies welcomed me enthusiastically at lunch time, but they had to get right back to dispersal; a big fighter sweep over France was on for that afternoon. The sorry news, told to me by Uncle Sam, was that my very young and good friend, Tommy McGerty, had been shot down and killed on 17 September. It happened on a bomber escort mission, a circus. No one really seemed to know exactly how it occurred, except that Tommy got separated from his section leader in a big dogfight and was bounced by a couple of 109s. It was assumed that Tommy and his Spitfire fell into the North Sea. Damn it to hell, Tommy, I'm sorry. He was just nineteen years old when he met his death in battle.

Uncle Sam also told me that Red Tobin had been killed in action during a fighter sweep near Boulogne, France, on 7 September. Andy "The Mad Russian" Mamedoff was killed in an aircraft accident on the Isle of Man on 8 October. Andy was leading a flight, including three new boys, during very bad weather, when they all crashed into a high hillside. So all of the Eagle Squadron's three original members—Tobin, Mamedoff, and Keough—had bought it in the service of Great Britain. There were a lot of new faces in No. 71 Squadron.

Following lunch at the mess, I went out to our dispersal hut to pick up my clothes and other personal belongings that had been cleared out of my room the day after I got clobbered. There it all lay, stuffed into a parachute bag, in a puddle of water on the hut floor. Thanks a lot, you bastards! Opening the bag, I picked out what remained of my kit: my best uniform all crumpled and soaked through, a couple of dirty shirts, my ruined new cap, my few toilet articles. All my socks, underwear, towels, neckties, clean shirts, and handkerchiefs had disappeared into some light-fingered SOB's kit. No one in the squadron, including the adjutant whose job it was to take care of my stuff, seemed to give a damn. Yes, I was somewhat pissed off.

Among other things, I found out that Chesley Peterson and Gussy Daymond, the guys Robbie was pushing for promotion to squadron leader and flight lieutenant, had been awarded the Distinguished Flying Cross during my absence in the Hospital. For what? Pete only had two victories. Gussy didn't get his fifth victory until 19 September, nearly a month after I shot down my fifth and sixth enemy aircraft. What about my victories—didn't they count? It seemed as if my distinguished flying achievements had been purposely overlooked. After I got shot up and chucked in the hospital they decided to forget all about me. The DFC was normally awarded to a fighter pilot with five victories. I'm sure, but I can't prove it, that Robbie, our intelligence officer, who was also a Member of Parliament and very influential at Air Ministry, worked the DFC gongs for his two fair-haired boys. I never did get a silver British DFC, just some bullet and cannon-shell holes awarded by my German opponents.

Later, however, Pete and Gussy did make some pretty good scores. Pete got six Huns confirmed, three probables, and six damaged, was promoted to squadron leader of No. 71 Eagle Squadron, and was later awarded the British Distinguished Service Order (DSO) as well as the DFC. Gussy got eight confirmed victories, plus one damaged, was awarded the DFC and Bar (a second award of the DFC), and became squadron leader of No. 121 Eagle Squadron, the second squadron to be formed. Years later, in the U.S. Air Force, Peterson became a major general. Gussy ended his service career as a lieutenant colonel in the USAF Reserve. They both did a hell of a fine job during the war and deserve their honors.

There was no doubt that I was somewhat piqued by this slight. The news media were also, at that time, writing up Gussy as the "first American ace," which was not true. Years later Air Ministry official records, and British and American historians of the Second World War, proved without a doubt that the honor of being the "first American ace of the war" belongs to me. Combat reports were verified by Air Marshal Sir Patrick Dunn (no relation) and W.J. Taunton of the Air Historical Branch, Royal Air Force; by Colonel William F. Curry and Royal D.

Frey of the United States Air Force Museum; and by Colonel Raymond F. Toliver and William N. Hess of the American Fighter Aces Association. AFAA research concluded that I was the "first Eagle Squadron pilot to shoot down an enemy aircraft, the first ace of the Eagle Squadron, and the first American ace of the Second World War." Having had my victories confirmed for the second time should settle this matter once and for all. (Sorry, Gussy, no hard feelings.)

So, on this note of discord, I said goodby to No. 71 Eagle Squadron—for good—that same afternoon. The squadron's record at the end of 1941 was 45 enemy aircraft confirmed destroyed, 15½ probably destroyed, and 24½ damaged. Not too bad; however, we had lost eight pilots killed in action, three were missing in action, and six were prisoners of war. Our worst record was the number of guys who were killed on active service; seventeen died in flying accidents. Six of our guys who "got the wind up" were returned home.

Catching some transport back to London, I returned to Wendy's waiting embrace. A couple of days later I reported to the seaport at Greenock in Scotland, where I boarded the French passenger liner *Ile de France,* now serving as a troopship, sailing for Halifax, Canada. The first leg of my sick-leave journey to the United States had begun. I told Wendy before our parting that I would return to her one day soon, and I'm certain she knew that I meant it.

In midwinter the North Atlantic can get pretty rough and cold. The *Ile de France* was supposed to be stabilized in heavy seas by some sort of gyro arrangement. Well it was, sort of. The ship didn't pitch and heave with the waves; it just met them head on and banged and shuddered and shook its way through them. A Royal Navy cruiser escorted us about halfway across the Atlantic, until two little Canadian Navy corvettes took over. I'd certainly have hated to be a swabby on either of them. They were like corks in the heavy seas, rolling almost halfway over from port to starboard, and sometimes they'd actually disappear from our sight in the deep troughs between the mountainous waves.

By the way, the captain of our ship called all of us officer passengers together one day, when we were in mid-ocean, telling us that our vessel carried only enough lifeboats and rafts for about half the people on board. If we got torpedoed some of us would have to swim or sink. A calculated risk, he said. Now who in the hell made that calculation?

Some Admiralty staff weenie, no doubt. Anyway, after a week of bouncing around on the submarine-infested high seas, we made safe port at Halifax. The rough passage had made everyone, including the ship's sailors, a little green around the gills.

Roy, my stepfather, had been recalled to active duty as a lieutenant colonel in the U.S. Army Air Corps and was at that time supervising the installation of some underground fuel tanks at Wright-Patterson Army Air Field near Dayton, Ohio. Upon my arrival at my folks' home in Dayton we split a good bottle of real American bourbon whiskey—all three of us, my mother, Roy, and me. It was a grand reunion, lasting until the wee hours of the morning. Roy showed me the message he had received from Air Ministry in London on the day after I got shot up. It read:

"Immediate from Air Ministry, Kingsway, 05545, 28/8/41. Regret to inform you that Pilot Officer William Robert Dunn is reported to be seriously wounded as the result of air operations and admitted to the Royal Victoria Hospital, Folkestone, today 27 August 41. Any further information received will be communicated to you immediately. Under Secretary of State, Air Ministry, 0452."

The message, of course, panicked my mother because it said I'd been seriously wounded and the Air Ministry didn't send a follow-up message with further details. Roy tried to find out more from Air Ministry, but without luck. They finally got the whole story in a letter from me—my wounds weren't so serious after all. Then they read a newspaper article about my fight and saw a picture of me in my hospital bed smoking a cigarette.

On Sunday, 7 December 1941, I heard on the radio the astonishing news that the Japanese had attacked Pearl Harbor in Hawaii! President Franklin Roosevelt had declared that the United States was now at war with the Axis Powers. The attack was called a detestable act by a cowardly enemy. Hell, it was a well executed surprise attack, and the United States was simply caught with its pants down. No one will ever make me believe that U.S. intelligence sources didn't have some idea that such an attack would occur. I'm sure the information was there; they just didn't know how to collect and evaluate intelligence data and apply it to the trend of military events. That's one thing the United States has always lacked—adequate military intelligence—and when they do gather such vital information, half the time they won't believe it.

They have another great failing—underrating and belittling the capabilities of the enemy. Years later on Okinawa, I met and talked to the man who planned the Pearl Harbor attack, General Minoru Genda of the Japanese Self Defense Force, and let me tell you he knew his business. Yes, the United States got caught with its pants down, and it has happened several more times. (As examples: the Battle of the Bulge, the fall of the nationalist Chinese Government, the Communist Chinese offensive in the Korean War, the Tet offensive by the Viet Cong and North Vietnamese Army in Vietnam, the Soviet invasion of Afghanistan.)

With the United States declaration of war things began to pop. Dimouts and blackouts were put into effect. Civil defense measures, such as air raid warnings, civilian evacuation plans, and casualty first aid, were practiced. Spy hunts were conducted, and security tightened on military and industrial complexes, communications centers, and transportation terminals.

Some of the spy hunts were planned and executed by bloody idiots. In the initial panic following Pearl Harbor they rounded up the Japanese people living in the United States and dumped them into concentration camps. It didn't make any difference if they were American born citizens, old people, or babes in arms—all were considered to be possible enemy aliens. How stupid! A lot of unnecessary misery was caused to the poor Japanese-American people because of an unreasonable and unrealistic government policy. We did almost the same thing as the Germans with their concentration camps. A hell of a lot of the Japanese-American boys proved later to be excellent, loyal, and brave American soldiers on the European battle fronts, where they fought valiantly for their country—the United States of America.

About a week before my leave was up, I received orders posting me to No. 31 Bombing and Gunnery School at Picton, Ontario, Canada, where I was assigned to assist in the training of Canadian (RCAF) and British (RAF) aircrew members. I had by this time quit using my cane, although I still limped on my bum right leg and foot a bit. I was happy to get the Canadian assignment, to get back to active duty and flying, as I was terribly bored with nothing to do at home.

Picton was a small town on Prince Edward Peninsula, on the north shore of Lake Ontario between Wellington and Prince Edward Bays. The airfield, operated by the Royal Air Force, was located on a large flat-topped hill above and behind the town. Our aircraft were old Fairey Battles, and when I say old I really mean ancient. My job was to fly the aircraft while a couple of air gunner students did practice firing at a drogue target towed on a long cable by another elderly Battle over the lake. It proved to be monotonous work, but it was flying—about five or six hours' worth of twenty-minute flights each day. On 7 February 1942 I was promoted to flying officer (first lieutenant).

These old Fairey Battles were very much underpowered for their size, hard to maintain because of their advanced age, and could get tricky, especially on the ground. To begin with, they caught fire a lot from priming the engine to start. Their brakes were operated by air-bottle pressure, which was usually low or leaky, and invariably, just when you were taxiing between two rows of parked aircraft, the damned brake pressure would fail. This situation could really get your undivided attention, causing a considerable amount of pilot panic as well as a scattering of ground crew personnel for safety. There was only one solution: give the Battle enough throttle so that its faster movement caused more airflow control over the big rudder, thereby providing a very limited steering capability.

They were spooky old crates, those Fairey Battles, but they had seen honorable and valiant service in the prewar RAF and during the hectic days of the 1940 Battle of France, where, as part of the Advance Air Striking Force, they provided air support for the British Expeditionary Forces. And they were veterans of the air battles over the beaches at Dunkirk. Age, not defeat, had caught up with them, and in the end they were relegated to student training and drogue towing at No. 31 Bombing and Gunnery School. I'll never forget my first flight in one. The Battle had a two-position pitch propeller, which no one told me about; there I sat up in the sky trying my damnedest to adjust the prop pitch like a constant-speed propeller.

Since I hadn't received a letter from Wendy for some time, I wrote to Uncle Sam Mauriello at North Weald, asking him to give her my new address in Canada and to see how she fared. A couple of weeks later Sam replied to my letter. Her block of apartments in Kensington had been badly hit by bombs during an enemy air raid. Wendy was dead! I couldn't believe it. I read and reread Uncle Sam's letter several times. Sam also told me where Wendy was buried, and, like the good guy Sam always was, he went to the cemetery and placed a bouquet of flowers on her grave in my name. I hurt inside, in my heart, for a long time. Goodby forever, dear Wendy.

Well, those of us still living must go on our way through this earthly existence. Some months later I met and fell in love with a beautiful, dark-haired girl named Martha Alton-Mouck who lived in Picton. Both she and her brother were orphaned when they were very young. Martha's brother had gone to sea in the Merchant Navy and was lost when his ship was sunk by a German U-Boat in the North Atlantic. Martha lived with her Uncle Hugh and Aunt Agnes McWilliam in a small house on John Street near the Picton docks. Uncle Hugh, in his younger days, had been a sailor; during a flash fire on board his vessel, he had been terribly burned on his face and hands.

On Wednesday afternoon at 5 p.m., 13 May 1942, Martha and I were married in the Picton United Church, Captain, the Reverend J. F. Reycraft officiating. Wedding music was played on the church organ by Professor F. E. Walden during the ceremony, and Miss Helen Yarwood sang very sweetly the song "Because." Martha's bridesmaid was Miss Bernice Kingsley, and my best man was Pilot Officer P. T. Edwards. A reception followed at the Picton RAF Station Officers' Mess, which, so the newspaper account of the affair stated, "was bright with spring flowers." Our brief but delightful honeymoon was spent in Toronto. We were a very happy couple, and Martha began the difficult task of knocking the rough edges off me.

Shortly thereafter I was transferred to No. 1 Operational Training Unit at Bagotville, Quebec. This newly formed OTU was to train Hurricane fighter pilots for the Royal Canadian Air Force, and since few Canadians had yet returned from England with combat experience, we RAF types became the first group of instructor pilots. The first station commander was none other than "Lovely" Parker, now a group captain. The chief instructor, the CI, was Wing Commander Edwin Reyno, a Canadian who had just completed a combat tour with the RAF in England. Squadron Leader Al Schwab was the chief flying instructor, the CFI, and Squadron Leader Charley Woolich was the chief ground instructor, the CGI. I was made the flight commander of B Flight and, with four other instructor pilots, was given a dozen RCAF student fighter pilots to train.

Our Hurricanes were Mark IIAs, but built in Canada by the Canadian Car Company. They were equipped with Hamilton Standard propellers, instead of the De Havilland or Rotol props, which the Hamilton Company, for some reason, would not guarantee with a prop spinner installed. This caused a restriction in the performance, especially the speed, of our Hurricanes, but they weren't too bad to fly. Their Merlin engines were built under license by the U.S. Packard Company, and, to be frank, ran a lot rougher than those built by Rolls-Royce. Packard mass produced the engines; Rolls-Royce made each engine by hand.

Every morning my first job was to test fly each of my eight Hurricanes before I permitted my student pilots to fly them. We taught the students everything we'd learned in air combat, especially air fighting tactics. We did a lot of air gunnery practice over Lake Saint Jean, where our Westland Lysander aircraft towed drogue targets for us. On October 1, 1942, I was promoted to flight lieutenant (captain). About that same time I found and rented a small house in neighboring Bagotville so that Martha could join me at the station.

The summer months in northern Canada are pretty nice, but it gets damned cold in the winter, twenty or thirty degrees and more below zero day after day, and the snow gets rump-deep to a tall Indian. Flying in such freezing weather was miserable. If one of our guys went down in that vast, sparsely inhabited brush country, every second counted in finding him before he bloody well froze to death. We were always blowing oil lines in the Hurricanes during such cold weather; the oil would get as thick as grease and it took a considerable amount of slow engine running time to thin it out each day. All our aircraft had to be hangared in wintertime or we'd never have gotten them started.

During the fall of 1942 I heard that most of the Americans in the RAF's three Eagle Squadrons (71, 121, and 133) had been transferred to the U.S. Army Air Corps to form the 4th Fighter Group of the 8th Air Force. Americans in the RCAF were also being transferred to the Air Corps. I can't say I was enthusiastic about the possibility of my being transferred; I was very happy with my situation in the Royal Air Force. I talked the matter over with Group Captain Parker. He told me that if I'd stay with the RAF, he'd arrange for me to command a fighter squadron and for my promotion to the rank of squadron leader. True to his word, he gave me command of No. 130 Fighter Squadron, based at Bagotville, and had me promoted to acting squadron leader; the "acting" in RAF terms meant "temporary, on probation, unpaid."

Martha wasn't very happy in Bagotville. The place was really just a small village in a bleak wilderness. The French-Canadians weren't friendly toward us, there wasn't any sort of social life or entertainment, and it was as cold as a witch's teat on a frosty Friday. The nearest town of any size was Chicoutimi, about fifteen miles distant. It wasn't a very pleasant life for her, stuck out in the boonies, I must admit, and besides, she was now pregnant. So I sent her back to Picton, to her friends and to civilization. Maybe things would work out better for us in the future so we could be together again. I continued with my tasks of bringing No. 130 Squadron up to strength and preparing it for combat operations in anticipation of moving the unit overseas soon. It was not intended, however, that I would be its leader in combat.

Early in 1943, about February I think it was, the United States Inter-Allied Personnel Board queried me about transferring from the RAF to the U.S. Army Air Corps. It was sort of implied that if I didn't agree to a transfer, they'd come and get me. I understand that the British Government had agreed on sort of a reverse lend-lease arrangement for us. If we were experienced in combat operations, the United States paid the British a fairly high sum of money, or credit, for our return to U.S. service. The United States at that time needed our wartime talents. The more combat experience we had, the higher the payment. The function of the Inter-Allied Personnel Board was to get all Americans serving with the British and Canadian armed forces returned to U.S. military service—some 40,000 men in the Air Force, Army and Navy were involved.

The letter I received from the U.S. War Department stated I'd be given equal rank in the Air Corps, and I knew the U.S. pay and allowances far exceeded that of the RAF. The Canadian Army and the Royal Air Force had been very good to me, and, I believe, I had in turn served them well and honorably. But Martha seemed pleased with the offer, so I agreed to the transfer. On 15 June 1943 I was released from the RAF to the U.S. Army Air Corps, being assigned to Mitchell Field, Long Island, New York, as a first lieutenant. There I exchanged by RAF blue uniform for the "pinks and greens" of the U.S. Army.

My orders were screwed up right from the start: no pilot's rating at all, and first lieutenant was hardly what I'd call equal rank for a squadron leader. So I went down to the War Department at Washington to see the chief of the Inter-Allied Personnel Board, Major General Guy V. Henry. Henry was the son of the famous Indian fighter, Major

Guy V. Henry, 3rd United States Cavalry Regiment, who, among many other battles and skirmishes of the Indian War period, also fought at the Battle of the Rosebud in June of 1876 in Montana Territory. In that battle our troops, under the command of Brigadier General George Crook, were defeated and retreated before the same horde of hostile warriors who, several days later, wiped out Lt. Colonel George A. Custer's 7th Cavalry command at the Battle of the Little Big Horn.

I found General Henry's office with some difficulty in the maze of the headquarters staff's organized confusion, where I asked a little old scrawny guy wearing a GI (government issue) shirt and trousers, and who was sitting behind a desk that had seen better days, if I could please speak to the general.

"Who the hell do you think I am?" he roared at me.

"How the hell do I know who you are?" I countered. "I don't see any rank badges on your uniform, and I'm not too damned good at guessing games."

He—General Henry—laughed loudly and, I thought, happily. He shook my hand, asking what he could do for me. I explained my pilot rating and rank problem. I told him that I'd be damned if I was going to fly number two guy for some Air Corps joker who had never heard a shot fired in anger. The general told me to sit down, he'd be back in a few minutes. Twenty minutes later he returned, handing me a set of orders as a pilot and a promotion order to captain. How about that?

"That's the best I could do," he said, meaning the captaincy. "And I'll tell you one thing," he continued. "If you had come in here crying on my shoulder, I'd have kicked your can clear up to your collar. I like people with a little spunk who stand up for what they think is right. I hate yes men. However, I must warn you, Captain Dunn, to be careful of your tongue. You may be able to cuss now and again at an old major general—but be damned careful how you address some of our young ninety-day wonder majors. One other thing. You're going to run into a lot of Air Corps types who will be jealous of your RAF service and combat experience, and they'll try to shoot you out of the saddle, mark my words."

I liked this little old general. He was a soldier's soldier, an unforgettable character. We talked together for perhaps thirty minutes more. I learned that he had been retired from active service several years before the war in Europe started, was about sixty-five years old, and, when the war started for the United States in 1941, had wangled to get back on active service in his present capacity as chief of the Inter-Allied Personnel Board. Like his father before him, he was a cavalryman. He was interested in my past experiences while living on an Indian reservation, and in my personal association with Indians and their customs.

Finally, when I thanked him for his kind assistance and prepared to leave his office, we again shook hands. I knew he liked me because he said, "In the old days you'd have made a good cavalryman, but now, these days, I can see the spirit is still there with you airmen. Good luck to you, and good hunting. Keep a deep seat in your saddle and a tight rein. So long, my boy."

I think, in the old Army days, I'd like to have served with Guy V. Henry, either the father or the son.

On 23 June 1943 my son, Gerald Roy Dunn, was born at Picton, Ontario, Canada. (He was named Gerald for Martha's brother, Roy for my stepfather.) I couldn't get leave to be with Martha at Jerry's birth because of my recent transfer between military services. Quite naturally, that didn't please Martha at all, but it was just one of those things we had to put up with in wartime. Also, I had received my first Air Corps assignment to the 53rd Fighter Group at Page Field, Fort Myers, Florida, as assistant group operations officer and fixed aerial gunnery instructor. In late July Martha and Jerry arrived at Fort Myers where, not far from the gulf beach and next to a mosquito-infested swamp, I managed to rent a small cottage for an exorbitant price. At least we were together again.

The commander of the 53rd Fighter Group, a full colonel, was a real weirdo. He wore riding breeches and riding boots (no spurs), carried a riding crop, wrapped a white silk scarf around his neck, never flew a group aircraft to my knowledge, and didn't particularly like young fighter pilots. He piled all sorts of ridiculous ground training on the "fly boys," but held back on actual flying training time. He and I soon had a go-round when I suggested the group's pilots should spend many more hours in the air on combat tactics and air firing. He wanted me to increase their classroom hours with tactical and gunnery theory. I lost, and off he strode, slapping at his polished riding boot at each stride with his riding crop. He knew what training was required—he was an expert in such matters, he informed me.

The 53rd Fighter Group was equipped at that time with Bell P-39

Airacobras, which had been nicknamed "the Allison time-bomb with a Curtiss Electric fuse." I certainly felt sorry for the poor SOBs that had to fly those damned things in combat against real fighter aircraft. With their tricycle landing gear, the P-39s were just great for taxiing. The known bad habits of all aircraft were collected together and developed into the P-39s' flying characteristics: flat spins, tail plane (stabilizer) stalls, tumbling, to mention a few of the most dangerous. The Allison engine was behind the pilot, which threw the CG (center of gravity) way off, and the propeller shaft ran between the pilot's legs to the three-bladed prop in front.

The Airacobra's engine ran rough most of the time, overheating all the time. There was always the worry that the prop shaft would seize, split apart, and castrate the unlucky pilot. If you got into a flat spin or tumble with the damned thing—and it was easily done if you weren't very careful—there was nothing to do but bail out of it. (My kid brother, who trained on P-39s in the class of 43G, bailed out of three of them—two flat spins and one tumble.) As an example, if you were practicing firing at a ground target and pulled up sharply after your pass, the tail plane would stall without warning and the rear end of the P-39 would fall out from under you with a frightening snap. If you were too low, there wasn't a chance of recovering—you went in with the kite. Trying to trim the Airacobra, even in level flight, was like sitting on the head of a pin, where you could fall off in any direction at any time.

In the beginning of the war the RAF, short of fighter aircraft, ordered 675 P-39s from the Bell Aircraft Corporation at Buffalo, New York. Their order was soon reduced to 80 aircraft because of mechanical problems and the Airacobra's failure in action against German fighters. It was a miserable kite to fly, and a lot of good guys busted their butts in the P-39. We should have set fire to them all; however, we gave them to the Russians. No wonder they're still mad at us.

Luckily, the group was soon re-equipped with the North American P-51A Mustangs, the "Spam Cans." Unluckily, they too had Allison engines, which limited a fine airframe to about 18,000 feet altitude. Later on, when the Allisons were replaced by Packard-built Rolls-Royce "Merlin" engines, the P-51 Mustang finally came into its own as a truly great fighter aircraft, one of the very best in the war.

While I'm bitching about some of the Air Corps equipment, I must mention their 70-mil reflector gunsight. It certainly took a real idiot to design such a sight, and another idiot to accept it for purchase and installation in American fighter aircraft. A gunnery problem: If an enemy aircraft is crossing 90° in front of you at 1,000 feet range at, say, 380 miles per hour, quickly figure out your deflection shot. How many times does 70 mils go into 380 mph? Well, it figures out to about 5.5 radii, but by the time you've figured it out, the enemy kite is long gone. Of course, different ranges and different attack angles, requiring deflection variations, added to the confusion. Now the British used a 100-mil reflector gunsight, and given the same problem, you knew in an instant that the radii deflection was 3.8 and you fired.

In October of 1943 I heard that the 406th Fighter Group was being formed at Congaree Army Air Field, Columbia, South Carolina, for immediate service in Europe with the 9th Air Force. I volunteered for the 406th (the 53rd had become an RTU, a Replacement Training Unit), was accepted as assistant group operations officer by Colonel Anthony V. Grossetta, the group commander, and departed the full colonel expert's school of theoretical warfare knowledge for the real war. Grossetta was an honest-to-goodness fighter group commander, a flying leader who knew his business. He built the 406th, with its 512th, 513th, and 514th Fighter Squadrons, into an outstanding military unit that achieved tremendous success in the European air war. Martha and Jerry moved with me into a small apartment in Columbia. She wasn't at all pleased by my volunteering to go back to war with the 406th but, like I told her, that's what I was hired for. It went over like a lead balloon.

The 406th was equipped with Republic P-47 Thunderbolts, a large and heavy aircraft, but a powerful, well-armed fighter. Its big Pratt and Whitney R-2800 radial engine could turn out 2,000 horsepower, and its eight .50-caliber machine guns put out a terrific firepower. In addition, the P-47 could carry 5-inch HVAR rockets, bombs, or external fuel tanks—or it could carry the whole works at once. Without a doubt, the P-47 was the world's biggest single-engine fighter/bomber. Like all other fighters, the P-47 received its share of nicknames: Repulsive Scatterbolt, Jug, Thunder Mug, Bucket of Bolts, T-Bolt, Big Ugly, and Cast Iron Beast. The Jug was a good and honest aircraft that performed every mission assigned to it effectively and efficiently—a real war bird, she was. As we found out later, it could also take a hell of a beating and still get us safely home.

Shortly after I joined the 406th my kid brother, who was then finishing P-39 RTU, asked me to get him assigned to the group. I talked it over with Colonel Tony Grossetta and the transfer was soon arranged. I explained to my brother in no uncertain terms that if he pulled his own weight he'd stay with the 406th; if not, I'd be the first one to fire him. I was responsible to Grossetta for recommending his assignment. Of course, when our mother heard about it, she was very much upset. All three of us—her two sons and her husband, Roy, who was now fighting Japs in Burma—would be in combat at the same time. She wrote to me, imploring me to take very special care of my kid brother, her "baby."

Well, as it happened, things didn't work out well for my brother. His flight and squadron commanders reported to me that he didn't always obey their instructions, acted a bit of the "hot shot," and, in their opinion, he wasn't ready for combat flying. So, I fired him, and for many years thereafter he never spoke to me. At least I kept him from getting his or someone else's rear end shot off. Maybe I was right, maybe I was wrong; my mother was pleased that he didn't go with our group. I wasn't happy about the way things turned out, but Colonel Grossetta said that the decision was mine, so I made it. My brother was later sent to Alaska, again flying P-39s, where he at least survived the war. I honestly think he'd have been quickly clobbered in the European air war.

The day in March, 1944, finally arrived when the 406th Fighter Group began its move to England and the war. Again I packed Martha and Jerry up and sent them back to Picton to await my return from this combat tour of duty. (A combat tour in fighters was 100 missions. Bomber crews did 25 missions per tour.) Before Martha left me at the train station she gave me one of Jerry's toys, a small calico dog named "Pancho," to carry with me for good luck. Pancho flew on every mission with me, strapped to the back of my flying helmet during the rest of the Second World War. (Years later he flew with me in Vietnam, and I still have my old and somewhat battered Pancho.)

We sailed from New York on board the French ship *Louis Pasteur* and, after a week or ten days of zigzagging across the Atlantic to avoid the German submarines, landed in England. From the port we took a troop train to southern England, to our new airfield at Ashford in Kent. Here, living in tents, messing in field kitchens, washing and shaving in our tin hats, and bathing in mobile canvas showers, we began the final operational training of the group.

I was issued a P-47D-15 Razorback, painted a dingy olive drab camouflage color, and with the identification marking 4P-V. Technical Sergeant Henry "Chief" Jones, who was a full-blooded Cherokee Indian from Oklahoma, was my crew chief. The Chief and I hit it off real good right from the start. When he said my Jug was serviceable, it was serviceable without a doubt. Sometimes, unexpectedly, I'd take Chief up for a local flight with me, which isn't easy in a single-seat aircraft. Chief would sit in the cockpit seat, then I'd place a wooden ammunition-box cover across his knees for me to sit on, and off we'd go into the wild blue yonder. You can bet my Jug was always serviceable, since neither of us had parachutes. And Chief never knew when I'd say, "Let's go for a ride and find out for sure." I flew over seventy-five missions before I had a single abort, which must be some sort of a record for a P-47 crew chief in wartime.

To begin the group's combat training, we sent the squadron commanders, flight commanders, and operations officers to other operational fighter groups, where they flew a dozen or so combat missions. Several others of us were sent to the Royal Air Force's Fighter Leader School at Milfield airfield in Scotland for ten days. There we were given special training in leading fighter groups (three squadrons) and fighter wings (three groups or nine squadrons) into air combat, in developing tactics and techniques for attacking a variety of ground targets, in the employment of special weapons, and in air force close support and cooperation with our ground troops. This special training for selected combat leaders was in preparation for the soon-to-come invasion of France.

When we U.S. types graduated from Fighter Leader School, we were authorized to wear a special insignia or identification: a gold-bordered rectangular blue cloth patch behind the pilot's wings on our uniforms. This indicated to all that we were specially trained as fighter leaders, were combat experienced, and, regardless of our ranks, were authorized by 9th Air Force to lead fighter groups and wings in combat. It was an honor to be selected for this very important combat leader responsibility, and shortly thereafter I was promoted to the rank of major.

I should mention that we all took our own aircraft to the Fighter Leader School. Since there was a great variety of pilots—RAF, RCAF, RNZAF, RAAF, SAAF, USAAF, Poles, Czechs, Free French, Norwegians, Belgians, Dutch—we had an equally great variety of fighter aircraft—Hurricanes, Spitfires, Typhoons, Tempests, Mosquitos, P-38s,

P-47s, P-51s. One the last day of the school we were all permitted to check out and fly any or all of these other aircraft. It was a bloody madhouse, let me tell you, and damned dangerous as well. A quick cockpit check, a short briefing (if you could understand the other guy's language), fire the aircraft up, and go.

I don't know why somebody wasn't killed or maimed in the wild melee that ensued. The propeller and engine torque in a U.S. fighter was the opposite to that in some British aircraft, such as the Typhoon and Tempest. So off they'd go, one careening to the left, another to the right. I understand the RAF station commander took one frightened look at the gaggle in the sky, went into his office, closed the door, shuttered the windows, and said "the hell with it."

Well, we all survived somehow without busting our cans or breaking the various aircraft. I got to fly a Spitfire Mk IX, a Typhoon, and a P-51. Someone had painted on the Typhoon's engine cowling the instruction: "If this engine catches fire on starting, don't just wave your arms at the pilot—try putting the bloody thing out." A Pole and two Free Frenchmen took turns flying my Jug. Only one guy, a Dutchman flying somebody's USAAF P-51, scraped off a wing tank on a tree during a low buzz job. The tank had been modified by the American pilot and his crew chief to carry their clothing and a tool kit. So, after the too-low pass, clothes adorned the tree branches and tools were scattered all over that part of Scotland.

Following my return to Ashford, I took a three-day pass to London. While there I went out to the little quiet cemetery where Wendy was buried. I put a small wreath of flowers on her grave with a prayer for her. Then I took the red paper poppy I'd picked up in 1940 at the Westminster Abbey grave of the British unknown soldier, scooped out a little bit of earth beside her headstone, and buried the poppy with her. I'm certain that Wendy understood my thoughts, my feelings, my memories.

8. Air Offensive Europe

The 406th Fighter Group entered the fray with a fury that was spurred by Colonel Grossetta's words as he opened his fighter's throttle on takeoff to lead the first full group mission: "All right guys, here we go! Remember, no guts, no glory!" An hour later we sustained our first combat casualty—Major Bill "The Green Hornet" Merriam, who was senior group operations officer. We had flown into northern France, our mission to dive-bomb and strafe a German airfield. The airfield was defended by all sorts of flak guns—heavy, medium, and light—and after the first section of four Jugs went screaming down from 12,000 feet on their dive bombing runs, the Krauts turned it all on.

Merriam, leading the second section, yelled over the R/T: "Here goes the Green Hornet!" and down he dove flat out through the hail of flak. I witnessed the whole thing as it happened. I was circling above the enemy airfield taking strike photos of the action with a new camera that had been installed in my Jug's fuselage belly. Just as Merriam dropped his 500-pound RDX bombs he got hit in the engine by several 40-mm cannon shells. His P-47 began to smoke, streaming oil, and then it began to burn. He pulled out of the dive, picking an open field to try to belly in his kite. He was too low to bail out. Merriam's voice came again to us over the radio, "That's all for me, boys. Guess I'll get captured. So long." I watched Merriam's Jug touch the ground, slide across the small field in a cloud of dust and smoke, and then in a sheet of flame it blew all to hell. The Green Hornet never got out.

We continued our attack on the Hun airfield until it was practically reduced to a mass of rubble. Columns of smoke from burning buildings, fuel storage tanks, destroyed aircraft, and exploding ammunition dumps attested to the plastering we gave the place. We must have destroyed at least thirty or forty enemy aircraft dispersed around the airfield perimeter and in sand bagged revetments. It was indeed a shambles when we finished our attack and returned to our home base at Ashford. Major Littleton C. Selden assumed Bill Merriam's group operations job.

The group was now flying at least two combat missions daily, sometimes three, which is pretty tough on pilots. Each mission duration averaged about three hours, striking targets in France, Belgium, and Holland. I don't think many fighter pilots enjoyed dive-bombing. It seemed that special targets were always selected for Thunderbolt pilots: well defended targets like railway marshalling yards, airfields, communications centers, factories, and critical bridges. The concept of our employment was simple. The inline-engine fighters couldn't take the heavy flak, the big 88-mm cannons, 40-mm rapid-firing "Chicago pianos," 20-mm and 7.9-mm light flak. One round through the coolant system and a fighter like that was a dead duck. But the good old lumbering cast iron Jug could take it all and survive. You'd be absolutely amazed at the P-47s that made it home after being literally shot to pieces—cylinders blown completely off engines and streaming oil, great rents and holes blasted through wings, fuselage, and tail planes. A great percentage of those tough old war birds were Class 26ed (junked) after bringing their pilots safely home.

Armed recce suited the Jug pilot better; targets of opportunity, as they were called. Shooting up railway trains in enemy territory was by far the most exciting. Dive down at about a thirty-degree angle to the train's route of travel to give the Hun antiaircraft gunners a deflection shot, which they usually missed. Now squirt the locomotive with your eight .50-caliber guns firing API (armor piercing incendiary) ammo. A few good hits on the boiler and up would pop a geyser of white steam and smoke. Now you had the train stopped and could beat it up at your leisure. If it proved to be an ammunition train, some caution had to be exercised in case it blew up under you on a firing pass. One of our 406th boys had to fly through the debris of such an explosion, and an 88-mm shell case smashed into the leading edge of his starboard wing and stuck there.

Shooting up enemy airfields caused the old adrenaline to flow, too. There was always a lot of heavy and light flak around them, and since you had to really low-fly, you were continually in the thick of it. Here again was the hazard of the enemy aircraft target or a fuel dump blowing up in your face—a great red fireball, and you were so low and close that you had to fly through it. But the tough, reliable Jug would generally make it.

I suppose, all, told, I've helped shoot up a dozen or more enemy airfields in France, Belgium, and Holland, and I've gotten my fair share of flak and bullet holes out of it. (I was credited with the confirmed destruction of twelve enemy aircraft on the ground, during such attacks, and damaged several more.) We lost a lot of good guys on those missions in the months just before D-Day—the Air Offensive Europe, as the historians called that period of operations—but the Germans lost most of their air force. The trick to stay alive and airborne was not to duel with the Hun antiaircraft gunners, to make no more than a couple of passes at the target, and then get the hell out of there. Many times, when I've heard the crack of shrapnel and bullets hitting my kite, I've thanked the good Lord that I had a Thunderbolt strapped to the seat of my pants.

Escorting bombers, prior to D-Day, was a mission that fell more to the 8th Air Force fighter pilots than to us 9th Air Force types. However, every now and then we'd get shanghaied by the 8th for an assist. By an intricate scheduling system of fighter group relays, the bomber boys could be assured of Thunderbolt and Mustang escort and protection all the way to targets deep in Germany and back home again.

I should add here that numerous times we were required to combine three missions into one flight: escort the bombers bound for Germany until relieved by another escort relay of fighters, then dive-bomb some preplanned target, and then do armed recce until we departed Hunland for our home base in England. The only trouble with that type of operation was that the staff weenies started counting them as three sorties, equal to one combat mission credit. On that basis, a 100-mission combat tour required about 300 sorties to complete.

There was one real hazard to us on bomber escort operations—even more dangerous, sometimes, than enemy flak and fighters—and that was friendly air gunners aboard our bombers. Someone forgot to teach them aircraft recognition, so those trigger-happy characters took a squirt at everything that flew. Of course, at a distance and in a head-on position with our radial engines, we might have been mistaken for enemy Focke-Wulf 190 fighters. We were always very careful never to approach the bombers with the aircraft nose pointed toward them. We used to fly parallel to them, a safe distance away, and tip up our wings so the bomber crews could see their shape and U.S. insignia. Even with this friendly gesture, a few .50-caliber tracers would come whizzing in our direction. Yes, we lost a few friendly fighters to our air gunner comrades-in-arms.

Air gunners were a pet peeve with me. One of them might get lucky and shoot down an attacking German fighter; then fifteen air gunners would all blast away in that same general direction, and all would claim the unlucky Hun as their victory! When, for example, an Me.109 made an attack on our bombers, the pilot usually broke away after his firing pass by half-rolling his kite and then doing a split-S. At that point of the break, the Kraut pilot would "pull the teat" and the 109 would emit a trail of black smoke—naturally—yet you'd be surprised at the number of air gunners who would claim they had shot it down.

I remember one time in early 1944 when an RCAF B-25 got shot up by enemy fighters and was limping home, oil spewing out of its engines and spattering all over the fuselage and gunner's turret. Well, one of our P-47 guys, trying to be helpful, flew up alongside to provide the Canadian B-25 safe conduct to its home base. The air gunner let loose with his machine guns broadside at about a 50-foot range and punched a few holes in our hero's Jug. Our pilot backed off, but followed the B-25 to a safe landing, where he too landed. Climbing out of his cockpit, this feisty little fighter boy let it be known that he was going to poke the air gunner right in the nose. The Canadian gunner emerged form his B-25, and besides being about eight axe-handles tall, he was exceedingly broad of beam and had fists like two sledgehammers. Apologies were quickly made for not being able to distinguish the P-47's bulk through the oil-covered turret, an invitation to the mess bar was extended, and the great alliance was preserved.

Now how did I get on the subject of air gunners? Oh yes, we were discussing bomber escort missions. If we were lucky and were assigned to the more distant fighter relays along the bomber routes, we generally got a crack at flushed enemy fighters. If we were unlucky and were assigned to the near relays—cross the North Sea, overfly Holland, and terminate at the German border—we'd get stuck with the dive-bombing and armed recce bit.

In May 1944 we lost the commanders of the 513th and 514th Fighter Squadrons in action. The 513th CO, Major Gordon W. Fowler, was shot down in France while shooting up ground targets on an armed recce mission. He belly-landed his P-47 and was observed by other squadron pilots to get out of his kite uninjured. He was never reported by the Huns as a POW. Months later we found out, through Free French intelligence sources, that just after Fowler got out of his Jug some Kraut infantry troops attempted to capture him. Fowler pulled out his Colt .45 automatic pistol and started his war all over again by firing at the Huns. The result was as could be expected. He was shot several times and, after being bayoneted several more times, died of his wounds. A gallant, fighting airman, Major Fowler fought to the last against impossible odds until he was outnumbered, overwhelmed, and killed in action.

The CO of the 514th, Major Gene L. Arth, met his death while attacking a German ammunition train in northern France. He made one pass at the train's engine, firing a long burst into its boiler, which exploded in a great geyser of steam. Now, with the train at a complete standstill, he began to systematically beat up the individual railway cars, each exploding with a terrible roar and flame as Arth's .50-caliber bullets set off the ammo cargo. A couple of passes at the train would have been OK, but in this case he made one too many runs on the target. The train carried, at each end, railway flak cars manned by some of the best Hun antiaircraft gunners. Major Arth started dueling with them, which was an absolute no-no, since the chances were very high that the fighter pilot would come out second best. They hit his Jug hard, several times. It burst into flames and, diving straight into the deck, exploded in a ball of fire.

The 512th Fighter Squadron commander, Major John L. Locke, survived all the group's combat operations, was promoted to command the 406th a year or so later, and eventually became a USAF general officer.

Another of our guys, a young lieutenant, was killed in action a few days after Arth met his death. We were dive-bombing a marshaling yard in France, and again the flak was heavy, intense, and accurate. His voice, weak and gasping, came to us over the radio, "I've been hit in the stomach by a cannon shell. My guts are spattered all over the cockpit. I'm going in." And with the abrupt and shocking end of his radio transmission, we all witnessed him put his Jug into an almost vertical dive. Roaring straight down to the ground, his engine at full bore, he crashed and exploded right in the middle of a Kraut antiaircraft gun position!

They got the lieutenant, but he took at least two 88-mm guns and twenty Squareheads with him.

During the 1942-43 period, when I was gone from the European theater battle scene, the Germans made operational an advanced version of the Me.109 and developed the new Focke-Wulf 190. Replacing the older Me.109Es and some 109Fs, they put the Me.109G into war service. The G model had a more powerful engine, greater firepower, could climb more rapidly and fly higher. Basically the Me.109 airframe design remained much the same; but the F and G aircraft had rounded wing tips instead of square tips, the stabilizer struts had been removed, and the prop spinner was larger.

Their newest fighter, the FW.190, called in German "Würger," meaning "butcher-bird," was powered with a BMW radial engine, was considerably larger and heavier than the 109, was armed with two 13-mm machine guns in the upper engine cowling and four 20-mm cannons mounted in the wings, and was about 50 miles per hour faster than the 109. We met two versions of the FW.190 in air combat. Since we didn't know the Hun model designations at that time, we simply called them "short nose" and "long nose" FW.190s. (Their models were FW.190A and 190D.)

Although the Germans had this new and very much improved fighter in service, it seemed to me that the flying skill of the enemy pilots had decreased considerably from those we fought during the first years of the war. Some of them, when you got on their tails, didn't seem to know what to do in the way of taking evasive action. Some of their maneuvers, instead of being a violent reaction to get out of your field of gunfire, were almost gentle banks, permitting you to nearly climb up their rear ends before giving them the blast. It seemed such a shame to waste an outstanding aircraft—even if it was a Hun kite—by letting a poor pilot fly it. Of course, the enemy fighter commanders, the old boys, were still damned good at the air fighting game, and I believe that most of those guys survived the war. There was no doubt in my mind that, by mid-1944, the enemy was running short of good fighter pilot material and their new boys just weren't fully trained for air combat.

Before D-Day, during the Air Offensive Europe period, I fought FW.190s in half a dozen separate engagements. I had no trouble at all staying with the 190s in my Jug, and this included speed, turning radius, diving, and climbing. Unfortunately for me, two of the FW.190s

I shot down were declared "unconfirmed" victories; a third FW.190 was assessed as a "probable." Oh well, what the hell. I knew they went down, I even had some pretty good gun-camera films of these fights, but that's the way it sometimes goes, especially when they go down over their own lines.

With regard to my statement concerning the deteriorating skill of the German fighter pilots by 1944, our group got into a scrap with forty Me.109Fs and 109Gs over the French-Belgian border area one day in lousy weather conditions. We saw them coming toward us just below a thick cloud deck at 14,000 feet; they hadn't seen us. We bounced them good, shooting down eleven of them without a single loss to ourselves. Following this engagement I knew that our fighter pilots were now much better than theirs, and that we had finally achieved air superiority in the European skies. I think I felt a bit sorry for some of the Kraut new boys. Years later I was informed by several ex-Luftwaffe fighter pilots that in those war days many of their young pilots only lasted a week or ten days in combat.

Early in the morning of 14 May we received a field order for a mission to dive-bomb another railway marshaling yard in northern France. This type of operation didn't excite much enthusiasm among our pilots any more. The Huns, proud of these locations, surrounded them with great quantities of flak weapons. It was very difficult for us to break through these antiaircraft defenses, especially when in the target area we had to line up our aircraft with the target for a short period of time to aim and release our bombs. That period of time— although it was just a few seconds— when you couldn't take any evasive action was very dangerous; you were most vulnerable, and it seemed like every Kraut flak gunner was banging away at you personally. L.C. Selden and I had been up since 4 a.m. planning the mission: the route in and route out, altitudes, armament required to assure target destruction, number of strike aircraft to be employed, communications frequencies, recall code words, probable enemy reaction by fighters and flak, withdrawal support, study of target photos—a multitude of very important factors that must be considered to insure a successful combat mission.

Since both L.C. and I were in group operations, we agreed that we would take turns flying on these missions. Today was my turn. On the flight line I checked over my Jug, marked 4P-V, with Chief Jones. She was ready, as always, to go to Hunland. Armament that day for each P-47 on the operations was eight .50-caliber machine guns, ten 5-inch HVAR zero-rail rockets, one auxiliary belly gas tank, and two 500-pound RDX bombs. After the dive-bombing, we planned to do a bit of armed recce on our own coming home, so we were carrying a full load of trash to scatter among the Squareheads.

We were lined up in such a manner that we could take off two Thunderbolts at a time, by sections. L.C. was at the runway control truck signaling us when it was our turn to take the runway and go. I'd guess about a dozen Jugs had taken off the piece-plank runway at Ashford when it came my turn to go, with my wingman Lieutenant Hughes.

Pouring the coal to our heavily weapons-loaded P-47s, we roared down the runway in a cloud of dust. Suddenly there was a hell of a bang! My Jug's nose abruptly pointed high in the air, the aircraft slewed around to the left, there was a flash and a lot of smoke, and my face was being pelted by all sorts of debris. Out of the corner of my eye I saw that Hughes's kite was on fire. I yanked back the throttle, opened the canopy and, in my frantic rush, forgot to undo all the radio cords and oxygen tubes before I went out and over the cockpit side. I got upended, landing first with a shocking crash on the Jug's left wing-root, then sliding off to fall with an equally hard crash from the wing's trailing edge to the ground. I really wasn't hurt much, I guess, but my face was bleeding from many cuts. Besides having the wind knocked out of me, it sure scared the bejesus out of me! Almost in a daze, I sat there on the steel runway planks staring at my Jug, which was blown completely in half just behind the cockpit!

"What the hell happened?" I shouted at L.C. as he came running toward me, followed by a flock of medics.

"Your landing gear hit a bomb that fell off the Jug that took off just before you!" he informed me. "Great God, are you lucky it didn't blow you to hell and back."

We both looked at the shambles that had once been my favorite P-47. She was full of shrapnel holes, besides having her rear end blown off. The fragments that had cut up my face were from the blast-shattered plexiglass canopy. Rescue guys had now gotten Hughes out of his burning kite, which was set afire by the 500-pound RDX bomb blast. He had been hit in the thigh by a shrapnel splinter and was rushed off to the first aid tent.

L.C. continued to describe the event to me. "I was standing by runway control when the bomb went off. It blew me flat on my can. As I lay there on the deck I could see the whole tail section of your bird sailing through the air directly at me. I ducked out of there and it hit the ground right where I got knocked down. We were both lucky, Bill."

The medics started checking my face, which was pretty well cut up, especially my left eye, then they took me to first aid. There they fished out the plexiglass splinters, including one that severed my upper left eyelid and cut the eyeball. My face, when I got a chance to view it in a mirror, was a chopped-up mess, which the medics soon stitched back together again.

By damn, that was all of that combat operation for me! Blown up by one of our own guys before I even got off the deck. The piece-plank runway was rougher than a cob, and the bomb had broken loose from its brackets. RDX was an extremely sensitive high explosive; my landing gear striking the bomb on the runway could easily explode it, which is just what happened.

The dive-bombing mission did not stop because of this unfortunate incident. Although the bomb did blow a hole in the runway we had been using, the remaining Jugs waiting for takeoff were diverted to our second runway, continuing their launch in a slight crosswind. Hughes was sent to an Army field hospital with his serious shrapnel wound; I went back to duty in group operations to sweat out our guys' return from the mission.

Next day Chief Jones came to the operation tent. He had a funny grin on his kisser. "We got a new kite for you. She's a brand new model, a P-47D-25, even got a bubble canopy." Then he continued, "A funny thing happened. This Jug was delivered by a female ferry pilot from the Air Depot, and she marked in the Form 1 that she'd used the relief tube enroute! Now how the devil do you suppose she did that? She's not built that way—no outside plumbing." I'd still like to know the answer.

We drove back to the flight line in my Jeep, and there, in all her proud and shining glory, sat my new Thunderbolt. No dingy camouflage paint, just bare naked, silvery metal skin.

"They don't camouflage them any more. They say she's faster by about 10 or 15 miles per hour without the paint," Chief informed me.

I walked around to the left side of my new Jug, where my mouth must have dropped open with astonishment; on the engine cowling was painted a sort of cartoon-type raunchy pilot, bent over, and covering his rear end with a steel helmet. Below the cartoon were painted the words "Posterius Ferrous." For those of you who are not Latin scholars, the words translate to "Iron Ass." I could hear Chief laughing quietly behind me. An appropriate name was provided for my new kite and me by my friendly crew chief. The event of the previous day was not a total loss, after all.

Although I hated to lose my old Razorback—she had served faithfully to the bitter end—my new Thunderbolt, bless her, carried me through a lot of tight spots in the months to come, and occasionally she felt the hot touch of the enemy on her "Posterius Ferrous."

Because of my eye and face injuries, I was taken off operations for a couple of days. (Later I lost my left eye.) During that period I visited an old RAF friend of mine, Warrant Officer Allen Deller, who was now flying with a Typhoon squadron. I just happened to mention the 70-mil gunsights we had on our Jugs, and that I wished I could get hold of a British 100-mil gunsight. Allen thought something might be arranged— what did I have for trading material? Well, I had a sheepskin-lined leather flight jacket (Type B3) I could part with.

"Good enough," grinned Allen, "you got a gunsight," which, through some hook or crook, he produced from his squadron's stores within the hour. Allen said more trades might be arranged, if we could collect more jackets.

Back at Ashford airfield I told the other pilots about my trade, holding up my new gunsight like a trophy for all to see. Later that same day, with a weapons carrier full of B3 jackets, I headed back to Allen's airfield. Again, through some devious process known only to RAF warrant officers, an equal number of 100-mil gunsights were produced and delivered to me within a couple of days. Before the week was out our armament types had modified our sight mounts and electrical wiring, installed the British sights, and harmonized them with the guns in our aircraft. Next time I saw Allen Deller and his mob, they were at an airfield near Caen in France, from which they were beating up German tanks and infantry with their powerful "Tiffies." Never did see Allen again—but thanks, old buddy, from me and the 406th Fighter Group pilots.

For some unknown reason Tony Grossetta decided his Thunderbolt should have some sort of distinguishing markings, so he had the rudder and wingtips painted a bright red. His kite sure looked pretty to us, but it looked even prettier to the fighter pilots of Hitler's Luftwaffe. On his first flight into Hunland, Tony's Jug attracted a great deal of attention—a crowd of Me.109s and FW.190s, each vying to get a squirt at the Thunderbolt with the pretty red rudder and wingtips. They didn't get Tony—we had him well covered—but upon landing at our home base, he instructed the aircraft maintenance officer to remove the distinguishing red markings. Distinguishing markings draw unnecessary attention to your kite, which can be very hazardous to your health. Of course, there was a German outfit, the Abbeville Kids, that had the noses of their Me.109s painted bright yellow, but there were about fifty of them. And there was an American P-51 group in the 8th Air Force that sported checkerboard-painted noses, but there were about seventy-five of them. At least if you were flying as a part of a gaggle like that you could sort of disappear into the crowd.

Later Tony told me that in the melee he had gotten on the tail of a 109, but in the excitement he couldn't find the gun-firing trigger—his mind went blank. He said he pushed and pulled everything in the cockpit, but no bangs. The 109 split-Sed and departed the scene, leaving a confused Tony still searching for the gun trigger, which was right under his finger on the control stick. Things like that do occur. It's the fighter pilot's version of buck fever.

The British have a real sense of humor, and occasionally they show it with a great flair. Over in occupied France the Krauts were going to great lengths to build a secret airfield. Their camouflage was nearly perfect, but a RAF photo recce pilot spotted the place. Photo interpreters confirmed the airfield construction and civil engineers determined how long it would be before the airfield became operational. No strike action was taken against the place, but periodically aerial photos were taken to determine the exact construction progress. Finally the day arrived when the Hun airfield was about to become operational. Lo and behold, when the German staff weenies were inspecting and congratulating themselves on their finished product, an RAF De Havilland Mosquito swept in on the deck across the secret airfield and dropped a huge wooden bomb right in the middle of the place. Shortly thereafter, RAF Bomber Command aircraft gave the airfield its wartime indoctrination with numerous loads of incendiary and HE bombs. The Squareheads never did get to use the airfield.

As I have mentioned previously, the Thunderbolt could take a lot of punishment and still bring its pilot safely home. I witnessed several miraculous incidents of this type, but one in particular is worthy of note. One of our guys returning from a fighter sweep, his Jug shot up and on fire, managed to reach Ashford airfield where he decided to belly land his burning kite. Now in a belly landing the SOP (standard operating procedure) is to land gear up, flaps down, cut the master switch, and turn off the gas tanks just before you touch down—and keep your shoulder straps and seat belt tight so your body doesn't slam into the instrument panel. The cockpit canopy would normally be opened, but when you are on fire it must be kept closed so that the flames don't burn you to a crisp.

Well, this guy did everything bass-ackwards. He made his approach low, the Jug trailing a long stream of fire and smoke. He opened the canopy and released his shoulder straps and seat belt. He put the gear down, but he forgot the flaps. He neglected to turn off the master switch and gas cocks. Smoke filled his cockpit, he couldn't see his landing approach, he missed the airfield completely, he flew right into the ground, and the whole works blew up! There wasn't much reason to rush over to the crash site. The Jug was just a mass of twisted junk. Exploding ammo was popping off in the burning wreckage.

We solemnly stood a reasonably safe distance away while the crash crews tried to put out the flames. There was absolutely nothing we pilots could do. No doubt the guy had bought the farm, and what was left of him was burned to a cinder. You can imagine our surprise when, about fifty yards away in the brush, the Jug pilot staggered to his feet, somewhat worse for wear, but still alive and kicking! He was skinned up, had a bit of a flash burn, but no broken bones, not even a black eye or bloody nose.

How could he possibly have survived the terrible crash? It was simple, he told us. When his P-47 hit the deck and exploded, it blew him clear of the cockpit, sending him sprawling in the brush. If he hadn't done everything wrong, like opening the canopy and releasing his shoulder straps and seat belt, he'd still be frying in the debris of his Thunderbolt. What bloody great luck! Next day he was off on another combat mission to Holland.

During the latter part of May and the first few days of June rumors began to circulate concerning the imminent Allied invasion of France—very strong rumors this time. Where was it to take place on the Channel coast? The flying weather over England had been lousy for the past several days, but it wasn't too bad over the Continent. Colonel Grossetta, Lt. Colonel Les Bratton (the deputy group commander), Major L.C. Selden, and a few other people were suddenly withdrawn from combat operations. They were called frequently to 9th Air Force Headquarters for briefings and soon became known as "bigotted personnel," whatever that meant. Yes, something was brewing. You could feel the tension building up.

All the 9th Air Force fighter groups, including the 406th, were directed to step up combat operations in France, especially armed recce missions. Hunt down and kill everything that moved was the field order—railway trains, trucks, automobiles, river barges, coastal vessels, anything that might support the German ground troops—shoot or blow the hell out of it. We were also directed to do a lot of bridge busting, strike heavy flak gun positions, and knock off flak towers.

This last bit, the flak towers, was a very dangerous business. The enemy gunners were encased in steel-reinforced concrete towers about fifty feet high, with all sorts of automatic weapons pointing, it seemed, in every direction. Since our .50-caliber machine guns didn't do too much damage to these towers, except knock off a lot of concrete chips, we soon learned to employ our 5-inch HVAR rockets against them. To get a rocket hit we had to get in pretty close because of the rocket's slow velocity and dropping trajectory. To divvy up the flak tower's return fire, we would attack the tower simultaneously from two or three directions. When we were within firing range, we each let go a pair of rockets. Then we spent the next couple of seconds ducking the other firing aircraft and the rocket bursts. A very tricky business. I might add that we did make several mistakes in tower target identification, blowing the hell out of some French village's water supply towers. C'est la guerre!

On 5 June I flew with a 513th Fighter Squadron mission in the morning for two hours and ten minutes to beat up some canal barges in Holland. It was a quickie, but we did shoot up and sink at least forty laden barges. When we landed we were informed that the group was in a "stand down" status until the next day. A stand down usually meant something big was cooking, since all aircraft were grounded for extensive maintenance during that period. The normally overworked ground crews were still laboring like mad when I hit the sack at about 10 p.m.

9. D-Day and Operation Overlord

It seemed I had barely fallen asleep when I was suddenly awakened by the sound of multitudes of aircraft engines overhead. Ours or theirs? I lay in my canvas cot and listened for a moment. The engines didn't have the unsynchronized throb of the enemy's bombers; must be ours. I looked at my watch; just past midnight and raining. L.C. wasn't in his cot. He must be at group operations. I figured I'd better go find out what the hell was going on, so I quickly dressed and went slopping through the downpour to ops. When I arrived, there was Tony Grossetta, Les Bratton, L.C., and the commanders and ops officers of the 512th, 513th and 514th Fighter Squadrons. They had evidently been at group operations for some time, as the air was blue with cigarette smoke.

"What's going on, guys?" I inquired.

"We are just getting our frag order on the teletype," said L.C. "Looks like this is the big show—the invasion. Everything I've seen so far, including the code words, say 'Go.' We were going to let you get a couple more hours of sleep before we called you over here, but since you're here now we might as well get cracking on this thing. Those birds you hear overhead are gooney birds (C-47s) towing airborne troops in Waco CG-4A gliders and hauling paratroopers. There's a flock of our bombers out ahead of them pounding the Huns in the invasion area and drop zones. We're going to hit them here," continued L.C. as he pointed to the ops map board, "on these Normandy beaches. The Army's invasion force is already at sea, about here, and will hit the coast at daybreak. We're going to launch all three squadrons at 4:30 this morning; we're to provide fighter cover over the invasion beaches."

Colonel Grossetta handed me a piece of paper. "Here, Bill, read this," he said. "It's your personal invitation to the biggest war party in history." The paper was from Supreme Headquarters, Allied Expeditionary Force, and read:

Soldiers, Sailors and Airmen of the Allied Expeditionary Force! You are about to embark upon the Great Crusade, toward which we have striven these many months. The eyes of the world are upon you. The hopes and prayers of liberty-loving people everywhere march with you. In company with our brave Allies and brothers-in-arms on other Fronts, you will bring about the destruction of the German war machine, the elimination of Nazi tyranny over the oppressed peoples of Europe and security for ourselves in a free world.

Your task will not be an easy one. Your enemy is well trained, well equipped and battle-hardened. He will fight savagely.

But this is the year 1944! Much has happened since the Nazi triumphs of 1940–41. The United Nations have inflicted upon the Germans great defeats, in open battle, man-to-man. Our air offensive has seriously reduced their strength in the air and their capacity to wage war on the ground. Our Home Fronts have given us an overwhelming superiority in weapons and munitions of war, and placed at our disposal great reserves of trained fighting men. The tide has turned! The free men of the world are marching together to Victory!

I have full confidence in your courage, devotion to duty and skill in battle. We will accept nothing less than full Victory!

Good luck! And let us all beseech the blessing of Almighty God upon this great and noble undertaking."

The paper was signed by General Dwight D. Eisenhower, Supreme Commander, AEF. (I still have the copy I was given that morning of 6 June 1944, a treasured memento to remind me of those desperate and glorious days.)

"Well I'll be damned," said I, "Ike really means it. Today we finally go—but couldn't he have picked some better weather for the beginning of our great and noble crusade? It's raining like hell; even the ducks are walking." According to the latest bulletin on the weather board I noted the clouds were solid from 1,500 to 15,000 feet in our part of England.

"Maybe it will blow over before dawn," commented L.C. "Let's get to work on this frag. We haven't got too much time before we all become heroes."

The frag order for "Operation Overlord," the code name of the invasion plan, listed a large number of fighter groups assigned the mission of beach cover that day, all in timed relays so that fighter support for the ground troops would be immediately available. There were a lot of new code words to be memorized. Special communications between air groups, naval ships, and army units had been set up, as well as lateral communications between the Allied forces landing on the several designated invasion beach areas. Recce photos of the Normandy battle zones were studied so that we could positively identify our assigned patrol area. Antiaircraft defenses—ours—were plotted on maps. Anyone who flew into those defense zones, friend or foe, would be shot at. Orders were issued to Captain Wilbur Smallwood, the group armament officer, to rapidly up-load the required munitions—machine gun ammo and rockets—on our aircraft. Major Larkin, intelligence officer, dug through his files to compile all enemy reaction data available. Group operations was soon a madhouse, activity of all sorts being generated to prepare the 406th for its D-Day participation. A full-scale briefing of all pilots was now scheduled for 3 a.m.

"Who is flying from group this morning?" I inquired.

"Well," said Grossetta, "the bigotted types can't go yet. They've all been briefed on the Overlord battle plan. Can't risk any of them getting shot down and captured. I guess, for this first mission, you'll have the honor, Bill."

This was surely my lucky day! Raining cats and dogs. At 4:30 a.m. the skies were still blacker than the inside of a cat's rectum. Solid overcast up to 15,000 feet, and who the hell knew who was going to be flying every which direction through that murky stuff.

Colonel Grossetta, directing the briefing in our large mess tent, gave the word to the guys—the invasion had finally begun. After all the whooping and shouting had died down, the sequence of the briefing continued: our missions for the day, three of them, were to fly beach cover; intelligence presented an outstanding briefing on the overall D-Day plan; then weather, armament, and communications gave their data. Tony also told everyone to note the special markings that had, in the past twelve hours, been painted on all our Jugs. Black and white stripes on the wings and around the center of the fuselage. All Allied aircraft had been painted with the same markings; any kite without these zebra stripes was a Hun—shoot it down. Lastly, mission times were given: cockpit time, start engines time, takeoff time, time over target—which each pilot wrote down in ink on the skin on the back of his left hand. You could misplace a piece of paper, but it was usually difficult to misplace your hand. By 4 a.m. we were all climbing into our Thunderbolt cockpits, the dark skies still sending down rain. Start engines time was 4:15, with takeoffs to begin at exactly 4:30 a.m.

Now climbing a full fighter group of three squadrons on a max effort up through a solid overcast some 15,000 feet thick is not easy. Then again, fighter pilots are generally not the world's greatest instrument flyers. Things could get pretty hairy, and usually did. To accomplish this first ticklish part of our mission, the three flights of the first squadron to take off entered the cloud at five- to 10-degree variation from each other's climbing course. This was to give them lateral separation so they didn't ram each other on their climb out. Five minutes later the second squadron entered the cloud with flight separation, followed five minutes later by the third squadron. The squadron time delays and flight separations, if executed properly, should have eliminated the possibility of midair collisions. However, when there are about sixty P-47s climbing up through the thick, dark clouds, there are usually a couple of aborts—engine or communications trouble, with those aircraft now letting down, unseeing, flying blind, to return to base. There's nothing that can excite you more than to be climbing through the cloud, the world outside your cockpit a dark gray void, and suddenly have your kite violently rocked by some other aircraft's slip stream! More brown-ring twitch!

By 4:25 we had all taxied into position, ready for the takeoff signal. I glanced behind my Jug's tail at all the other Jugs in line, props whirling and navigation lights blinking in the steady downpour. Surely we'll get a delay—they won't send us off in this lousy weather. The hell they won't! The greenish glow of the takeoff flare arched up into the rain and the Aldis lamp at runway control began to blink its "go" signal. We're on our way!

I poured the coal to my aircraft and off we went with a clatter on the pierce-plank runway. The tail is up, the gear is lightly bouncing, and we're in the air, skimming over the dark mass of trees and then the tent camp surrounding the airfield. We circle below the cloud base to gather our sections into flights and squadrons, then point our noses up into the English pea soup to begin our climb out in the direction of

Normandy. The cockpit instruments glow in the dark; now set up the climb rate, check compass heading and directional gyro, carefully watch the needle and ball, coordinate with the artificial horizon, keep the air speed steady. I glanced quickly at the two Jugs tucked in formation off my wing tips. I know the eyes of the other two pilots are watching every move of my aircraft. I'm flying instruments for all three of us; they depend solely on my skill, when we're in tight formation, to lead them through the cloud.

What was actually a few minutes' climb seemed to take an hour. Then, as the cloud tops began to lighten with the coming dawn, we suddenly broke out to a clear blue sky above us. Flights of 406th Thunderbolts began to pop up through the dense overcast; there were some narrow misses. In a couple of minutes the group was gathered together again. Reformed, we continued our flight toward France.

About midway across the Channel the clouds began to thin out and disperse. Soon we could clearly see the water 16,000 feet below us. The sight of the massive invasion fleet was absolutely amazing! The Channel seemed to be literally covered with ships of all sorts and sizes, all heading toward Normandy. The skies around us, now bright with sunlight, were filled with aircraft—fighters, bombers, transports. They were ours, all easily identified by the black and white painted zebra markings. What a tremendous sight it was to witness the incredible might of the Allied invasion force in motion! Unbelievable! And here I am, in my kite, a very small part of all this free-world power.

The 406th arrived on station over the Normandy beaches a few minutes before 6 a.m. Not a single Hun aircraft had come up to challenge us in air battle. I couldn't really blame the Krauts. The air was absolutely saturated with allied fighters from the deck to 25,000 feet. Far below us we could see the bright flashes from the guns of Navy warships, their shells bursting just beyond the sandy beaches. Infantry, supported by tanks, had already landed and were fighting their way inland. Paratroopers and glider infantry had landed just beyond the beachheads during the night and early dawn, capturing and holding key positions behind the German front lines. Enemy artillery, mortars, machine guns, supported by infantry, blasted away at our invaders from reinforced concrete bunkers and pillboxes. Fighter/bomber aircraft, flying in direct battlefield support, pounded the Hun positions with bombs, rockets, machine gun and cannon fire. The German Army, so I heard later, fought savagely for every foot of ground they lost. The high casualty losses of our invading troops testify to the ferocity of the battle for the Normandy beaches.

Our patrol period ended uneventfully as far as enemy aircraft reaction was concerned. No one came up to fight us, but what a marvelous event in world history we had witnessed. So we returned to our airfield in England, passing hordes of other Allied aircraft outbound to take up their battle positions. The 406th flew a second and a third beach cover mission on D-Day, but none of us fired a shot.

I understand that two German FW.190 pilots, Oberst Josef "Pips" Priller, commander of JG 26, and his wingman, Feldwebel Wodarczyk, did make a strafing pass over the beaches that day—Heil Hitler!—and then got the hell out of there. Their attack came as such a surprise that they got away with it. Hardly a shot was fired at them. Historians of the war have recorded that the Allied air forces, on D-Day, operated with a strength of some five thousand fighters and three thousand bombers.

A bit of interesting news I heard about this time was that Carroll W. "Red" McColpin, who served in our RAF Eagle Squadrons, was now a colonel commanding the 404th Fighter Group, another 9th Air Force Thunderbolt unit. Welcome back to the war, Red. There was also some sad news: Wee Mike McPharlin, another ex-Eagle friend, was killed in action on D-Day while dive-bombing in a P-47. So long, old buddy.

During the several days that followed D-Day, the 406th continued flying daily missions to Normandy. Now that the ground troops were slowly fighting their way inland from the bloody beaches, these missions were mostly close air support—strafing, rocketing and dive-bombing enemy strong points. A system was employed that we called "cab ranks." Four of our Jugs, as an example, would be assigned to cover a portion of the front lines. If the ground commander in that sector required an air strike on an enemy position that was tough to crack, he could call the cab rank in the air by radio for a cab to make the strike. The enemy target was identified for us—sometimes by terrain features, sometimes by colored smoke shells—and down we'd dive to bomb, rocket, or strafe, depending on the type of target. As a safety factor, so we didn't mistakenly hit our own troops, the infantry guys laid out panels of fluorescent orange cloth on the ground to indicate our front lines. There were cab ranks scattered all along our front, and they were constantly replaced as the fighters used up their munitions and fuel. This system for providing close air support worked very well, especially when our troops were punching through the Normandy hedgerows.

We also did a couple of escort missions for American bombers to strike industrial targets in France and Belgium. One typical mission, on 11 June, was close escort for about a hundred A-20s, A-26s and B-26s. The bombers were strung out over a ten-mile area of sky at 15,000 feet—a bomber stream. Where wasn't any Hun fighter reaction to speak of, but there was a hell of a lot of heavy, intense, accurate flak. It seemed almost stupid for these bombers to fly straight and level through the bursting shells. There was nothing we, in fighters, could do to protect them from the flak, so we flew out to one side of their formation and watched them get shot up.

A direct hit. The bomber, a B-26, is blown to bits. No survivors. Another hit. The A-26 sheds a wing and starts its death dive to earth. The bodies of two men fall clear of the stricken kite; their parachutes pop open. Another crew member, most probably the pilot, didn't get out. Several bombers are trailing smoke. One is on fire with a blazing engine. And still they go onward through the flak, unmindful, it seems, of their high losses—more guts than brains. Like sticking your head in the barrel of a cannon and pulling the firing lanyard yourself. Thank God I was flying a fighter! What a bloody waste of bomber aircraft and aircrews. Too bad the American bomber commanders wouldn't accept the advice of the RAF Bomber Command aircrews, who had over four years of combat lessons learned under their belts. Daylight bombing at that altitude, in a ragged bomber stream, and in straight and level flight—perfect targets for enemy flak gunners—was a killer. Bomber losses on that particular mission were twelve aircraft and about thirty-five or forty airmen, most of them unnecessary losses.

The next night, 12 June, England experienced its first V-1 attack. The V-1s were flying bombs, soon called "doodlebugs" and "buzz bombs." The letter "V," I understand, designated them as Hitler's "Vengeance" weapons. A V-2 weapon was used later on, which was a rocket-propelled missile with a large warhead, but I never saw any of the latter weapons in operation. This first attack on England with V-1s wasn't the greatest success. A whole batch was supposed to be launched, but because of technical difficulties only ten got off the ground, four reached England, and just one struck London.

Launched from the French coast toward London, the V-1s began flying overhead when we were still at Ashford airfield. They were something of a mystery the first couple of days, as no one had ever employed pilotless flying bombs before. You could hear them coming quite a way off, their pulse-jet engines making a sort of odd, deep popping sound. As long as the motor could be heard running, it was reasonably safe for persons below the bomb's flight path. But when the motor stopped, there were a few seconds of deadly silence as the V-1 dove downward, then a bloody awful explosion when it hit the ground. They seemed to fly on three tracks, which we named A, B, and C. A track was just north of Ashford, B track crossed directly over the airfield, and C track was a short distance to the south.

The V-1 had a wingspan of 17½ feet, a length of 25 feet, and weighed about 4,000 pounds, including the 1,870-pound high explosive warhead. They normally flew at an altitude of 3,000 feet and at a speed of around 400 miles per hour. Soon the V-1s were being launched by the Krauts both day and night. They were supposed to create a feeling of terror, but really they were just annoying. A V-1 could, however, get your undivided attention if its popping engine went silent overhead.

To counter the doodlebugs, the RAF formed the Defense of Great Britain Group. This group flew Spitfires, Typhoons, and the new jet-powered Gloster Meteors, each aircraft stripped of all unnecessary weight so that they would have a greater overtaking speed when chasing V-1s. The idea, of course, was to shoot the damned things down before they reached their London target, which, as it soon proved, was very dangerous to the RAF pilot and his pursuing aircraft. A few good hits on the buzz bomb with 20-mm cannon fire and the nearly one ton of HE warhead blew up in the chase pilot's face, making a hell of a big fireball explosion!

One Spitfire pilot who blew a V-1 up was so close to the explosion that he had to fly through the blast. The intense heat of the explosion burned all the paint off his Spit—seared it, to be more exact—clouded his windscreen and canopy, and sealed him in the cockpit. He landed safely at Ashford, where we had to pry the burned canopy off to get the guy out of his kite. The RAF, as expected, soon came up with a solution to the problem. Fly up alongside the doodlebug in formation, then, with your aircraft's wing tip, flip the buzz bomb over and topple its gyros. Down it would go to explode harmlessly in an open field, it was hoped. Pretty tricky, eh? Typical RAF thinking and ingenuity—

less chance of blowing your aircraft and yourself to bits.

As you would expect, all fighter pilots now wanted to knock down a V-1. Soon, when a V-1 was incoming toward England and the Defense of Great Britain Group aircraft were being vectored after it, the sky was filled with every kind of fighter trying to get to it. This, of course, made the intercept dangerous for everyone, and obstructed the DGB Group fighter's mission. A directive was soon issued to all fighter units: the DGB Group would handle the buzz bombs; all other aircraft stay clear of the action. Well. it was fun chasing the damned things while it lasted.

There wasn't too much enemy air reaction over the Normandy invasion beaches, as I have already stated. But on 18 June I had the good luck to engage an Me.110 that was shooting up one of our ships off the French coast near Cherbourg. The Hun pilot saw me coming flat out and turned toward me to make a head-on pass. I had ten 5-inch rockets on board, and as I wasn't particularly fond of head-on attacks, I salvoed the whole lot at him.

The rockets didn't hit him, but they must have scared the bejesus out of him, for he did a steep turn to starboard. I pulled my Jug hard to port, ending up about fifty yards behind this Squarehead's kite, where I let him have the full blast, all eight .50-caliber machine guns. I had never seen an aircraft, unless it exploded, completely disintegrate in the air the way this Me.110 did under the pounding of my guns. It just turned into shattered bits and pieces. No one got out. The ship's crew confirmed this victory for me a day later.

Most of the air combat action during the month of June took place farther inland in France and Belgium, where 9th Air Force fighter and bomber groups were engaged in continuous strikes on the enemy's transportation system and airfields. By 30 June, 9th Air Force combat reports confirmed that 187 Hun aircraft had been shot down, 33 were probably downed, and 63 were damaged. In addition, 34 were destroyed on the ground and another 15 were damaged. Our 9th Air Force losses during that same period of heavy fighting were very high—203 fighters, 39 bombers, 43 troop carriers, and 17 recon aircraft. Most of our fighters were lost to enemy flak while we were striking ground targets deep in enemy territory. Something else to be considered is that during June our fighter force flew nearly 31,000 sorties against the enemy—a thousand sorties each day!

The story of the bitter fighting by our Army troops to get off the Normandy beachhead and gain sufficient ground so that they would have room to maneuver against the enemy has been told in considerable detail by others. Soon they fought their way across the peninsula, thereby dividing the strength of the German forces in that area. At Cherbourg, where a large number of Hun troops had dug in and barricaded themselves in the city's fortress, the German general declared he would never surrender, but fight to the bitter end. The bitter end came a hell of a lot sooner than he expected. On 22 June, about noon, ten squadrons of RAF Typhoons and Mustang fighters rocketed and strafed enemy positions. We, 557 fighters of the 9th Air Force, then dive-bombed the place with 500-pound RDX bombs, some 520 tons. The Allied ground attack began about 14:00 hours, supported by 375 9th Air Force medium bombers, which dumped another 590 tons of bombs on the Kraut positions. By July 1, after a nine-day battle, the enemy surrendered Cherbourg, which included a large seaport to support Allied resupply requirements. Our 9th Air Force losses in the battle for Cherbourg were 30 aircraft shot down and 132 aircraft damaged, all by Hun flak.

Now we turned our attention toward a breakthrough out of Normandy and into the open French countryside. We bombed the hell out of Saint Lo twice in twenty-four hours, on 24 and 25 July, employing just about all the bombers and fighters we could muster. Almost like units parading in a great air formation, each group flew in turn straight across the target area, dumping their bombs in a saturation pattern. Saint Lo was reduced to clouds of smoke, numerous fires, and rubble. We learned a good lesson from this massive air attack: too much bombing can be a very real hindrance to the advance of our ground troops. So much so that with all the streets and roads demolished, plus the shattered and collapsed buildings, our tanks, infantry, artillery, and supply support columns had a difficult time getting through the wreckage of this completely devastated city.

About this time the 406th Fighter Group moved from England to Normandy, to a primitive airfield carved out across some French farmlands by U.S. Combat Engineers near the little village of Ste. Mere Eglise. At the very beginning of the invasion campaign three crash strips had been built near the beaches; A-1, A-2 and A-3 were their designations. Our airfield, A-6, had a single runway made of chicken wire and tar paper. The combat engineers brought in their bulldozers, leveled a strip of land for a runway and taxi ways, and overlaid the raw ground first with pegged-down rolls of chicken wire, and then laid sheets of tar paper over the wire, sealing the tar paper edges with hot tar so that the runway surface wouldn't pull apart so easily. You had to be very careful when you ran up your aircraft's engine before takeoff. The aircraft, even with brakes full on, would slide forward and bunch up the tar paper in front of your wheels.

Our runway at A-6, besides being short, was almost on the beach, so that if you took off toward the north you had to turn sharply and climb like mad to get over the barrage balloons of the invasion fleet ships. Take off to the south and you were over enemy lines before you could get your gear up. We had the same problems when landing—over the balloons or over Hun lines. During taxiing and takeoffs the airfield was covered with a dense cloud of dust. In rainy weather it was a sea of mud.

Our encampment was all tents, except for a couple of large house trailers we used for group operations and communications. Since German bombers, mostly Ju.88s, made a number of sorties at night to bomb the beaches, it was a damned good idea to dig yourself a foxhole. When the Hun kites were overhead, our antiaircraft guns fired up a lot of flak at them, much of which fell back to earth. You could actually hear it come whistling down and smack into the ground near you. Being an enterprising guy, I dug my foxhole under the operations trailer— good cover from all sides and above.

We had all come to France to liberate the place; there were a few Frenchies, however, who sided more with the Krauts than with us. For example, during the daylight hours, French girls who probably had German soldier boyfriends would come riding their bicycles around the perimeter of our airfield and the positions of other American units. They would spot where we had dug our foxholes, then at night creep silently up and toss grenades in our general direction. I soon fixed a string line about 10 inches above the ground in a 12- or 15-foot circle around my foxhole. I put a few pebbles in a number of old C-Ration cans, which I attached to the string line. This device would give me a little warning if someone touched the string in the darkness, rattling the pebbles in the tin cans. My old infantry training was put to good use. Soon most everyone at A-6 adopted my C-Ration can alarm.

Living in a tent camp can get pretty old, especially after living that way for four months with four or five guys sharing each tent. Washing, shaving, and bathing in cold water out of a steel helmet isn't the greatest either. Everyone washed his own clothes, colonels and privates alike, and soap was at a premium. Our uniforms, being of wool or gabardine material, we dry-cleaned by soaking them in aviation gasoline. Of course, you smelled like a gas truck, and some care had to be taken when lighting a cigarette.

Our field messing consisted of K-Rations, C-Rations, and 10-in-One Rations, all of which really weren't too bad if you could find some way to heat them up now and again. One way was to cut off the top of a five-gallon gasoline can, fill it with sand, pour in some aviation gas, and set the whole works on fire. It would burn for ten or fifteen minutes, long enough to heat up your food and some water for a cup of coffee or tea. The British troops had a field ration that was covered with some kind of wax impregnated with a material that burned. They just set a match to the ration carton and in a couple of minutes they had a hot meal. Our food, however, was much better than their bully beef.

One day L.C. and I gave a French farmer some of our extra C-Rations. From the stories we'd heard back in England, we thought he and his family were probably on the verge of starvation. The kind farmer invited us to dinner that evening at his nearby home, where we figured we'd at least be served hot C-Rations. Not so! You can imagine our pleasure, and chagrin, when we dined on beefsteak and potatoes fried in country butter, carrots, hot rolls, dessert, coffee—the whole works. What a bunch of BS propaganda we'd been fed—that the poor French were being starved by the Huns! They had more and better food than we did, at least in Normandy.

During our brief stay at A-6 airfield we learned another trick of the trade from our neighboring RAF allies, a Typhoon squadron based near Caen. Periodically they'd send a kite with a clean belly tank back to England, where the tank was filled with beer. A flight back to France at an altitude of about 15,000 feet and the beer arrived nice and cold. We soon followed their lead, with our 150-gallon belly tanks. Those British types sure knew how to take all the comforts of home to war with them.

Our friend the French farmer gave us a keg of calvados, which we set up on a small table next to the admin tent. Now calvados is some powerful drink—a couple of sips and it starts creeping up on you. A couple more sips and the lights go out. Within an hour the sipping admin staff had to hang on to the grass to keep from falling off the earth. My advice to anyone regarding calvados is to leave it alone.

A couple of weeks later we moved to an airfield previously used by the Luftwaffe, Cretteville, which we designated A-14. This airfield was a most dangerous place. Before they departed, the retreating Germans mined and boobytrapped everything. Our combat engineers found and dug up hundreds of mines, yet you still had to be careful where you walked and what you touched. Reach for a German P-38 pistol, a machine pistol, a Squarehead helmet or Mauser rifle, lying on the ground and you were sure to blow yourself to hell.

In the latter part of July fresh army troops and much-needed supplies began to pour into the Normandy battle zone. These troops were the 3rd U.S. Army, commanded by General George S. Patton, "Old Blood and Guts," as he was nicknamed. The XIX Tactical Air Command of the 9th Air Force was assigned the mission of providing air support to Patton's 3rd Army. We, the 406th, belonged to the 303rd Fighter Wing of XIX TAC.

Patton's tactics were simple: if the enemy is in the field, go clobber him, and don't let up until you've kicked the living hell out of him. His military philosophy for the battlefield soldier was equally direct and to the point: "No bastard ever won a war by dying for his country. He won it by making the other poor dumb bastard die for *his* country!" Shortly thereafter, Patton made himself most unpopular with the air force units supporting his command. He directed us all to wear our steel helmets or helmet liners, and to wear those damned canvas leggings, like a bunch of infantrymen. Who the hell did this tin-star general, with the cowboy pistols, think he was? We soon found out why he was called Old Blood and Guts.

I had an odd experience one evening when I was flying home after a dive-bombing mission. Since my route took me on the outskirts of Paris, I decided to go have a quick look at the place. It looked beautiful from the air, wide tree-lined boulevards, the glittering Seine River, the famous Eiffel Tower landmark—and an Me.109 diving down from the darkening skies to clobber me. I poured the coal to my Jug, turned into the Kraut, and so we began our duel by flying tight circles 6,000 feet above Gay Paree. We took turns squirting at each other, but neither of us could out-turn the other for a good deflection shot. Around and around we went, banging away at each other until, almost at the same instant, we each saw the white star insignia on the other's aircraft. The Me.109 turned out to be a lost 8th Air Force P-51. He thought my P-47 was a FW.190! That was a close one. We then joined up in formation, flying back to A-14, where the P-51 pilot got his kite refueled and then headed off in the general direction of England. It was the 8th Air Force kid's first mission, a bomber escort. He got separated and lost, and had been boring holes in the French skies for a couple of hours all by his lonesome. It was absolutely amazing to realize he hadn't been scrubbed by the Huns during all that time over enemy territory. I'll bet that was a mission he damned well won't forget.

On 28 July we had a long and rough mission to rocket and strafe a German airfield deep in France. As usual, the flak was heavy, intense, and accurate. We had to really get down low on the deck, sometimes below the tree-top level, to make our attacks. Now, flying so low at high speed, sighting a parked enemy aircraft, trying to duck the flak, squirting a blast at the target, then sweeping upward in a steep climb to get clear of the exploding aircraft's debris isn't so damned easy.

We caught the Squareheads flat-footed—all their kites on the deck— and we shot the hell out of them. We also shot up their hangars, buildings, fuel and ammo storage areas, vehicles—anything that moved or didn't move. The airfield was a mass of wrecked, exploding, and burning aircraft and facilities when we victoriously departed the scene. We were credited with destroying at least thirty enemy aircraft, of which number I got four. Several of our guys got shot up by flak, but managed to limp safely home to A-14.

The success of this particular raid was brought to the attention of General Eisenhower through his headquarters staff briefings, which pleased Tony Grossetta very much. Tony was sitting in the ops trailer, proudly grinning from ear to ear, when I walked in and said in a loud voice for all to hear: "Did you hear what General Eisenhower said about me today?"

"No," said Tony, his curiosity aroused, "what did he say?"

"He said very distinctly," I continued, "Who?"

When I and the others present began to laugh, Tony ran me out of the ops trailer with a following shout of "Smart ass!"

10. The Battle for France

Operation Cobra, which was the code name for the massive air attack on Saint Lo, was, as I've already mentioned, carried out on 24 and 25 July 1944. Saint Lo was the location selected for our armies to break through the German lines and begin their liberation sweep across France. On 1 August General Patton's armored columns smashed through the enemy positions beyond Saint Lo and began their rapid advance along the Loire River and on toward Paris. Patton was moving so fast that he hadn't the time to protect his right flank from the large number of German troops south of the Loire. That problem, protection of his exposed flank, was left to us fighter pilots.

The 406th Fighter Group now achieved a distinction unique in the annals of air warfare. In the Chateauroux-Issoudon area, south of the Loire, and advancing to attack Patton's 3rd Army flank through the Belfort Gap, we found an entire German armored column that was 15 miles long. After hitting this column with our full group strength three times during the day, with bombs, rockets, and strafing, the road was jammed by burning, exploding and destroyed tanks, trucks, and armored personnel carriers. The German commanding general asked to surrender—but only to the air force unit that had entirely destroyed his army group. If I remember correctly, Colonel Grossetta did the honors by accepting the German surrender at a bridge across the Loire River. The 406th received a Distinguished Unit Citation for this most unusual action. (The group received a second DUC later at Bastogne for the close air support provided, in very bad weather, to the besieged American toops in the Battle of the Bulge.)

On 11 August, just east of Montrichard, we destroyed a complete railway train and its cargo, sixty German Tiger tanks. That same day we hit two more trains—one made up of fuel tankers—which we left in a fiery shambles. On the 13th we attacked and destroyed six more enemy supply trains in the Argentan area. Near Paris, on 16 August, we fought an air battle with 30 FW.190s. We had no losses; they lost four kites. Later in the afternoon we again engaged another batch of enemy fighters with the loss of one P-47 for two of their FW.190s.

While all this air activity was going on, our ground troops were slowly surrounding a German force of some hundred thousand men in what was called the Falaise Pocket. From 17 August to the 20th we were directed to make continuous strikes against the Hun troops in this pocket. It was like shooting fish in a barrel. The roads were absolutely jammed with enemy transport vehicles and tanks, all of which we methodically destroyed. The end soon came for these Germans who had witnessed the massive strength of battlefield air power. Although about forty thousand did manage to escape from the Falaise Pocket, some fifty thousand were captured and over ten thousand corpses were strewn over the killing ground.

On 25 August three of us—Lieutenants Howard M. Park and Lewis W. Hall and I—were scrambed to hit some enemy shipping in the harbor at Brest. Flying over the area at about 8,000 feet, we observed the German army trying to evacuate their troops by sea. The flak was bloody terrific and one Jug, from some other group, had already been shot down in the drink. The pilot had evidently bailed out without a Mae West and was paddling around in the middle of the harbor. Some other Jug pilot had managed to get out of his parachute harness in the cockpit and had taken off his Mae West. Then he flew very low and slow over the water, through all sorts of flak, and threw the life vest over the side to his buddy in the water. This brave P-47 pilot got shot up a bit but returned safely to his home base. The guy in the water got the Mae West and, so we were later told, was picked up by friendly troops. That brief episode was something to see. We all provided flak suppression for this bold and heroic effort.

After this the three of us picked out ships to hit with our HVAR rockets. Park and Hall made a furious attack on one vessel, holing it twice at the waterline and once below the waterline. They made a second determined attack on another ship and fired their rockets, but they were driven off by the heavy flak before they could observe their hits. I witnessed both attacks and confirmed two good hits on the second ship's hull.

The target I selected was a loaded 4,000-ton troopship at anchor in a small bay just below the city of Brest. Twice I tried to make low-level attacks on this vessel, but each time I was driven off by the intense and accurate flak. Little white-hot balls of fire zipped past my Jug's canopy and kicked up geysers of water all around my aircraft. Finally I climbed up to 4,000 feet, shoved everything forward, and dove flat out on the target ship. I must have been doing close to 500 miles per hour when I leveled out just above the water and salvoed my rockets. Four of them hit the ship dead center, exploding inside the hull; two hit just below the waterline; and two went skidding across the ship's deck. Two rockets didn't fire; the pigtails had been knocked loose by ejected .50-caliber cartridge shells when we were suppressing the flak for the guy in the water. I was so low that I collided with some of the ship's top rigging as I pulled up and over the enemy vessel. I hedgehopped over another ship, which I squirted with my guns, and then pulled straight up. When I reached 5,000 feet I was still doing 280 miles per hour.

We three sank three enemy ships (confirmed) with our rockets, and each of us was later awarded the DFC for that bit of action. We all got holed by the heavy flak we flew through; my Jug had eighteen battle scars to prove it, but the faithful old girl got me home all in one piece. As we were departing the Brest harbor area we saw a terrible thing occur. An 8th Air Force B-17 was bombing German positions when a P-47, making a dive-bombing run from high above, dove right through the B-17. The shattered wreckage of both aircraft littered that piece of sky before crashing to earth. I didn't see any parachutes.

A few days later, on 29 August, we fought another air battle with some thirty-five or forty Kraut Me.109s and FW.190s. We lost two of our guys, but we shot down six of theirs plus three damaged.

For 38 years I've kept a piece of paper in my personal files, and now I finally have the chance to use the information it contains. It's a statistical data sheet concerning the combat operations of the 406th Fighter Group for 167 missions during a three-month period ending 1 September 1944. During that period we flew 5,006 sorties in 13,847 flying hours, dropped 905.9 tons of HE bombs and 68.5 tons of fragmentation bombs on the enemy, fired 914 rockets and 1,967,607 rounds of .50-caliber ammunition.

With all that shooting and bombing we destroyed fifty-eight enemy aircraft, probably destroyed another nine, and damaged thirty-seven in air-to-air fighting. We wrecked an additional thirty-three enemy aircraft during airfield attacks, damaging another eighteen on the ground. The havoc wrought by our fighter group was as follows:

TARGET TYPE	DESTROYED	PROBABLY DESTROYED	DAMAGED
Military vehicles	943	16	397
Tanks	168	24	112
Locomotives	55	11	87
Railway cars	820	90	873
Bridges	12	5	28
Gun emplacements	60	20	52
Fuel/ammo dumps	20	2	3
Aircraft hangars	8	1	3
Factory buildings	44	21	59
Road cuts	11	1	7
Railway cuts	184	6	28
Vessels/ barges	21	1	35

In addition to the above we attacked railway marshalling yards sixty-one times, attacked airfields seventeen times, and struck enemy troop concentrations eight times. We were pretty damned busy. That's the "stat dope" for just one fighter group from D-Day to 1 September 1944. Multiply those figures by the number of fighter and bomber groups employed in all these operations and the result in destruction heaped on the German enemy is absolutely astounding and appalling.

Lieutenant Kenny Knowles and I were directed to take a few days' rest from air combat operations. While we were resting, we were further directed to take a Jeep, go to the front lines, and find a new location for the combat engineers to build an advanced airfield for the group. Off we went, following General Patton's 3rd Army route toward the southeast to the Loire River. From Angers we drove to the little town of La Fleche. There we found a most suitable spot, and set the engineers to work making another chicken wire and tar paper airfield.

Since there wasn't much for us to do for the next few days, Kenny and I decided to see if we could liberate an automobile for our personal use. It was quite normal in those days, when you got an occasional day off duty, to go to the front and capture a vehicle of some sort. In order to be successful, it was necessary to go up with the forward infantry troops, well ahead of the artillery units. The infantry guys were too busy to mess with enemy vehicles they bypassed, but the artillery types took everything on wheels, so you had to get between the infantry and artillery lines. Our group already had quite a few liberated Hun vehicles—German jeeps, half-tracks, a couple of staff cars, and a small bus. All these vehicles changed sides by simply having the black crosses painted over and white stars stenciled on them.

Kenny and I, in our jeep, with our tin hats and our .45-caliber pistols at the ready, started out on our search for wheels. We did get a bit lost. When we hadn't seen any of our troops for the better part of an hour in our wanderings, we parked our jeep on a dirt roadway and sat down on the edge of a small stream to rest and find our location on a map. Soon about a dozen U.S. infantry toops came down to the other side of the stream. They asked us if we'd seen any Krauts. "No," we replied, but we got to wondering just where in the hell we were.

"You're in front of our front lines," a staff sergeant told us. "You airdales are damned lucky you didn't get killed or captured." ("Airdale" was Army slang for Air Force types. We, in turn, called them "dogfaces.") We asked the sergeant if he'd seen any good cars nearby for us to liberate. Yes, there was one about half a mile back in the barn of a French farm.

The infantry platoon then crossed over the stream, cautiously advancing down the roadway. Right behind the platoon came several other guys with mine detectors sweeping the ground. They were also laying narrow white cloth tapes along the roadside.

"Stay away from the taped areas," they warned us. "The whole place is heavily mined."

Kenny and I got the hell out of there but quick, heading for friendly territory.

We found the farmhouse mentioned and drove into the yard. An elderly farmer and his wife came out of the house to see what we wanted. We finally made them understand, by our fractured French, that we wanted the German car in their barn. Oui, oui, we could have it, they said, but they kept repeating the word "Boche," which means Germans. Kenny and I figured there were Huns in the barn too, so we hauled out our trusty .45s, kicked open the barn door, and jumped quickly inside, just like John Wayne always does in the movies.

Bill Dunn,
age ten, 1926.

Seaforth Highlander
Sgt. Dunn, 1940.

Sgt. Dunn in gun pit with Lewis machine gun, 1940.

Seaforth Highlanders pipe band on parade, Delville Barracks, England.

Sgt. Dunn with his mortar crew, Delville Barracks, 1940.

Red Tobin, Shorty Keough, and Andy Mamedoff show the badge of the newly formed Eagle Squadron of the RAF, 1941.

Bill Dunn beside his Hurricane fighter; note Eagle Squadron insignia and victory score.

Hurricane with eight .303-caliber machine guns.

Fighter Control Operations Center, Uxbridge, Middlesex.

Pipsqueak on the stabilizer of Bill Dunn's Hurricane.

Squadron scramble, North Weald airfield.

Above: Heinkel He.111 over London.
Below: He.111 shot down in England, 1940.

Gun camera film of Me.109E taking hits.

Wreckage of
Me.109E downed
in England, 1940.

Shot down Ju.88 blows up in English Channel.

Ju.87 Stuka dive bombers.

The "short nose" FW.190.

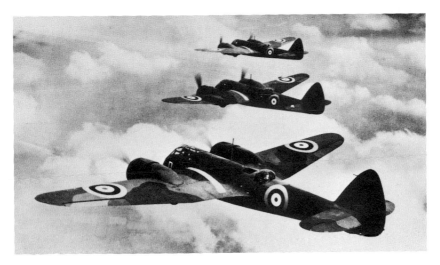

Bristol Blenheim bombers. The Eagle Squadron escorted many
of them to enemy targets.

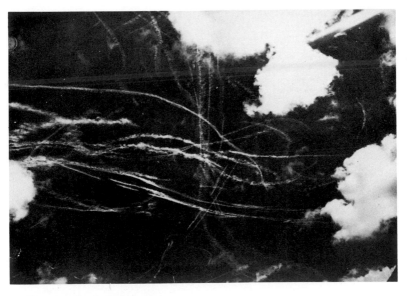

Vapor trails of an air battle.

Pilot Officer Dunn in Spitfire Mk IIA, 1941.

Flight of Spitfire Mk IIAs.

The Ace. Dunn's portrait was drawn in 1941 by an RAF friend, F/Lt. Hyden.

Flying Officer Dunn and
Martha Alton-Mouck
were married at Picton,
Ontario, 1942.

Dunn with son Jerry,
born 1943.

Some of the Americans of the Eagle Squadron who transferred to the
U.S. Army Air Corps in 1942. Uncle Sam Mauriello is standing on the
right, Red McColpin standing on the left, and Wee Mike McPharlin
kneeling on the left.

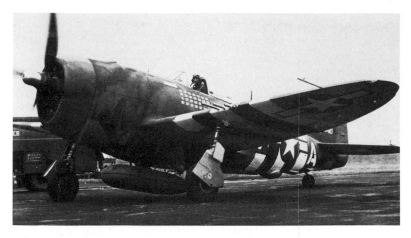

Ace of Aces "Gabby" Gabreski in his 56th Fighter Group P-47 Thunderbolt; note invasion stripes.

Farewell party for the 406th Fighter Group before going overseas, March, 1944. From left, Lt. Dudolski, Lt. Hughes, Capt. Dunn (with cigar), Lt. Marusiack; Capt. L.C. Selden in front.

Col. Grossetta, commander of 406th Fighter Group, on left, with Lt. Col. Winslett, air base commander, 1944.

P-51D Mustang, nicknamed the "Spam Can," 1944.

Maj. Adolf Galland,
the famous German ace.

Below: Messerschmitt 109E.

France, 1944. *Above,* a village is liberated; *below,* German prisoners under guard.

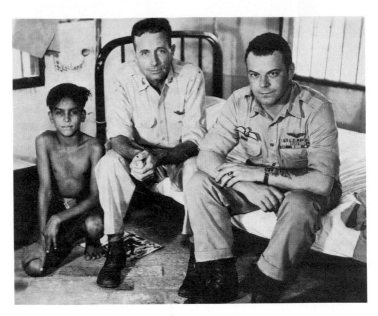

Roy Harding and Bill Dunn together in Burma, 1945.

Elephant power used to haul 1000-pound bombs to American aircraft in Burma.

Yanks with captured Jap flag and sword, China, 1945.

C-54 loaded with
Chinese troops to be
flown to Shanghai for
occupation duties.

A-1 Skyraiders on a close air support strike in Vietnam. U.S. Air Force photo.

Napalm and bomb strike on enemy targets in Vietnam. U.S. Air Force photo.

Evelyn and Bill Dunn (with Evelyn's sister Edie on the left)
celebrate their wedding in Dallas, 1947.

Evelyn and Bill Dunn at his retirement ceremony at Air
Defense Command Headquarters, Colorado Springs, 1973.

Lt. Col. Dunn (U.S.A.F. retired) proves he can still fit into a Spitfire cockpit at Eagle Squadron reunion, England, 1976.

The "Boche" were two very young German soldiers lying in the hay on the barn floor, both dead. Whoever had placed their bodies there laid them side by side, pillowed their heads on their rolled overcoats, crossed their hands on their chests, and closed their dead eyes. They couldn't have been more than seventeen or eighteen years old. So very young to die. What a bloody awful crime against humanity war is. I started to walk over toward the two dead boys, but the farmer quickly stopped me and made me understand that the bodies were booby-trapped. Wouldn't you know some Kraut son-of-a-bitch would do something like that, the bastards.

The car we were looking for was in a corner—a French Peugeot 302 with only 3,000 kilometers of use—nearly brand new! "Gestapo," said the farmer. When we pushed it out of the barn we saw that our beautiful black car really did have Gestapo markings on the outside door panels. Again the farmer made us understand it was mined. I gently opened a door, saw that the driver's seat was loose from the floor boards, and also saw a piece of dark yarn cord attached to a seat spring. Lifting just a corner of the seat ever so little, I saw a land mine attached to the other end of the cord. I cut the cord with my pocket knife, then Kenny and I gently lifed out the car seat to expose the big, round, ugly mine. Even more gently I slowly lifted the mine, while Kenny checked all sides of it to make sure no more trip-cords were attached. Just as gently I deposited the mine in a ditch a hundred yards from the farmer's house.

Hooking the Peugeot by a rope to our jeep, we towed it back to La Fleche. I drove the jeep while Kenny steered our liberated prize. At the airfield we showed off our proud possession and then began to clean her up. The battery was low, but we finally got her started; she ran pretty good on 100-octane aviation gasoline. We drove our little beauty over to the combat engineers camp. It was there that one of the engineers, viewing our new car, noticed another piece of dark yarn cord near a corner of the back seat. Yes, it was another land mine trip-cord, but this time an Army ordnance officer removed the mine safely. Finally, after going all over the car, he declared it safe for us to drive. Twice our luck had held on the same day. We could have been killed or captured at the front, or we could have blown ourselves to hell with the mines. I guess God really does watch over fools.

While Kenny and I were off on our adventure, a patrol of Kraut infantry managed to get into the hedgerows on one side of our new airfield and began taking pot shots at the U.S. combat engineers. The engineers were very busy digging up the landscape, and weren't pleased with this interruption of their work schedule. A couple of bulldozer drivers lifted the heavy steel blades on their machines to protect themselves from the rifle and machine gun shots, put their huge bulldozers into high gear, and drove clattering down on the Hun position. Several of the Squareheads broke and ran before these charging iron monsters. Those that didn't run were dug under or flattened right then and there. Those combat engineers were a fearless bunch of characters. They had a job to do, and no one was going to stop them from doing it.

I sent a message to the group telling them the airfield would be ready to take aircraft in three days. A confirmation reply told me the 406th would arrive on the planned date. Since Paris had been liberated by the Free French troops on 25 August, Kenny and I decided we'd make a quick trip there to see the sights. We gassed up our Peugeot, loaded a couple of extra five-gallon Jerry cans of gasoline, some C-Rations, and headed out.

While we were minding our own business driving along the road, an MP jeep passed us and motioned us to stop by the roadside. We did as directed. Out of the jeep hopped a feisty little MP major from the 1st Army, who, officiously, wanted to know what we were doing in his area and where we got our car. The major's driver was a tech sergeant, who remained seated in the jeep, but who had his hand on a ready carbine. I told the MP officer our story, to which this little dusty butt said, pompously, he'd have to confiscate our Peugeot—1st Army orders.

I got out of our car, put my hand on my .45 Colt automatic, and, with several cuss words, told the little SOB something of his parentage. Further, I told him the whole damned 1st Army wasn't going to take our car away from us, and for him to buzz off. He got red in the face, said he'd see about that, he'd report us to our CO, then he got into his jeep and drove away. Before the MPs left, the sergeant grinned back at us, giving us a little "thumbs up" sign his major didn't see. Makes you wonder, sometimes, whose side the MPs are on. So we continued our journey without further incident.

On the outskirts of Paris we saw a sight that really touched us. An Army liaison aircraft had crashed and burned, but the skeleton of the airframe was still intact. The French people of the neighborhood, God bless them, had completely covered the airframe with multitudes of flowers—all of it, wings, tail plane, and fuselage. A beautiful gesture! We never did find out what happened to the liaison pilot and his observer.

In the city we drove around completely lost, but it was fun just to see it. Paris had been liberated on 25 August, but the fighting had not completely ceased. There were still quite a few pockets of German troops holed up in various buildings. The Free French were slowly eliminating them, block by city block. During the time we had been in Paris we hadn't seen a single American soldier—not even an MP, and those bastards are generally the first to get into a liberated city or town, which they promptly make "off limits" to all real combat troops.

Kenny and I sat down at a table in a little sidewalk cafe and ordered a brandy each. There were quite a few other customers, all French, who smiled and nodded welcome to us. Just as we took our first sip, some Kraut down the street fired a machine pistol, sending a spattering of bullets in our general direction. Being well trained troops, Kenny and I were under the table in a flash. The Frenchies rushed out into the street, where they jabbered away excitedly and pointed toward the building the gunfire came from. Several French troops, with their sub-machine guns, took off to rout out the Hun holdouts. We heroes of the air, Kenny and I, regained our chairs and, with the other cafe customers, returned to sipping our drinks. We knocked back several brandies, which we paid for with invasion money, which was all we had.

There was a small hotel next to the cafe, so we decided to check in there for the night. The hotel manager was most pleased to see us, giving us the best room in the place. The room had a large window, directly in the line of fire from where the Huns had shot at us earlier. Now in this room the toilet was located in a corner, no screen or anything around it. Well, after our several drinks in the cafe, the hotel manager brought up a big bottle of cold champagne, compliments of the house. We sopped this up, and it so happened that we both got the urge to use the can at the same time. Being somewhat of a gentleman— I wouldn't pull rank on Kenny—I graciously told Kenny to use the regular can while I used this other thing that looked sort of like another toilet. Kenny had no problems, but when I pushed the flush button on the can I'd used, a bloody great stream of water came whooshing out and squirted me right in the face! My education concerning French latrines increased a bit when I learned, the hard way, what a bidet was for.

That evening we went back to the little cafe for dinner, and a very delicious meal we had. The bill came, which we paid with our scrip money, but the waiter wanted something else from us. We couldn't understand what it was. Then a Frenchman who spoke some English told us the waiter wanted our "bread coupons" for the bread we had eaten (bread was rationed by the Germans). Of course, we didn't have any coupons and said as much, whereupon the waiter began to yell at us like we were bandits. Soon all the Frenchies in the place were on their feet, shouting back at the waiter, telling him the Huns were gone, tearing bread coupons out of their ration books, which they threw at him. We got the hell out of there ASAP.

Next morning, when Kenny and I were ready to depart Paris for La Fleche, the hotel manager refused our payment and gave each of us a small present. Mine was a set of gold embroidered major's leaves and Kenny's was a pair of silver lieutenant's bars; all had been made for U.S. officers during the First World War! I still have my set.

The 406th ground echelon began arriving at La Fleche the next afternoon, with the aircraft landing the following morning. Soon thereafter Colonel Grossetta called me to his tent office. Looking very grim, he said, "Bill, you're in real trouble. I want an explanation for this, and it had better be good." Tony handed me a paper, written in French, with my signature at the bottom. The group medic, Major Howell, and an MP captain were standing behind Tony. Both were livid with rage and glared daggers at me. A very grim situation was in the making.

"Well," I began, "when we first arrived down here the mayor of La Fleche came out to see me, telling me he wanted us liberators to enjoy our stay at his town. There was a place in town the German troops used during their leisure time—a sort of USO type canteen, I was told—but the MPs were clamoring to shut it down. The MPs, as you know, are always putting things 'off limits,' except for themselves. The mayor had this piece of paper," I continued, "which said in French that I, as senior officer in the immediate area, authorized the place to remain open for the enjoyment of our troops. So I signed the paper for him. What's the big flap?"

"You dummy," said Tony, then he began to laugh like mad. "You authorized the local whorehouse to stay open for business—and the mayor owns the damned place! You were had."

Major Howell and the MP didn't think it was so funny. The place, they said, was the busiest spot in town. The mayor was making a mint of dough. My action could cause a VD epidemic in the troops, Doc warned—and besides, whorehouse authorization was his responsibility alone. I suppose my authorization order was promptly countermanded. Well, that's the way it goes some days, especially when you don't understand the language. I ought to have had an interpreter assigned when I went to La Fleche. I found out a couple of days later that the mayor of the town had an identical authorization paper in his hands, but signed this time by Doc Howell and the MP captain.

Following that fiasco, I went back to my regular job in group operations and combat flying—hours and hours of sheer boredom relieved by moments of stark terror. We continued with our beating up of the German army, dive-bombing, rocketing, and strafing wherever we found the enemy. Their losses in men and materiel were terrible. Allied air superiority soon became so powerful that the enemy only moved troops during the night hours. General Patton's 3rd Army was charging across France so fast that the enemy on his front was soon disorganized and in full retreat. Our group successes in supporting Patton with accurate and devastating air strikes brought us the nickname "The Raiders." Now we painted our Thunderbolt cowlings and rudders red, so all— friends and enemies alike—would know just who we were.

Our stay at La Fleche airfield lasted only a couple of weeks before we were ordered to move forward to Mourmelon-le-Grand airfield (A-80) near the city of Reims, northeast of Paris. This airfield had previously been used as a permanent Luftwaffe base. It had concrete runways, barracks, shops, hangars, all that good stuff. Our quarters were good cement and brick buildings, but they were absolutely bare of any furniture. The infantry, when they captured the place, burned it all as firewood to keep warm and cook their food. We slept on the floors until our canvas cots arrived with the group's ground echelon.

The weather began to turn sour in the latter part of September— thick fog, lots of rain, dense clouds nearly on the deck with tops at 20,000 feet. This, of course, curtailed some of our support operations with the army, but we still managed to fly nearly every mission assigned to the 406th. One day, when the weather was particularly bad and the forecast wasn't any better, the group was given a stand down for a twenty-four-hour rest period. Someone suggested we have a big bash, a party in the mess.

Since the city of Reims was famous for the production of outstanding champagne, we dispatched a weapons carrier to the Mums winery to obtain a couple hundred bottles of their best. Two six-bys were sent into town to collect any young ladies who might wish to attend our gala and consort with our heroes of the air. The three vehicles returned a couple of hours later, each fully loaded with its appropriate cargo.

The party really turned out to be a fine affair. Lots of good food, drink, and companionship. Music for dancing was provided by a small French orchestra we managed to hire for the evening from a city hotel. Tomorrow was a full day off duty, so why worry, plenty of time to recover from hangovers. I happened to be the operations duty officer, so, of course, I couldn't drink too much of that wonderful champagne; what a bloody shame, I thought, as I sipped my single glass.

It must have been about 2:30 or 3:00 in the morning when I was called to the ops telephone—urgent call, the operator said, from wing headquarters. As I stood with the receiver to my ear, watching all the fun and frolic, I heard the words I feared: "Return the group to full readiness at 05:00 hours. Sorry to cut short your rest period, but there is a flap brewing. Be prepared for takeoff at first light. Further operations details are forthcoming in the teletype Frag Order. Hope your boys did get a bit of rest yesterday afternoon and last night." If that guy from wing ops could have seen what I was seeing at that moment, he'd have had a hemorrhage.

I got the word to Colonel Grossetta and L.C. straight away. The grand party came to a screeching halt. Wing operations was roundly denounced by all concerned. The squadron pilots hit the sack for a couple hours of shuteye, but we group types went to work. Lots to be done before 5 a.m.

At the 5 o'clock briefing the weather was foggy; the pilots in the briefing room were a bit foggy as well. Our mission was to bomb and rocket a batch of Kraut tanks that were holding up our troops' advance. What was the weather like over the target area? Bloody awful—no fog, but clouds nearly on the deck. Well, that's what we were hired for, so off we went into the wild gray crap. I told the guys to start sopping up pure oxygen when they got into their cockpits. It would clear most of the cobwebs from their brains, but it wouldn't do a thing for their cotton mouths. I knew most of them felt like the Russian army had marched across their tongues, barefooted.

Since I was in the best physical shape, I led the gaggle of 406th air-craft up through the soup and on to the cloud-shrouded target. The forward controller in one of our tanks identified the enemy positions for us, and down we went on the deck to exact a terrible punishment on those Huns who had ruined our earlier festivities. We bombed them, rocketed them, strafed them—in general, we kicked the living hell out of them. Mission accomplished, we straggled back to Mourmelon-le-Grand, landing in the lousy weather. One pilot forgot to put his gear down, bellied in on the runway, but luckily slid off onto the grass.

Back in group operations I got a phone call from the wing ops offi-cer. He wanted to know how I was certain I had hit the right target in such bad weather. A bit browned off, I replied, "I went down to 25 feet, saw the black crosses on their tanks and the square heads of the troops, so I shot the bastards." End of conversation. It was a month before we got another day off operations.

Despite the poor flying weather, we continued to support the ad-vancing army ground forces in October. It was hard work, playing the role of airborne artillery. There was none of the fighter-pilot glamour of the early war days. Close air support strikes were nothing more than flying directly into the firing barrels of hundred of antiaircraft cannons and machine guns, with the chances about one in five you'd get hit, one in ten you'd be shot down. As the German army was gradually com-pressed by our Allied forces into smaller defense pockets, so their flak was also compressed, with many more guns now defending each target area. This sort of flying, after awhile, is no longer exciting fun—it's bloody tough and extremely dangerous work. With several missions each day, the heavy flak, the lousy weather, the very low flying to get into the target and make a successful strike, the mounting losses of pilots and aircraft, all wore on your nerves. After you had completed 100 missions, which sometimes required as many as 250 or 300 sorties, you get tired, short-tempered, worried about when your number was coming up, and, I suppose, you lost some of your original combat aggressiveness.

So it occurred in mid-October that Colonel Grossetta informed me that I had finished my tour of combat operations with the 406th Fighter Group. I would soon be reassigned, he continued, to other duties. I hated to leave the 406th. It was an outstanding unit with a very proud combat record—and Tony, its leader, was without a doubt the best fighter group leader I ever had the honor to serve under. I should also say, in all truth, that I was somewhat relieved to be taken off combat flying for a well deserved rest period.

I went to see the group personnel officer, Major Weinberg. What was available for my reassignment? He told me—and this is almost unbelievable—that the USAAF had just implemented a new policy for fighter pilots who had completed their combat tours. They could volunteer to go with the army for six months as forward controllers, riding in the second tank of an advancing armored column, or they could volunteer to do another 100-mission combat tour in the Far East! Some choice! I promply volunteered for a Far East combat flying tour. At least, I figured, I'd get to go back to the States for maybe a month's leave with my family, Martha, and little Jerry, before I headed out again to fight the Japs.

My combat record in the European war area wasn't too bad when I reviewed it all. I had flown two combat tours, one RAF and one USAAF, for a total of 234 combat missions in 519 combat flying hours. I had shot down 15½ enemy aircraft in air-to-air fighting—8½ were confirmed victories, 4 were unconfirmed, 3 were probables; an additional 4 were damaged. I was also credited with the destruction of 12 enemy aircraft on the ground. So, in the air and on the ground, I destroyed a total of 27½ enemy aircraft. In other air support attacks I destroyed 168 enemy vehicles, including tanks, railway trains, and trucks. At Brest harbor I sank a 4,000-ton enemy troopship. For these actions, I was awarded the British European Star, Aircrew Star, and Defense of Great Britain Medal, and the United States Distinguished Flying Cross, the Bronze Star, and thirteen Air Medals.

On the other side of the scoreboard, I had been shot down once, shot up several times, and wounded in action four times. I had served fourteen months on air combat operations—some 420 days—meeting and fighting the Hun enemy nearly every day. I had survived it all, beating the odds in the gamble on the length of a wartime fighter pilot's life span. No, it wasn't too bad a combat record. Now I'd have to give the Japs a chance to see what they could do.

11. War in the Far East

I got my leave in the States all right—one whole week with Martha and Jerry! Martha seemed a bit fed up with me going off to war again so soon, but it couldn't be helped. It had been a long war—nearly five years—and it would prove to be still longer. My next assignment, before going to the Far East, was to attend the Command and General Staff School (Air Staff Course) at Fort Leavenworth, Kansas. This course, in peacetime, lasted for a year, but in wartime had been compressed into three months, and they were still teaching tactics and techniques that had been outdated for several years. I managed to get through the course by applying school-approved solutions to school-developed situations, and graduated in the top ten of my class. I've always wondered why I was sent to that school; surely no one was planning to make a general officer out of me. At the end of the course they had a three-day simulated war exercise. I was appointed to be the air commander, and employing current air operations tactics won our side's war in less than twelve hours; we celebrated our victory in Kansas City for two days.

School finished in March 1945, I was off on an Air Transport Command C-54 for North Africa, then Cairo, then Karachi, and finally Dum Dum airfield at Calcutta. India was stinking hot and humid; I sweated like a stuck hog twenty-four hours a day. My quarters consisted of a canvas cot in an abandoned jute mill that the U.S. Army converted into a BOQ. Having served in well organized European commands, I'd never seen anything to compare with the disorganized, mismanaged, apathetic China-Burma-India (CBI) Command. No one seemed to know what was going on anywhere, and coordination of effort was about nil. None of the air staff knew how to pour urine out of a boot—even if the directions were written on the heel. I was asked to join the air staff as fighter operations officer. My reply was not only "no," it was "hell no"; I asked to be shipped on to Burma or China ASAP.

Roy Harding, my stepfather, was now a full colonel commanding the
51st Air Service Group at Myitkyina (pronounced Myi-che-na), Burma.
I knew he was a Scotch drinker, so I scurried around the officers'
messes in Calcutta until I found a jug, which I purchased at an out-
rageously high price. Off to Burma in a troop carrier C-47 "Goony
bird" I went with my kit and Roy's whiskey. At the Myitkyina airfield
a guy with a jeep gave me a ride to Roy's quarters, a basha made of
bamboo walls and a grass roof.

I beat on the screen door, yelling "Hey, Harding! You got a visitor!"
and stood there with the bottle of Scotch held at arm's length. The
basha door flew open. Roy glanced at me, then at the bottle, grabbed
the Scotch and disappeared inside the hut. I followed him inside, where
he was stuffing the jug down into the bowels of a footlocker, which he
then padlocked. After the giggle soup was safely secured, he turned to
me and said, "Where the hell did you come from?" I briefed him on my
assignment to the CBI. He was sorry about my bad luck, but maybe it
wouldn't last. That evening we sat on the banks of the Irrawaddy River,
killed a quart of Karoose Booze, soaked off the bottle label, dried it,
and then wrote a brief letter to my mother on it.

After waiting ten days for a Burma assignment, I was instructed to
go across the Himalayan hump to Kunming, China, and report to Headquarters, 14th Air Force. There was some talk of an offensive soon to
drive the Japs from the areas they had conquered in eastern and
southern China during 1944. I was most anxious to participate in this
offensive, which would no doubt be a vital step toward terminating the
war in the Far East.

To provide a brief situation background on the conduct of the
Burma and China campaigns, we must review the events from 1931 to
1944. The Japanese invaded Manchuria in 1931 and then China in July
of 1937. Before the invasion, the Chinese armed forces were in a sad
state of preparedness, equipment, and training. A group of German
Army officers, retired from active service, began to reorganize the
Chinese Army in 1932. An American, Colonel John Jouett, retired
from the Air Corps, with nine other American pilots, assumed the task
of building the Chinese Air Force during the years from 1932 to 1934.
In 1934 Jouett's services were terminated, and an Italian air mission of
about 140 personnel took over the job. In April of 1937 Claire L.
Chennault, another retired U.S. Army Air Corps officer, was requested

by Generalissimo Chiang Kai-Shek, president of China's Nationalist government, to review the Chinese Air Force capabilities and report on its combat readiness to defend China against the Japanese. (Chiang had several nicknames—CKS, Gimo, Jack, and Chancre Jack.) Chennault was in the midst of his inspection report when the Japs attacked China in July. The Italians quickly withdrew their services and support from China. Since the Chinese Air Force (CAF) pilots were still inexperienced and ill equipped, they were powerless to defend against the vastly superior Japanese Air Force.

To strengthen the CAF, an International Air Squadron was formed, composed of "pilots of fortune" from many nations. The Japs soon chewed this squadron up and spit it out. In August of 1937 the Russian Air Force sent four fighter squadrons and two bomber squadrons to fight the Japs in China and to test and evaluate their own equipment and tactics. The Russians also provided some 400 military aircraft to the CAF. The Russian airmen could not stop the Japanese advance into northern and southwest China, so it was proposed that an American Volunteer Group (AVG) of fighter pilots be hired and organized as part of the CAF.

Chennault, now commissioned a colonel in the CAF, was directed by Chiang Kai-Shek to procure pilots, mechanics, aircraft, and support equipment from the United States. By June 1941 he had obtained 100 P-40B fighters. Four hundred had been requested but couldn't be supplied at that time by Curtiss-Wright. He also managed to recruit about 100 pilots and 150 mechanics, most of them trained in the U.S. military. The AVG, after arrival at Rangoon, Burma, in July, began operational training at Kyedaw airfield near Toungoo. Their planned home air base at Kunming, China, was not yet ready. On December 1941 came the Japanese attack on Pearl Harbor and the United States entered the war. Shortly thereafter, on 23 December, the Japs launched their initial air raid on Rangoon, and the AVG went into action for the first time.

On 20 January 1942 Japanese Army forces invaded Burma in a furious and rapidly moving campaign, which resulted in the defeat of Allied forces—Burmese, Indian, and British. The Gimo, Chiang Kai-Shek, sent Chinese Army troops to support Allied forces in Burma on 28 February 1942, but to no avail. By July the Japanese had completed their conquest of Burma and closed the Burma Road supply route. The

Allied forces were evacuated, some to India, some to China. The AVG, during the Battle of Burma, was credited with the destruction of some 300 Japanese aircraft and damaging a like number—an excellent combat record resulting in their nickname, the "Flying Tigers."

Lieutenant General Joseph "Vinegar Joe" Stilwell, who commanded the United States CBI forces, worked out an agreement with Chiang Kai-Shek and Chennault for the transfer of the AVG to the China Air Task Force (CATF), a component of the U.S. Army's 10th Air Force. Chennault was now recalled to active U.S. service and promoted to brigadier general commanding the CATF. Very soon there was discord and a lack of cooperation between Stilwell, Chennault, and Brigadier General Bissell, who commanded the 10th Air Force. The CATF was expected to provide the air defense of China, but was always on the short end of the stick when it came to CBI logistical support of CATF operations. For several months in the latter part of 1942 the CATF had only 47 aircraft capable of flying combat operations. Japanese combat aircraft strength in China was 500. However, with their few aircraft and minimum support, the CATF pilots did provide air defense for the "hump" air supply route, air strikes on Jap coastal shipping, and battle-field support for the Chinese Army units fighting in eastern China. Every gallon of gasoline, every bullet, every spare part, every pair of socks to support the CATF had to be flown into China over the hump route. Chiang Kai-Shek requested that President Roosevelt give General Chennault a command separate from the 10th Air Force. Roosevelt agreed, promoting Chennault to major general and creating the 14th Air Force in China. Provision of air crews, maintenance personnel, and logistical support began to improve somewhat with this change, which led to the addition of B-25 and B-24 bomber units and several more fighter squadrons. A B-29 squadron, stationed at Chengtu airfield, but not under the operational control of the 14th Air Force, was assigned the mission of flying long-range bombing attacks on the Japanese home-land islands. They used too much of the precious aviation fuel airlifted over the hump, so the unit was sent elsewhere.

In February of 1943 a Japanese force of 100,000 troops attempted the conquest of China by starvation. They destroyed rice crops and burned granaries, and the Chinese endured terrible privations. On 17 April 1944 Japan's North China Army launched an offensive planned to capture and destroy 14th Air Force bases in eastern China, to unite with Japan's Southern China Army, and to seize the railways between Peking-Hankow, Canton-Hengyang, and Lingling-Kweilin-Nanning. At about this same time the Burma Campaign was launched by combined American, British, Indian, and Chinese forces to drive the Japs out of Burma and from India's Bay of Bengal area. Most of the supplies originally destined for 14th Air Force operations in China were diverted by General Stilwell to the Burma offensive.

Both Chiang Kai-Shek and Chennault asked Stilwell for sufficient supplies to defend against the advancing Japanese armies in China and were refused. The rift between the Gimo and Chennault on one side, and Stilwell on the other side, grew in hostility until 18 October 1944 when, at the insistence of Chiang, President Roosevelt relieved General Stilwell of his CBI duties and recalled him to Washington. Both Stilwell and Chennault were aggressive, outspoken, and abrasive; both were great soldiers. It was too bad they had to bump heads on battle management problems of the China-Burma-India theater of war. Stilwell was replaced by Major General Albert Wedemeyer, with Major General George Stratemeyer, commander of U.S. Army Air Forces, CBI, providing air support operations. These two generals were known to us as the Meyers brothers—Wede and Strate. Now you're up to speed to the events of 1945.

China is different from the rest of the whole world. I don't mean just foreign—I mean alien, strange, like belonging to another world. The moment I got off the goony bird at Kunming airfield I could sense China's strangeness. The air had a sort of spicy aroma that was pleasant to breathe. And the Chinese people were different; smiling broadly, happy-faced, and all jabbering away in their singsong language. I knew I would like the place, the people, and the new adventure I was about to begin.

One of the first people I met was a colonel in the Chinese Army, an Australian named Gil Stewart, who looked and acted like Erroll Flynn, the adventurous and flamboyant movie actor. Stewart had, a short time previously, with his Chinese bings (soldiers), driven off a force of Chinese rebel troops of a local warlord that tried to capture Kunming and its airfield. The fighting had been hand-to-hand, a bloody affair that lasted for two days. The defeated and captured rebel officers and NCOs were immediately executed. The rebel private soldiers were "transferred" to Colonel Stewart's command. Stewart took me to Headquarters, 14th Air Force, and provided my introduction to its staff personnel. I should note here that the 14th now had received quite a few P-51 Mustang fighters to replace the worn out P-40s. There was even a group of P-47 Thunderbolts in China, commanded by Colonel Ollie Cellini, a friend of mine from the 3rd Air Force. The Jugs, however, were gas-guzzlers, which limited their employment.

Several of us new boys to the China war zone were briefed on 14th Air Force combat operations conducted during the past few days. After European war service, this briefing was almost pathetic to hear. There was very little air combat—a few dozen sampans shot up on a river, a couple of villages strafed, some supply trucks bombed and set afire— nothing more. Everything seemed to be on such a reduced scale of operations. Of course, at that time, none of us realized the critical shortage of aviation fuel and munitions that existed in China. There was no place for me, a major, in any of the fighter units. For a change they were fully manned with field grade officers. I was assigned to Luhsien airfield, on the Yangtze River, about seventy miles east of Chungking, as deputy base commander.

Our building facilities at Luhsien were a mixture of tents, quonset huts, and mud and bamboo bashas. The thatched roof in my basha, like all the others, was infested with ugly, hairy, black spiders as big as your hand. At night, lying in bed, I would turn my flashlight on the ceiling and see the little beady eyes of the spiders peering down at me. Taking my .45 pistol, loaded with birdshot rounds, I would occasionally take a shot at them. Bang! One would fall, and the others would scurry deep into the thatch. Soon I was an ace spider killer.

An offensive, called Operation Alpha, was planned to drive the Japs from occupied Chinese territory. Phase I of this operation, in December 1944, required air attacks on Jap supply lines and an advance by the Chinese Army into southern and southeast China. Phase II was designed to disrupt the flow of enemy supplies by rail transportation in eastern China and began in January 1945. To counter 14th Air Force interdiction air strikes, the Japanese began a counteroffensive the same month. Their plan was to knock out 14th Air Force air bases and so reduce the air power assault on their supply lines; they successfully captured and destroyed half a dozen air bases in eastern China. A second Japanese attack, beginning in mid-April 1945, was directed against 14th Air

Force bases in central China, but it was defeated a month later by the combined Chinese and American forces. By June the Japs began to retreat from central and eastern China. Phase III of Operation Alpha now began—the advance of large Chinese ground forces to drive the Japs out of China.

Luhsien air base was a major installation for the receipt and distribution of supplies being flown over the hump. B-24 bombers and C-54 transports delivered much-needed aviation fuel in 55-gallon drums and in their own wing tanks. We drained every drop of gas out of them, except for just enough fuel to return over the hump for another load. Some B-24s were converted into tanker aircraft, designated C-109s—we called them C-one-oh-booms. C-46s and C-47s carried all sorts of other supplies: food, ammunition, bombs, clothing. But in all this huge supply airlift, there was not a drop of decent booze to drink for us hard-working types at Luhsien.

The Chinese made a fairly powerful alcoholic drink called "orange whiskey," sometimes "victory whiskey." They also produced a rice wine, which we called "ging-bao juice." The term means "air raid" in Chinese. If you've never tasted any of this stuff, you don't know what you're missing. And if you have tasted it, you know damned well what I mean. At Luhsien we had a small officers' mess made of mud walls and a bamboo-supported thatched roof. There were no mess dues but to join it was required that a person drink a coffeecup full of ging-bao juice. This stuff had a horrible smell when it was cold—like decayed flesh—but didn't smell so bad when heated. Of course, we served it cold to the new guy, with the suggestion that he not smell it, hold his nose shut, and gulp it down as fast as possible. Well, people never listen to good advice, so most of them would sniff it first. A horrified expression would cross the candidate's face, and, being a very manly type, he'd "down the hatch" with the foul stuff. Sometimes it came up nearly as fast as it went down. Some guys began to sweat and turn green around the gills and burp. The worst cases were the guys that had to take two or more swallows to get it down. One of them, after going through the sweat-green-burp stage, rushed out of our mess, taking the unopened screen door with him. Another fell off the cliff edge beside our mess, and we had to go rescue his skinned and bruised body from the dirt road about forty feet below.

Since my stepfather, Roy, ran a supply base over in Burma, I sent him samples of orange whiskey and ging-bao joice in empty atabrine bottles. "Taste this stuff," I told him in a note, "and see what you can do for us in the way of alcoholic libations." A few days later one of his C-47s landed at Luhsien loaded with cases of American beer! We divided it up, and it came to four bottles for every guy on the airbase.

One day a sergeant from South Carolina told me he knew how to make moonshine; he thought he could make it out of Chinese alcohol motor vehicle fuel. I told him to go ahead, but secretly. He stripped some copper oil lines out of a crashed B-24 to make a coil, got a field kitchen stove from supply, and a bunch of pots and bottles from the mess hall. Soon he was in business, producing a gallon of alcohol every two hours. I asked the base medics to test the stuff. Their report said it was about 150 proof pure alcohol, and good enough to be used for "medicinal purposes." Thereafter, deliveries were made of one gallon each to the officers' mess and sergeants' mess, and two gallons to the enlisted mess daily. Mixed half an ounce with some sort of fruit juice it was really good. Other bases soon heard of our accomplishment, so our South Carolina sergeant spent quite a bit of time on TDY (temporary duty with another unit).

While at Luhsien I got to fly twice in B-24s on bombing missions down near Canton. There was no Jap fighter reaction, the flak was minimal, the weather bright and sunny. The missions were a piece of cake. Imagine, a fighter pilot flying as copilot in a bomber just for the hell of it. The B-24, by the way, didn't fly; it waddled through the air. A P-51 landed for refueling at Luhsien one day and the pilot let me fly it for an hour around the base. For fun, I beat up the airbase and the town of Luhsien, scaring both the local population and myself, which displeased my boss, Lt. Colonel Joel Y. Ledbetter, the base commander. My stay at Luhsien was all work and a minimum of flying.

Word was received that the war in Europe ended on 8 May 1945 with the complete defeat of the Squareheads. Hitler, the TWX stated, had bumped himself off in his Berlin bunker, and Göring, plus a batch of other senior Krauts, had been captured. Good show! However, for us in the Far East, the war continued. On 14 June the air base at Liuchow was recaptured from the Japs by Chinese forces. This base had fallen to the Japanese on 11 November 1944. Very shortly after its recapture I was reassigned as the Liuchow airbase commander. At this base I had the 23rd Fighter Group (the redesignated American Volunteer Group), 4th Combat Cargo Squadron, and 7th Liaison Squadron, plus an Air Transport Command detachment for cargo aircraft handling—all in all about 1,500 American troops and several thousand Chinese troops and laborers. Liuchow was located just below the confluence of the Lung and Liu Rivers, and just above the Yungfu River, in Kwangsi Province.

The Japanese Army was just across these rivers from our air base, so we were occasionally shelled by their artillery. These shells blew holes in our runway, hence the large number of Chinese coolie laborers required to repair the damage by hand. I was promoted to lieutenant colonel when I took over Liuchow as commander.

One morning there was a hell of an explosion near the runway. It seems the coolies were digging in a pile of dirt and stones used for repair of the Jap shell holes when it blew up. There were eight or nine killed and maybe twenty wounded. The explosion was from a land mine hidden in the pile some time during the night by an enemy infiltrator. When the coolies began to dig, up she went. A widespread search began for the infiltrator, and by noon Chinese soldiers captured the guy. He was brought before me—a Japanese Army major, dressed in coolie clothes. He had been badly beaten by his captors, but he had guts. He never cowered when they pushed and struck him with rifle butts. A Chinese Army captain told me how the Jap major had been caught, then he gave me a Japanese flag the major had wrapped around his waist under his coolie clothes. Five minutes later the Jap was executed by a Chinese firing squad. The Jap was a brave man to carry on his war behind our lines, but he suffered the consequences of an occupational hazard. If he had been my prisoner he'd have been a POW. I still have the flag he carried.

Liuchow was a hub of air activity. The 23rd Fighter Group, equipped with P-51s, was providing air support for the advancing Chinese Army from dawn to dusk. C-54s and C-46s and C-47s were nearly always in the airfield traffic pattern hauling in supplies and troop reinforcements. L-5s of the liaison squadron were in the air every daylight hour, searching out enemy positions and directing Chinese artillery and mortar fire against them. During June and July, Liuchow was the front line of the battlefield.

On 6 July 1945 we received the unhappy news that our "Old Leather Face" boss, General Chennault, had retired from active service.

He was really forced out by a group of political generals who sat on their fat cans back in Washington. For eight years Chennault had done everything humanly possible to defend China in the air war, only to be shot down by a bunch of JCS weenies who couldn't fight their way out of a wet paper bag with a pitchfork. Some good news came on 28 July: the end of the Burma campaign and the complete defeat of the Japs in that area. The Japanese 15th, 21st, 28th and 33rd Armies had been annihilated. Their losses were 347,000 men.

During July and August I flew a number of close air support missions with the 23rd Fighter Group. They were not too exciting, as the enemy was fast folding up, first in retreat, then in rout. I never did see a Jap fighter in the air, but we did strafe a few on the ground. One time Lieutenant Jim McGovern and I, in our P-51s, spotted two Japanese twin-engine bombers (we thought they were "Sallys," Mitsubishi Ki-21s) but they got away in thick clouds before we could get within firing range. McGovern was quite a character, a huge man of over 250 pounds who could barely fit in a P-51 cockpit. He was nicknamed "Earthquake McGoon." More about him later.

With the dropping of the atomic bomb on Hiroshima on 6 August and on Nagasaki on 9 August 1945, the Second World War came to a screeching halt. The Japanese surrender came on 14 August, although the official signing of terms did not occur until 2 September, and orders were sent to all combatants to cease military operations on 15 August.

On 17 August we received the following message from the Commanding General, CBI Headquarters:

Japan has officially and unconditionally surrendered! No American, no freedom loving person anywhere, will fail to realize the deep significance of these words. The fight against the enemy has at last been won, and with it, the right to peace and world security.

Millions of Americans left their homes and risked their lives that this war might be brought to a successful conclusion. Among these, you who served in the China-Burma-India theater of war have turned in one of the finest performances. You have worked and fought with inadequate facilities, against time, and against the worst that nature and the enemy could offer. You have flown under conditions not found in any other parts of the world—over rugged mountains, treacherous jungles, and usually in icing and instrument weather. You have lived on the outskirts of civilization with primitive surroundings, in areas infested with disease. You have often been afflicted with the wet monsoon, the steaming heat, and other discomforts of the Orient. Yet your performance was so fine that it brought the highest recognition and praise from our comrades and from all Allied quarters throughout the world.

As each of you returns to his home you may do so with the certain knowledge that you have shared with great distinction one of the most difficult and important assignments of this war.

On 3 September 1945 I assembled all my troops at Liuchow and, following the general's example, gave them my thoughts on the war's end. I realize my speech was full of flag waving, mother, and apple pie. But what the hell, I had to say something.

Soldiers and airmen of the Armed Forces of the United States! This is a year of triumph for us and our allies. The United Nations have inflicted defeat in open battle, man to man, on our last enemy—Japan!

The eyes of the world were upon you during these past crusading years. The hopes and prayers of liberty loving people everywhere marched with you. In company with our brave comrades-in-arms on other areas of this front you have brought about the destruction of the Japanese war machine, the elimination of Japanese tyranny over the oppressed peoples of Asia, and security for ourselves in a free world.

Your task was not an easy one. Your enemy was well trained, well equipped, and battle hardened. He fought savagely.

Much has happened since the earlier victories of the enemy. The Allied Nations have inflicted great defeats upon the Japanese forces. Our air offensive destroyed their strength in the air and their capacity to wage war on the ground. The tide has turned. The free men of the world, blessed by God, are victorious.

Since the end of hostilities we have been given a new task, and this task will not prove too easy. There will be soldiers and airmen, as well as civilians, that will now become lax in their duties and shirk their responsibilities. This must not happen here! We must continue to be efficient and professional, to support and supply our comrades during the forthcoming period of Allied reoccupation of this nation, until we are withdrawn from the China Theater.

I ask you to cooperate in the final phase of this mission, and to realize that the more efficient you are, the quicker the job will be completed, the sooner you will go home.

Now that wasn't such a bad speech. At least the troops didn't boo me. (I hope General Ike didn't mind my lifting a few lines from his 6 June 1944 Normandy invasion message to the troops.)

With the termination of hostilities, the 23rd Fighter Group moved to Hangchow, not far from Shanghai. I, as Liuchow air base commander, was ordered to assist in the airlift movement of the Chinese 94th Army to Shanghai for occupational duties. For this operation, Air Transport Command sent me a whole fleet of C-54 aircraft, and we began hauling the Chinese troops day and night for nearly two weeks—some 25,000 men and their equipment. It was a miserable job, but we got it done on schedule. Yes, sometimes we stacked the Chinese bings in the C-54s like cordwood. We lost only one aircraft, which flew into a hill on a dark, rainy night.

When we began this airlift mission, I flew down to Kangwan airfield at Shanghai so I could get the picture of what was going on at that end. On our C-54 we also carried about a dozen Chinese generals, plus their staffs, who were to accept the surrender of the Japanese forces in the Shanghai area. I also put a jeep on board for my and the aircrew's use. It was amazing, after spending so much time in the backlands of China, to fly over the great city of Shanghai, look down at the buildings, streets and boulevards, teeming people, city traffic, and busy harbor—civilization.

After landing at Kangwan under the guidance of an English-speaking Jap in the control tower, we taxied to the ramp where a Japanese Air Force lieutenant directed the parking of our C-54. The Chinese generals were met by Japanese generals, and all were soon whisked off in staff cars to town. The Jap lieutenant asked, in near perfect English, what service we required, and he directed some Jap airmen to assist our crew chief. I told him we had a jeep on board we needed to get off. He brought a stake-body truck, backed it up to the C-54 door, we bounced the jeep out of the door and onto the truck bed. On the up bounce, you can easily move the jeep about a foot at a time, and then bounce it around a turn so you can get it out of the aircraft door. The Jap officer then drove the truck to a cut-bank of earth about as high as the truck bed, and we simply drove the jeep off the truck. I was surprised that we and the Japs both used the same SOP for unloading a vehicle.

The Jap lieutenant now escorted us into Shanghai. About every fifty feet along the roadway, for maybe a couple of miles, stood Japanese soldiers who, as we drove past them, bowed to us. I'd be willing to bet each one had a few unkind words for us under his breath. In Shanghai we were billeted at the Broadway Mansions, a beautiful European-style hotel. There was only one problem: the rooms had no beds. Japanese officers had been billeted there, and they didn't use our type of bed, just sleeping mats. We got in touch with the hotel manager, who soon had a flock of Chinese setting up beds for us. Our escorting Jap took us all to dinner that evening at a wonderful Chinese restaurant where, I would guess, we ate about everything on the menu. We, of course, paid for the sumptuous meal, which we shared with our ex-enemy escort, including a bottle of good British scotch.

All the facilities in Shanghai—electric power, water and sewage, traffic control, city transportation, telephone and telegraph communications, and harbor operations—were still being run by the efficient Japanese. The Chinese authorities permitted this situation to continue because they did not have any qualified people of their own. The Chinese are the world's greatest spitters, which the Japanese forbade them to do when they occupied Shanghai. Now the Chinese would spit on the street, right in front of a Jap policeman, and dare him to do something about it. Another thing, during the occupation, the Jap medics would suddenly cordon off three or four city blocks, check Chinese immunization shot records, and give needed shots right on the spot. The Chinese wouldn't take shots on their own, so to prevent disease among the local population, the Jap medics used this system. Actually, the Japs did many things of benefit for the Chinese, which the latter didn't always appreciate.

In the few days I was in Shanghai I learned about, and witnessed, the execution of some of the Chinese who had collaborated with the Japanese during the war. The executions were conducted at the

Shanghai race track. The condemned person's hands were tied behind his back, and he was forced to kneel down, then shot with a single pistol bullet in the back of the head.

By mid-October my job at Liuchow was terminated and the base was closed. I received a nice commendation from Lt. General George E. Stratemeyer, commander of Army Air Forces, China Theater, for my actions in the airlift of the Chinese 94th Army. Since a lot of our people were now being returned home to the United States, I figured it was about my turn. Not bloody likely! They had another job for me—director of all air transport services in China, based in the Chase Bank Building in Shanghai. For the next couple of months I organized the air movement of more Chinese Army units and supplies to various locations in China, where they took over from the Jap troops. I began to get frequent letters from my wife, Martha, wanting to know why I hadn't come home now that the war was over. She didn't seem to understand that, as a soldier, I did the jobs I was ordered to do. My married life was beginning to come apart at the seams.

On my birthday, 16 November 1945, I was sitting in a little Shanghai bar called The Black Cat, celebrating all by myself, when in walked Earthquake McGoon. He had had an unfortunate time in Shanghai during the past month. First, no one could find a U.S. army uniform big enough to fit him, so he went to a Chinese tailor and had a uniform made from Japanese Army material, which the powers that be frowned upon. Second, he had been assigned to repatriate Japanese troops by LST vessel from Shanghai to Japan. To properly perform this function with appropriate dignity, Earthquake purloined an admiral's hat and a bosun's whistle. When going aboard his LST, he would take off his fifty-mission Air Corps hat, put on his admiral's hat, and with his whistle, pipe himself up the gangplank. He departed his vessel in a reverse procedure. But the worst part of his brief naval career was when he got drunk one night, took the LST out into the middle of the Shanghai harbor, and opened the front ramp to the sea. He damned near drowned before he was rescued by some curious Chinese in a sampan. Third, he had been released from further repatriation duties—fired, to be exact.

On Christmas eve, 1945, I had managed to procure a bottle of Schenley's Black Label whiskey—Schenley's black death, we called it—

at the going rate of $40 U.S. I had just opened it in the officers' mess when I saw Earthquake coming over to my table. "Have a drink," said I to Earthquake. He picked up the full bottle, put it to his lips, and gulped, gulped, gulped. When he set it down it was half gone—$20 worth! Earthquake told me he was quitting the Army Air Force and going to work as a pilot for CNAC (China National Airways Corporation). The pay was good, he said, $1,000 per month, and besides he liked and wanted to stay in China.

That was the last time I saw Earthquake McGoon. During the French-Indo China war of 1950–1954, at the siege of Dien Bien Phu in April of 1954, Earthquake, flying a C-82 Packet and air-dropping supplies to the French forces, was shot down by Viet Minh troops and killed. A *Life* photographer took a series of photos from the time Earthquake's kite was hit, as it plunged earthward burning, and the explosion when it crashed into the jungle. Poor Earthquake made the pages of *Life* the hard way.

My air-transport job finished in Shanghai, I was reassigned, not back to the States, but to the 4th Fighter Group of the Chinese Nationalist Air Force as an advisor. There were two factions in China during and after the war, the Nationalist Kuomintang government of Chiang Kai-Shek and the communist government of Mao Tse-Tung. The United States tried in vain to get these two rival political factions to join together in a single government for China. The result was civil war between the Chinats and Chicoms, as we called them. I had just survived six years of the Second World War, and now some staff bastard in Washington had decided to stick my rear end right in the middle of another war! Maybe someone was trying to get rid of me. Anyway, our U.S. command was called MAGIC, Military Advisory Group in China. At least I'd be a fighter pilot again. MAGIC was commanded by General John P. "Big John" McConnell, who some years later became USAF Chief of Staff.

The 4th Fighter Group of the CNAF was located at Peking and, happily, equipped with P-51 Mustang fighters. My advisory unit included Major Hennick, supply and maintenance; Captain Keller, operations; and Captain Abbott, adjutant. To compensate us for this job, we were paid our regular U.S. Army pay, plus $400 per month by the Chinats. Our quarters, rations, transportation, and servants were provided free of cost to us. Not too bad a deal at that. The senior houseboy, named Yu, who was about forty years old, we soon discovered was a major in the Chinese intelligence service. His job was to report secretly on each of us and our actions to CNAF headquarters in Nanking. Major or not, he was a good guy, managing all our household affairs very efficiently.

Lt. Colonel Tsai, the 4th Fighter Group commander, was U.S. Army Air Corps trained. He spoke English fairly well and we got on nicely together. In the group were two American-born Chinese pilots, Lieutenants Shih and Ho, and a Canadian-born Chinese flight commander, Captain Sun. The commander of the Chinese Nationalist Air Force at that time was a number one fighter pilot, General "Tiger" Wong. The 4th Fighter Group was a damned good outfit, well trained, combat experienced, and they knew how to fly and fight. I was very happy with my new assignment, even though it meant a longer stay overseas for me. They gave me my own P-51, all nice and polished, and bearing the blue and white-twelve-pointed star insignia of the Kuomintang government.

The mission of our group was to provide close air strike support on the battlefields for the Chinat armies advancing to the northeast of Peking, toward Mukden and Harbin, against the Chicom armies. We were also to interdict Chicom supply routes and support bases, and to assist Chinat garrisons with our firepower, if needed. Although this was a large mission, it wasn't too difficult for us to handle. The 4th Fighter Group was composed of four fighter squadrons, with 25 aircraft in each squadron. In addition, we had operational control over two B-25 bomber squadrons, a C-47 transport squadron, and an L-5 liaison squadron. With this composite force we could do about everything: fighter strikes, saturation bombing, airlift of troops and supplies, and liaison and target spotting. All of our logistical support was provided by the United States.

The Chinese rented a big house for us Americans in Peking, a beautiful place, with a large courtyard, swimming pool of fair size, and black marble "moon gate" doorways. They also provided us with a huge German shepherd watchdog which, I'm certain, could tear a bandit limb from limb. We were issued a Chevy staff car and a jeep, and besides Yu, the chief houseboy, we had a cook, two housemaids, a wash woman, a second houseboy, a gardener, and four Chinese Army guards who slept most of the time. One morning I met the occupant of another house in our compound, who turned out to be Colonel Gil Stewart, the Aussie in the Chinese Army I'd first met at Kunming. Stewart was assigned as a liaison officer to the U.S. Military Commission in Peking. The Commission's task was to try to get the Chinats and Chicoms to cease fighting. Their huge four-story headquarters was known to Chinese and Americans alike as "The Temple of the Thousand Sleeping Colonels." They, of course, were not successful, so the civil war continued through 1946.

Like all—or most—fighter pilots, the 4th Fighter Group guys enjoyed a good drinking party now and again. Their primary effort at these affairs was to get us Americans swacked. I had a secret weapon: Captain Peter Abbott, the adjutant, whom we called Peter Rabbit. (Try it, say his name fast.) Pete had a cast iron stomach and a hollow leg that could hold a gallon of giggle soup.

Now these Chinese are pretty cagey people at a "gumbay" party. After a wonderful dinner of bird's nest soup, Peking duck, fried rice, candied grasshoppers, and all sorts of other exotic dishes of the Orient, everyone got down to serious hot wine drinking. As an example, a Chinese pilot would come to have a drink with me. He was followed by an orderly with a teapot, presumably full of rice wine. The orderly would fill the Chinese pilot's cup to the brim, to which the pilot would toast "gumbay," meaning "down the hatch." and toss off his drink. After about a dozen or so of these toasts, you could get pretty well bent out of shape. It wasn't long, however, before we discovered the Chinese were filling their cups with tea instead of wine. So, when asked to "gumbay," we'd tell them to exchange cups with us. They couldn't lose face, so we got their tea and they got our wine. Near the end of our party, when most of the Chinese guys had passed out, Pete would challenge all those still on their feet to a final "gumbay." Then he would fill a big rice bowl with wine and gulp it down. The valiant Chinese would try to duplicate Pete's feat, but ten minutes later Pete and I would carefully walk through the bodies of our fallen Chinese comrades, the undefeated victors.

All was not fun and games with the 4th Fighter Group. We still had a war on our hands. About fifty miles south of Peking a Chinat garrison, occupying the town of Pachow, was attacked and surrounded by Chicom forces. Until other Chinat ground troops could come to their aid, we were directed to provide air-dropped support to the garrison—ammunition, food, medical supplies. To do this, we sent a couple of C-47s once a day, sometimes twice a day, to make the drops. We escorted the C-47s with two P-51s. In the drop zone the P-51s would strafe the Chicom troop positions to make them keep their heads down, while the goony birds flew over the town and dumped their cargo from about 200 feet.

One morning one of the strafing P-51s was hit by 20mm antiaircraft cannon fire and its pilot badly wounded in the neck by a shell. By radio he managed to tell his section leader of his wound, the shot-up condition of his aircraft, and that it was necessary for him to belly-land just beyond the Chicom lines. He made a successful landing on a rather narrow strip of hard ground that was flanked by rice paddies. The pilot didn't get out of his P-51.

His section leader, Captain Woo, flew back to Peking balls out, landed, jumped out of his Mustang and into an L-5, and took off again for Pachow. We knew something unusual had occurred, so we scrambled two P-51s—mine and Lieutenant Wong's—to assist in the problem. We arrived before Woo's L-5, saw the downed P-51 with the pilot still in the cockpit. About 50 Chicom troops were advancing across the rice paddies toward the aircraft, so we began to discourage them by our strafing. Captain Woo arrived about this time in his little two-seater L-5, which he landed amid Chicom rifle fire beside the P-51. He ran to his wingman's aircraft, dragged the badly wounded pilot out and into the L-5's rear seat, and then took off for Peking. We shot up the downed P-51—she caught fire and blew up. Captain Woo's gallant rescue effort went for naught. His friend was dead on arrival at our airfield; half his neck had been blown away. Woo's L-5 aircraft had well over a dozen rifle-bullet holes in it.

The Russians, supporting the Chicoms, provided them with the nucleus of an air force—a batch of P-39 "Airacobras," originally given to the Russians by the United States during the Second World War. They also sent a few instructors to teach the Chicom pilots how to fly the damned things. To my knowledge, none of these P-39s ever flew a combat mission. Every one was destroyed on the ground, courtesy of the strafing 4th Fighter Group, Chinese Nationalist Air Force.

We, that is my advisory team, ran into a good deal one day when a U.S. Marine colonel from Tientsin paid us a visit. It seemed that the

Marines received regular shipments of American whiskey at the port of Tsingtao, but had no safe way to move the whiskey from the port to their troops in Tientsin and Peking. That, of course, was a terrible situation that must be alleviated at once. We had a C-47 available to us, which gave us the upper hand in the deal. We would haul their whiskey for them at the rate of one case of whiskey per aircrew member per flight. Our C-47 would require a crew consisting of a pilot, copilot, navigator, crew chief, and radio operator, which totalled five cases of giggle soup for each of four flights per month. Agreed! Now we were really living in the lap of luxury. We had some outstanding parties at our Peking home after this pipeline was opened. Some of them were noisy enough even to awaken the occupants of "The Temple of the Thousand Sleeping Colonels."

On my birthday, 16 November 1946, I received a message telling me that I had been awarded a regular commission in the U.S. Army Air Force. My previous commission was in the AUS (Army of the United States), which was a temporary commission issued just for war service. So, now I was a regular first lieutenant, but retained my active duty AUS rank of lieutenant colonel. About this same time I received word that my father had died in the Veterans' Hospital at St. Cloud, Minnesota.

Not long afterward a large Chicom army was discovered about eighty-five miles north of Peking, advancing in our direction. Air recon estimated its strength at about 10,000 troops, supported by a large number of artillery guns. A Chinat army force of about equal size was sent to do battle with the Chicoms. In the meantime, before the ground action could occur, the 4th Fighter Group began air attacks on the enemy column. Strafing and bombing as we did, sort of reminded me of the 406th Fighter Group attack on the German column at the Belfort Gap in France in the autumn of 1944. This Chicom force, caught as it was passing through a long narrow valley, was massacred, stopped in its tracks with a terrible loss of troops, and defeated by the strength of air power alone. When the Chinat ground forces arrived on the scene they captured the remaining Chicom troops, executed the Chicom officers and NCOs, and "transferred" the Chicom bings into the Chinat army. This system was employed after every battle, no matter who won. The poor Chinese private soldier would fight for whichever side fed and clothed him—the purposes of the civil war meant absolutely nothing to him.

One night, about midnight, when Pete Abbott and I were driving from the airfield to Peking, I saw a roadblock ahead of us. As Chicom infiltrators were active in the area, I always carried a .38-caliber pistol close to me on the car seat. This night, in the car's headlight beams, I could see several armed Chicom troops manning the barricade. They knew we would have to pass this way on our way into town. There wasn't much of a choice for Pete and me—we had to fight or get rubbed out.

I poured the coal to our old Chevy, heading for the barricade full bore with the horn blowing. Lots of noise makes for confusion in a situation like this. With my left hand on the steering wheel, I took the .38 in my right hand, stuck the pistol out the driver's window and, as we smashed through the barricade, began pulling the trigger. We went through them like a dose of salts, scattering Chicoms in every direction, and then barreled on down the road. I don't think they even got a shot off at us. We immediately reported the incident to the commander of the Peking Chinat garrison, who dispatched his troops to the scene. They found the barricade, but no Chicom troops; however, they did report that quite a bit of blood was scattered about the area.

This incident, of course, was reported to MAGIC headquarters in Nanking. A few days later I was ordered to withdraw my guys from advisory service with the 4th Fighter Group. There seemed to be a Chicom pattern set up for the assassination of all American advisors to the Chinat Air Force. The advisor withdrawal instructions, I was informed, came directly from General George C. Marshall of the Joint Chiefs of Staff in Washington, D.C. It's too bad the general couldn't see how his action would affect the near future of China, and the distant future of all of Asia.

I few eighty-two missions in the China-Burma-India theater of war, twenty-eight of them during the last month of my active service with the Chinese Nationalist Air Force. For this service I was awarded the Special Breast Order of Yun Hai with Ribbon on 20 August 1946. I received a second award of the same medal on 14 December 1946, and received the Air Force Mao Chi Medal, Class 1, Kind A, on 17 December 1946. President Chiang, himself, approved the first two "gongs," and General Chow Chih-Jiu, commanding general of the Chinese Nationalist Air Force, authorized the latter "gong."

In January 1947 I caught a ride on a war-weary C-54 back home to the United States. So ended my war—or rather two wars, the Second World War and the Chinese Civil War. I first entered war service in September 1939 and now terminated such war service in January 1947, well over seven years later. There had been some rough times, but I had survived.

Epilogue: The Later Years

When I arrived back in the States from China, a bunch of us went to the "Top of the Mark" hotel in San Francisco to celebrate. There we spent several happy hours with a glass of cold milk in one hand and a glass of bourbon in the other. I don't know which tasted better. Transportation arranged, I went to Picton, Ontario, to see my wife Martha and my son Jerry. The long years of waiting for me to return from the wars had somehow changed things between Martha and me. When she, Jerry, and I met, Martha was accompanied by a guy who, I guess, later took over and did a better job than I did. Jerry was a handsome young lad of four years, but I was a stranger to him, and he cried when I tried to embrace and kiss him. So, to solve the whole situation, Martha and I were divorced. That was a hell of a beginning for my homecoming.

My first assignment in the States was as chief of operations plans, Headquarters, 10th Air Force, at Brooks Field, San Antonio, Texas. At that time the entire Air Force was playing musical chairs for duty assignments. Being a staff weenie didn't suit me, so I managed to obtain an assignment as Senior Air Instructor to the South Dakota Air National Guard at Sioux Falls, where I flew P-51s and A-26s with the 175th Fighter Squadron. Joe Foss, the famous Marine ace and Congressional Medal of Honor winner, was the squadron commander. Joe had one of the finest squadrons I'd ever seen. All his troops were well trained, eager, ready to fight, and willing.

In Sioux Falls I met and fell in love with a beautiful little blonde lady named Evelyn Cecelia Rowley. After a whirlwind courtship, I talked her into marrying me on 23 September 1947. Evelyn had two sons from a previous marriage—Howard Dana, age twelve, and Gary James, age seven—so I acquired a wonderful ready-made family. I wasn't doing too badly, after all. Not long after our marriage I was assigned to Headquarters, 2nd Air Force, Offutt Field, Omaha, Nebraska, as Deputy Director of Operations. Then in early 1948, at the request of Colonel Bill Offutt, who I had worked with at times in China, I was assigned to his 82nd Fighter Wing at Grenier Field, Manchester, New Hampshire, as Deputy Wing Commander. About this time I heard the sad news that the Chinats were slowly being defeated by the Chicoms, and that my old 4th Fighter Group at Peking had been ordered to depart mainland China for a new home on the island of Taiwan.

In August of 1948, Air Force asked me to accept a special assignment as fighter advisor to the Imperial Iranian Air Force at Teheran. So I packed up my family and off we went to the Middle East. At that time the Iranian Air Force had one fighter regiment (like our group) equipped with my first love, Hawker Hurricanes. A second fighter regiment was to be organized and equipped with P-47 Thunderbolts. There was an RAF wing commander at Doshen Tappeh military airfield who was instructing Iranian pilots on Hurricanes. However, when the Shah, Mohammed Riza Pahlavi, reviewed my service records and noted that I had flown both Hurricanes and Thunderbolts, he directed the release of the RAF type and instructed me to train the pilots of both fighter regiments. I certainly enjoyed flying a Hurricane once again, and I was the culprit who occasionally buzzed Teheran and my family's home compound.

Sixty P-47s soon arrived from the USAF 86th Fighter Group in Germany; forty-five of them were to fly and fifteen were to be cannibalized for spare parts. What a way to run an air force! Some parts, of course, could be reused, but such items as gaskets, seals, hoses, etc., needed to be installed new. I began a long fight with USAF Headquarters supply people to give me a five-year level of P-47 spare parts to keep the kites serviceable. Some feelings were hurt and toes stepped on in our TWX exchange, but I finally got my spare parts. I checked out every Iranian pilot assigned to the 2nd Fighter Regiment in the Thunderbolt without a single accident. And this included the Shah of Iran himself, who was one hell of a fine fighter pilot. As a matter of fact, the Shah flew single-engine, twin-engine, and four-engine aircraft, and he set aside every Tuesday and Thursday for his flying.

Then in January of 1949 I received a TWX from Headquarters, USAF in Washington informing me that I had been passed over for promotion to regular captain. On 28 February I received a copy of my Officer's Career Brief, which should have been sent to me for review before the first Officer Promotion Board's decision to pass me over. There were thirteen mistakes and omissions on the career brief, plus information that belonged on some other guy's records. On 5 March I wrote a letter to USAF stating all of the mistakes and requesting that corrections be made before the career brief went before a second promotion board—my last chance. On 31 March I received a letter from USAF stating that the requested corrections had been made. Then on 15 July I was notified I had been passed over for promotion a second time by the board, and that I would be honorably discharged on 27 September 1949. The Iranian minister of war, General Razmara, and the commander of the IIAF, General Sepahpour, tried to retain me on active duty by personal letters to USAF—so did my commander in Iran, Major General Vernon Evans—but to no avail.

On 2 August 1949 I was terribly shocked to receive a message from Martha, in Picton, that my son Jerry had accidentally drowned that afternoon. The funeral was to be held on 5 August, and there was no way I could make it halfway around the world to Canada by that date. I have never cried much in my life, even when I was a small boy, but that night I couldn't stop the tears from flowing.

On 29 August I, with my family, returned to the United States. I visited Headquarters, USAF, Directorate of Military Personnel where I found that my career brief had *not* been corrected as stated in their 31 March letter. I took the entire matter to the USAF inspector general, General A.H. Gilkeson. His findings and recommendations were: "It was the unanimous opinion of the board [which gave me a regular commission in 1946] that his war record was so good that we had to integrate him into the regular service. My office has done its best and has made a recommendation (which we do not think will be followed) that the last board which acted on promotions be reconvened in order to reconsider his case in the light of his performances during and since the last war."

In reply to the inspector general, the USAF Director of Military Personnel stated: "The specific reasons why Lt. Colonel Dunn was not selected as 'fully qualified' for promotion are known only to the Selection Board, which has already adjourned. There is no provision of the Officer Personnel Act of 1947 whereby he may challenge the decision of the Board, nor is such action within the spirit of the Act." Wrote General Evans to General Gilkeson: "His case (Dunn's) should be reviewed from A to Z to insure that everything was in accordance with regulations, common sense, and justice. It may be okay, but it smells, from what I know. He (Dunn) is entitled to a turn at bat or in court. I ask no favors unless it be that you personally see that he gets justice and a square deal. I'd ask no more for myself." Ruled the USAF deputy chief of staff for personnel, "There is no recourse. Discharge Lt. Colonel Dunn."

Well, how about that—shot down in flames by my own Air Force personnel staff weenies. I wasn't even permitted to say a word in my own behalf. Democracy—military democracy—at work. I have an idea that my "over the hill" episode when I was in the Army back in 1934 may have had some bearing on my pass-over. Somehow I reasoned that all of my war service should have outweighed that earlier indiscretion of my youth, but maybe not.

I decided I might just as well stay in the air force in one capacity or another, so I went to see the personnel guy who was in charge of enlisting ex-officers. Usually an ex-field grade officer was given the rank of master sergeant upon enlistment. This guy sat in his chair with his feet on the desk while I explained my situation to him. He was a lieutenant colonel—an arrogant, gravel-agitator type—with a wise smirk on his face as he listened to my story. When I had finished, he said, "What the hell can you do besides fly an airplane?"

Somewhat pissed off, I replied, "I can do everything you can do, you son of a bitch, and still fly an airplane!"

His face turned about twelve shades of purple, he slammed his feet on the floor, pointed an anger-shaking finger at me and shouted, "Tech sergeant!"

"I'll take it," said I, and strode out of the bastard's office.

On 14 November 1949 I enlisted as a technical sergeant at Carswell AFB, near Forth Worth, Texas. That was quite a drop in rank—reduced nine grades in a month's time. Well, that's what sometimes happens to us war heroes when the peacetime troops take over running the Air Force. My fine wife, Evelyn, took it all in stride, never shedding a single tear for her ex-lieutenant colonel as she sewed my tech sergeant stripes on my uniform sleeves. Good girl!

Inspector General Gilkeson didn't give up on my case. Before it was all over, in 1956, Secretary of the Air Force W. Stuart Symington and his general counsel were involved, as were the USAF judge advocate general, General Hoyt S. Vandenberg, the USAF chief of staff, Senators Chan Gurney (South Dakota), Tom Connally (Texas), and Lyndon B. Johnson (Texas), the later president of the United States.

At Carswell AFB I was assigned as Operations NCO of the 42nd Bomb Squadron, 11th Bomb Group, 7th Bomb Wing, Strategic Air Command. My stay there was short; I applied to be an advisor to the Brazilian Air Force, was accepted, and after a six-month course to learn the Portuguese language, my family and I departed for Rio de Janeiro in February of 1951. There was another sergeant pilot already there, Master Sergeant George Holmes, who had also been a lieutenant colonel during the Second World War. As a matter of fact, George had been a captain in the First World War.

With the Joint Brazil-United States Military Commission I was soon promoted to master sergeant, and then to warrant officer. With this last grade, I was assigned to the job of plans officer for the Mutual Defense Assistance Program (MDAP) for Brazil. My function was to plan for the future requirements of the Brazilian Air Force—aircraft, logistical support, personnel training, and special schools. When the Korean War broke out I volunteered to go there, but my application was turned down—I was needed in Brazil, I was told. Oh well, I guess I could miss one war.

In April 1954, my Brazilian tour finished, I returned to the United States and an assignment as war plans officer with the 33rd Air Division of Air Defense Command, at Tinker AFB, Oklahoma. At this station Evelyn and I adopted two American Indian children, Marianne (age five) and John (age four) Bringing Good. They were half Cheyenne and half Arapaho. Also, I was promoted to chief warrant officer in the regular air force. And, of all things, on 13 June 1956, I was commissioned a lieutenant colonel in the Air Force Reserve, by order of the President of the United States, the order signed by Donald A. Quarles, secretary of the air force. Thank you, General Gilkeson, for having the intestinal fortitude to help me fight my battle to a just and successful conclusion. There were some real right guys in this air force after all.

It was at Tinker AFB that I got my first chance to fly a jet, a T-33, with my boss, Colonel Robert C. Brown, who was the Air Division's deputy for operations. Most of the T-33 flying was acting as a target aircraft for F-102 and F-106 interceptors, or making intercepts on EC-121 aircraft that trained in ground radar-jamming techniques. Flying a jet was a big change from our old prop fighters, but the target intercept procedures were still the same as in the war days.

After nearly four years with the 33rd Air Division, I was reassigned to the 51st Fighter Interceptor Wing, Naha Air Base, Okinawa. The 51st was equipped with F-86D Sabres when I first arrived there in early 1958. Later, in 1960, the wing was converted to F-102 Delta Daggers. Nothing much exciting happened there except the Taiwan Straits Crisis, another flap between the Chinats and Chicoms. Our 51st Wing was deployed to Taiwan to assist the Chinats, if need be. In the one big air battle that was fought over the waters of the Strait, the Chinat Air Force kicked the hell out of the Chicoms, shooting down a batch of their Russian-supplied fighters. My job at Taipei, during this flap, was fighter officer and intercept director at the Air Defense Control Center. While on Taiwan I had the opportunity to visit my old 4th Fighter Group, now called a wing, of the Chinese Nationalist Air Force. There were quite a few personnel changes, as might be expected after eleven years; however, I was happy to see that General Wong, the old "tiger" of the CNAF, was still alive and kicking. Tiger Wong offered me the rank of a full colonel in the CNAF if I would resign from the USAF, but I decided against it. I wasn't that fond of low pay, fried rice, and hot ging-bao juice.

In 1961 I returned to the States, to the Central Air Defense Force at Richards-Gebaur AFB, Missouri, again as war plans officer. After a very short tour in Uncle Sugar Able, I was off again to the Philippines with the 848th Aircraft Control and Warning Squadron of the 405th Fighter Wing. The next year, 1964, I went to Pacific Air Forces Headquarters at Hickam AFB, Hawaii, where, for three years, I labored as Southeast Asia Treaty Organization and PACAF war plans officer. Evelyn and our Indian children followed me to all these assignments, except to Taiwan and the Philippines. Evelyn was the perfect soldier's wife—part nomad, part gypsy, and a woman who could make a happy home for us anywhere in the world. Our son Gary was now a budding television program producer and director in Dallas, Texas, and Dana, who had joined the Air Force in 1954, was now a technical sergeant.

In late 1965, with the Vietnamese war beginning to gather steam, I went there as a member of a SEATO planning team to have a first hand look at things. In May of 1967 I received orders assigning me to head-quarters, 7th Air Force, Tan Son Nhut Air Base, at Saigon in South Vietnam, as a tactical weapons force plans officer. My job proved to be very interesting: I was to test and evaluate new weapons, tactics, and techniques, and to develop special warfare plans. Somehow I got to thinking of myself, and World War II, and my age. Here I was, fifty-two years old, off to war again. And then I remembered old Sergeant Archie Proudfoot of the Canadian Army Seaforths in England in 1940. My god, was that twenty-seven years ago? What the hell am I doing here, an old retread?

Vietnam was stinking hot and humid and filthy. It reminded me of India and Burma in 1945. The war itself was also a stinking and stupid affair, drawn into years of fighting because of idiotic operations planning and restrictions imposed on the capabilities of our troops. If you're going to have a war, then go at it hammer and tongs until it's won. One of our biggest problems in the whole Vietnamese affair was that we were plagued by politicians who wanted to play at being generals, and generals who wanted to be politicians. The entire war could have been won by us in six months if we had been free to apply proper military tactics and the full strength of our avilable forces. But no, said the Washington staff weenies, led by an ex-Edsel salesman, who sat on their fat cans 10,000 miles from the battlefields. You wouldn't believe the many ways they found to tie our hands to restrict our operations. The worst part of the whole thing was the unnecessary deaths and injuries, the unnecessary heartbreaks, to soldiers and civilians alike, all because of the ignorant meddling of incompetents in high places—and then, in the end, complete failure and rout and disgrace.

I thought to myself that we should never have abandoned the Nationalist Chinese in their fight against Communism. General Marshall was wrong to withdraw our support, both advisory and materiel. In the Korean War President Truman should have listened to and approved the plans of General MacArthur to strike Red China. Instead, an ex-reserve artillery captain of little military experience fired a man who had been a general officer for over thirty years. After the Second World War we ended up with two Germanys—now we had two Chinas, two Koreas, and two Vietnams. If, with 20/20 hindsight, we had taken positive mili-tary action against the spread of Communist forces in Asia in the begin-ning, we would never have had to fight the Vietnam war.

In Saigon I was billeted at the Air Force BOQ, in Vo Di Nguy street, about a mile and a half from Tan Son Nhut Air Base. Seventh Air Force Headquarters was on the air base, in a nice air-conditioned brick building. Not too far away was the headquarters of General Westmoreland, U.S. commander in Vietnam, called "Disneyland East." Our BOQ was an old Vietnamese hotel which had seen better days. There was inside plumbing, but most of the time we didn't have any water to flush the cans or to bathe properly. The place was high-walled and sandbagged, with two guard posts on the walls. The guards were sleeping most of the time. They were armed with three 12-gauge shotguns. I had a .38-caliber revolver, another guy had a .25-caliber automatic. Those were the only weapons in the whole place. My roommate was Major "Moose" Amos, a big guy who worked in intelligence for 7th Air Force. At night Moose and I used to go up on the BOQ roof to watch the fireworks. To the north of the city could be seen the flashes of artillery shell explosions. Off on the city's outskirt a "Spooky"(AC-47 gunship) could occasionally be seen firing its 7.62 machine guns at some Viet Cong (VC) position, a steady stream of fire from the aircraft to the ground. Then, nearly every night, bright flares were released by our aircraft, hanging in the sky to brighten the view of our infantry on the city's perimeter. Saigon was surrounded by the enemy, the VC and the North Vietnamese Army (NVA). In daylight the battlefield was ours; at night it was theirs.

My work involved the testing of infrared devices for locating enemy vehicles in the jungle by heat detection rays, low-level-light TV for use in night viewing of the ground from the air, "Sky Spot"radio beacon bombing, the use of CS gas, smart bombs, locator devices placed in the jungle camps of Special Forces troops, and several chemicals which turned dry roadbeds into quagmires. In order to properly test these things on the enemy, I had to fly 62 missions as an observer in A-1s, F-4s, RF-4s, B-57s, AC-47s, and AC-130s. Down south, in the U-Ming forest, the VC were in considerable strength with large stockpiles of munitions. We tried dropping napalm to burn them out, but the cans would burst on the treetops, sometimes 100 feet above the ground, so the fire never got to the VC supplies. We solved the problem by loading a C-130 aircraft with pallets of six 55-gallon drums of gasoline each, which we fused with thermite grenades. Over the target area we pushed out the pallets, which crashed all the way through the jungle canopy to the ground, where the grenades ignited the gasoline. At one time we set a fire in the forest hiding place of the VC that burned for over a week, with all sorts of secondary explosions. At Seven Brothers mountain, a VC headquarters, we dropped CS gas at the base where their tunnel entrances were located, and then napalm fire on the mountaintop to suck the gas up through the tunnels and caves. The VC came staggering out by the hundreds, which our A-1 aircraft then strafed. On the Mekong River the enemy came streaming down from Cambodia sanctuaries at night, their boats loaded with supplies and reinforcements. I worked out a plan to hit them using a B-57 equipped with IR, a flare dropping F-4, and a striking F-4. From detection to destruction took less than ten seconds. Well, that will give you some idea of my operations.

Saigon was not really the safest place to be. The city was full of VC sympathizers and active VC terrorists. Little kids, paid by the VC, would toss hand grenades into movie theaters. Two American soldiers, who went to a small bar with a couple of Vietnamese girls, were later found dead, their skin stripped off their bodies, and the corpses dumped into a latrine. And then there was the Dragon Lady, who rode around town on the back of a motor scooter. She carried a .45 automatic pistol, which she would fire into a crowd of American soldiers waiting at a bus stop, and then speed safely away. At Tan Son Nhut air base, without warning, the enemy's 122-mm rockets would strike with a hell of an explosion, spreading shrapnel all over the place. Occasionally there were booby traps and mines set by the VC for unwary American troops.

Dana, our son, took his turn serving in the Vietnam war with an air defense radar squadron. My niece's husband, Lieutenant William Seacrest, was killed in action in the Vietnamese jungles.

On 31 January 1968, the night of the Vietnamese Tet celebration, Moose Amos and I were up on the BOQ roof watching the fireworks, both of us sipping a soothing drink of bourbon and swamp water. Suddenly it began to dawn on me that besides the harmless fireworks bangs, there were some other bangs that whistled through the air around us and ricocheted off the BOQ walls. Within a very few minutes we learned through radio broadcasts that Saigon was under attack by huge forces of VC and NVA troops. The Battle of Saigon had begun.

Our BOQ in Vo Di Nguy Street was on the northeastern outskirts of Saigon, about a quarter-mile from a golf course. During the night the enemy, armed with light and heavy automatic weapons, RPGs (rocket propelled grenades), and mortars, had crossed the golf course and penetrated to our area to strike an ARVN (Army of the Republic of Vietnam) headquarters compound behind our BOQ. The enemy force for this operation numbered two hundred plus Viet Cong soldiers. There was another BOQ, belonging to the 460th Tac Recon Wing, nearer the golf course than we were. It was directly in the line of advance of the enemy, was overrun, and the American occupants zapped. Billeted in our BOQ were sixty USAF officers and five Red Cross personnel, two women and three men. We were armed, as I have previously mentioned, with three shotguns and two pistols. Our communications with Tan Son Nhut air base, a single field telephone line, was cut by the enemy during the night. The VC troops concentrated just ourside our BOQ walls, using the eastern wall to cover their left flank. At dawn a terrific fire fight began between the VC and the ARVN.

In an effort to determine our situation in this flap, I went up onto the BOQ roof for a look-see. I observed the enemy's positions as I peered through some little slits in the roof's two-foot-high brick edge. Then the VC saw me, and I was showered with concrete and brick splinters when their machine gun bullets smacked into the building near my observation spot. I think I was more worried about being hit by a sniper's bullet than by the VC fire from the ground. There were other buildings near our BOQ where an enemy sniper could easily survey the whole battle area.

An ARVN jeep speeding down Vo Di Nguy street drove right into a VC crossfire, overturned, and caught fire, its four occupants rubbed out. Then an ARVN APC (armored personnel carrier), just past our BOQ front gate, was struck by a VC-fired antitank rocket and put out of commission. The troops in the APC scrambled to get back to their own lines; some made it, some didn't. I'd venture to say there were a dozen or so dead ARVN soldiers lying in the street and on the sidewalk. A VC machine gun crew had now moved into a position where they covered Vo Di Nguy Street with their field of fire. By the way, they were using a captured U.S.-made .50-caliber heavy machine gun. The position of this enemy machine gun crew covered our only escape route from the BOQ, so we were pretty well surrounded.

I went from the roof back down to the BOQ gate, opened it, and went out into the street where I moved slowly and cautiously along the wall and a sewer gutter. There I met a U.S. Army sergeant named

Hansen, who was an advisor to the ARVN. He had a 40-mm grenade launcher. I explained the situation to him and told him about the enemy machine gun position. Hansen loaded his grenade launcher, and I went back up to the BOQ roof where I got sprayed again with concrete chips from heavy gunfire. Then, with my hand signals to direct his fire, Sergeant Hansen launched his grenades. Together we destroyed the VC machine gun nest and its gun crew. I never saw Hansen again, but, old buddy, thanks for your assistance and I hope you made it safely back to good old Uncle Sugar Able.

Throughout the morning hours, American helicopters orbited over our BOQ pouring machine gun and rocket fire into the VC positions, sometimes not more than fifty feet from our walls. Within our BOQ, the two Red Cross ladies made coffee and, of all things, tape-recorded the sounds of the ongoing battle. No one had been injured, luckily, even when enemy .50-caliber bullets blasted through the BOQ walls and shrapnel from exploding mortar shells showered our compound. Our Vietnamese Army guards had long departed their BOQ defense duty for parts unknown, leaving us their shotguns. A shotgun loaded with double 00 buckshot is a formidable weapon for street fighting or in heavy jungle fighting.

At this point one thing amazed me, a thing I'm not really certain I should record now. All of the American officers, some sixty in number (lieutenants to lieutenant colonels), did absolutely nothing in their own defense. They all huddled behind a pile of sandbags in the rear of our compound, waiting, it seemed to me, for the enemy to burst into the BOQ and rub them all out. I couldn't believe it. I know they all lacked combat training (most were technical and supply officers), yet to just wait behind the sandbags to be slaughtered by the enemy was unbelievable. There were only two guys ready to fight for their lives: Major Moose Amos and Major Sam Riddleberger.

About midafternoon the battle began to go against the ARVN troops and I could see they were beginning to pull back and out of our area. I knew then we had to get the hell out of the BOQ. I told Moose I was going to Tan Son Nhut for help, gave him my pistol, and asked him to hold down the fort until I returned. I put on a flak jacket, slipped out the BOQ gate, found an abandoned jeep, and sped off to the air base. I took with me a very young captain, who was hysterical. I shoved him down beside the jeep's back seat, where he sobbed with fear.

We made it safely to the base, which was also surrounded and under heavy attack. I rushed to the command post, told the duty major of our plight at the BOQ, and asked for immediate assistance. He said he had no troops or weapons to give me, but he did give me two six-by-six trucks and drivers. So, with the trucks following my jeep, I led the way back to our besieged BOQ. We weren't fired upon either going to or returning from Tan Son Nhut airbase. Amazing, because we drove right through the enemy lines flat out.

At the BOQ the trucks followed me right into the compound. Moose, Riddleberger, and I loaded the people into the six-bys about 5 p.m. and headed them out of the battle area to the safety of Tan Son Nhut. When Moose and I were loading the last truck we nearly got clobbered. Just as the truck started to pull out, some damned VC troop fired an AK-47 automatic rifle at us. With the bullets kicking up the dirt at our feet, Moose and I made flying leaps over the truck's tailgate and got the hell out of there.

Of the sixty officers I helped get out of that BOQ, only half a dozen ever thanked me for my effort. I think some of them were embarrassed by their lack of intestinal fortitude. Next day Major Riddleberger and I went back to the BOQ. We found that the VC had entered it and used it as a command post during the night. The place was shot up a bit, BOQ room doors were kicked in, but there was no looting by the enemy troops. We estimated that only twenty-five or thirty of the two hundred or more VC soldiers survived the Battle of Vo Di Nguy.

This incident—a small event in the furiously fought Battle of Saigon—was reported to and confirmed by my commander, General Jones E. Bolt, the director of in-country operations for 7th Air Force. He turned the story over to John Riddick, a war correspondent for the *Tucson* (Arizona) *Daily Citizen.* Riddick put the story on the news service wire on Friday, 9 February 1968, with the caption: "Old Soldiers Never Die. VC Attack Can't Slow Aging Hero." How about that—me, an "aging hero." Well, I'll confide one thing to you, I was a bit sore and stiff the next day. Maybe I really was getting a little too old for that sort of thing. I had, however, put my early infantry training of some thirty years back to good advantage. And, happily, I managed to keep my skin from being punched full of holes. I was awarded another Bronze Star medal by General William W. Momyer, Commander of the 7th Air Force.

My mother and Roy, my stepfather, who were then living in Mesa, Arizona, first read of the incident in the newspaper, so they knew I was still among the living in Vietnam. My wife, Evelyn, who had been watching the terrible Saigon battle scenes shown on the TV news programs, had no word of my whereabouts or safety until they telephoned her and told her about the newspaper account.

The Battle of Saigon continued for many more days until the last of the enemy troops were surrounded in the Cholon district, on the race track, where they were finally strafed, rocketed, and bombed into submission.

A short time later 460th Tac Recon Wing RF-4 aircraft spotted a huge gaggle of about 400 NVA supply trucks at a jungle transshipment point. We could not attack the trucks along that part of the Ho Chi Minh trail without special approval from Washington. Two days later that approval was given, but by then the trucks had scattered in every direction. Several nights later, when we were testing a new AC-130 gunship, equipped with infrared, four 20-mm cannons, and four 7.62 machine guns, we found a batch of the trucks and destroyed 46 of them. The next night we found some more of them, shooting up another 28 trucks. We could have easily gotten them all on the initial sighting, but Washington was running the show. That was the last time I was actively involved in a combat engagement in Vietnam.

In June of 1968 I returned to the States, to Headquarters, Aerospace Defense Command, at Colorado Springs, Colorado, where I was assigned once again as a war plans officer. Almost five years later, I received orders directing my retirement from active service on 1 February 1973. On 31 January I was honorably discharged as a regular chief warrant officer and, for one day, promoted to my highest-held rank of lieutenant colonel. On that last day, if nothing else, I was the most senior lieutenant colonel in the entire air force—twenty-two years in grade. Yes, I proudly pinned on my silver leaves once again, and a friend of mine, Lt. Colonel Don Zeine, gave me one of his service caps with—excuse the expression—silver embroidered farts and darts on the visor.

The British air attaché, Royal Air Force Air Commodore "Paddy" Harbison, came from Washington, D.C. with his staff officers to attend my retirement ceremony. RAF types who were instructors at the

United States Air Force Academy also attended. Paddy presented me with a framed copy of my 27 August 1941 combat report—when I shot down my fifth and sixth enemy aircraft. I gave him an RAF type salute—longest way up, shortest way down, with a spring in my arm—that made him and the RAF guys grin from ear to ear. Lt. General Thomas K. McGhee, ADC Commander, presented me with a specially designed metal plaque with my likeness embossed on it, a Spitfire chasing an Me.109, and the words: "Presented to William R. Dunn, first U.S. fighter ace of World War II, on the occasion of his retirement after 38 years of military service. From Lt. General Thomas K. McGhee, Commander, Aerospace Defense Command, and staff." The general also presented me with my second award of the Legion of Merit medal.

My bride of thirty-three years, Evelyn, and I have settled comfortably into retirement at Colorado Springs. Our son Dana has retired from the air force as a chief master sergeant. Gary is now a very skilled TV director and producer in Dallas. Marianne has married, and John is working as a restaurateur, both living in Dallas. And Evelyn and I now have seven grandchildren—imagine me called grandfather.

I have been asked several times in recent years what I thought about young men who refused to serve in the military in the defense of our nation. My thoughts are expressed completely in the following statement: War is an ugly thing, but not the ugliest of things; the decayed and degraded state of moral and patriotic feeling which thinks that nothing is worth war is much worse. A man who has nothing for which he is willing to fight; nothing he cares about more than his own personal safety; is a miserable creature who has no chance of being free, unless made and kept so by the exertions of better men than himself.

In recent years I've attended a couple reunions of the American Fighter Aces Association and several reunions of the Eagle Squadron Association. You know, I'm always surprised to see how much older those guys look than me. Well, that's my war story—the story of a has-been fighter pilot, which is a hell of a lot better than a never-was.

So ended my military career—thirty-eight years of service in the armed forces of three nations—Canadian Army, British Royal Air Force, and the United States Army and Air Force. I had fought in three wars, the Second World War, the Chinese Civil War, and the Vietnam

War. For this service I was awarded nineteen combat decorations, plus twenty-four service medals and eight major battle stars. I had achieved the distinction of being the first American ace of the Second World War, but not one of the greatest aces by far. Along the way there were bullet holes and bruises and scars, but what the hell, I made it.

Appendix: The War Birds

When someone finds out you were a fighter pilot during World War II, they often express an interest in the sort of aircraft you flew and fought against. And many times they'll say: "I understand the Me.109 was better than the Hurricane and Spitfire, and the FW.190 was better than the Spitfire, Thunderbolt, and Mustang." I haven't the slightest idea where they get the "understandings." If those Hun kites were so damned superior to our fighters, how come we won the war in the air?

When anyone comes out with the flat statement that, as an example, an Me.109 was better than a Spitfire, or a FW.190 was better than a P-51 or Jug, that person hasn't any idea of what he or she is talking about. Anyone who knows anything about military aircraft and wartime flying understands that each type of combat aircraft goes through a number of mechanical modifications and capability improvements during its service life. Therefore, on a given date, one fighter aircraft's capabilities and limitations are at a certain level and may be less, equal, or better than another type of fighter. An aircraft that is not quite as good as another will be modified—larger engine, improved armament, configuration design changes to increase maneuverability, speed or climb—and suddenly it's better than the opposing fighter. The other aircraft then goes through a series of modifications which, in turn, upgrades its capabilities. So when someone starts telling you one aircraft was better than another, just ask what version or model series he's talking about. Generally, they don't know.

Yes, it is true, the Me.109E was better than the Hurricane Mk I, but the Hurricane Mk II was about equal, and the Spitfire Mk II was better. When the Huns came out with the Me.109F version it was better than the Spitfire Mk II, but the improved Spitfire Mk V outclassed the 109F. The Me.109G and the FW.190A had an edge over the Spitfire

Mk V, then the Spitfire Mk IX entered service and proved to be better than both of the Kraut kites mentioned. And so the aircraft performance improvements went on, including many modifications to the P-47 Thunderbolt and P-51 Mustang: water injection and cold fuel injections for greater engine power; turbosuperchargers for high altitude performance; three-bladed propellers, which in turn were replaced by four, five, and six-bladed props. To flatly say one type of fighter was better than another is silly, unless the specific type, model, and series is defined.

Another thing that gets to me is how some so-called military historians arbitrarily change historical facts to suit their own misunderstandings. A perfect example is that these "historians," in the past several years, have designated the Messerschmitt Me.109 as the "BF.109." Yes, I know the abbreviation "BF" stands for Bayerische Flugzeugwerk, the aircraft factory that produced the Me.109, but that fighter was designed by Willy Messerschmitt and known to all who flew or fought it as a Messerschmitt 109, or an Me.109, or just a plain 109—not a BF.109.

This account is to acquaint later generations of military aviation enthusiasts with the several types of aircraft we fighter pilots flew during the war. I can, of course, only speak from experience about the aircraft I flew and fought against in air combat. Therefore, I will discuss the wonders, the warts, and the winning ways of the Hawker Hurricane, Supermarine Spitfire, Republic P-47 Thunderbolt, and the North American P-51 Mustang. My comments concerning the Hun fighters—the Me.109 and FW.190—will necessarily be limited to their observed performance when I fought them. It should also be noted that my comments may vary from those of someone else who flew the same aircraft; our likes and dislikes were not always the same.

For the reader's edification, I have thrown in a few technical, operational, and historical facts relating to the service life and times of each aircraft.

It is true that the Hawker Hurricane, that gallant war bird of the early years of the Second World War, provided the bulwark of the British Empire's air defenses, and, by struggling magnificently against staggering odds, turned the tide of the air war against the enemy. And the Hurricane continued to fight valiantly, on every front, until the final victory was secured.

In January 1934 Mr. Sydney Camm, of Hawker Aircraft, Ltd., began a private company enterprise to design the first monoplane fighter for Royal Air Force service. At that time RAF fighter squadrons were equipped with the Hawker Fury and Gloster Gladiator biplanes, both of which were made obsolete for air warfare by the more modern monoplane fighters then being developed and placed on active military service by the Germans, French, Italians, and Americans. On 4 November 1935 Hawker's prototype aircraft, which was christened "Hurricane," was rolled out of the assembly hangar at Brooklands factory airfield. On 6 November, piloted by Flight Lieutenant P.W.S. "George" Bulman, it made its first successful test flight, reaching a top speed of 312 mph at 16,200 feet. The Hurricane was the first fighter aircraft to exceed a speed of 300 mph in level flight.

This original version was powered by a Rolls-Royce PV-12 Merlin C engine, rated at 900 hp (a much improved development of the older Rolls-Royce Kestrel 600 hp engine), and a Watts fixed pitch, two-bladed wooden propeller. The entire airframe, except for the engine cowlings, was fabric covered. No armor plate was provided to protect the pilot and fuel tanks, nor did it have a bullet-proof windshield. Its design did, however, include landing flaps and a retractable undercarriage—but of most importance was its greatly increased firepower, a bank of four .303 caliber machine guns in each wing.

On 3 June 1936 the Royal Air Force Fighter Command contracted for the production of 600 Hurricane fighters. The Merlin C engine was replaced by the supercharged Rolls-Royce Merlin II engine, rated at 1,030 hp, which increased aircraft performance to a speed of 320 mph at 17,500 feet and the rate of climb to 2,450 feet per minute. Delivery of these aircraft, for service testing at RAF Station Martlesham Heath, began in October of 1937. A change of propellers, from the two-bladed wooden type to the three-bladed constant-speed type produced by the DeHavilland and Rotol Companies, further increased the Hurricane's speed to 328 mph. In December of 1937 the first production models, the Mark Is, entered active service with No. 111 Fighter Squadron, based at RAF Station Northolt. Squadron Leader John "Downwind" Gillan, commanding No. 111 Squadron, proved the Hurricane's outstanding performance in that day and age when he flew a distance of 327 miles at an average ground speed of 408.75 miles per hour.

No. 3 and No. 56 Fighter Squadrons were the next units to be equipped with Hurricane Mk Is in the latter part of 1938. By April of

1939 the Hurricane design had been considerably modified to include metal-covered wings, protective armor plate for the pilot and fuel tanks, a belly ventral fin to increase air flow over the lower portion of the rudder for better spin recovery, redesigned engine exhaust stacks to reduce night flying exhaust flash, and a faired-in tail wheel. Following the Munich Crisis in the fall of 1938, and with the very real probability of war with Germany occurring within the next year, the RAF requirement for Hurricane production was increased by awarding contracts to the Gloster Aircraft Company and the Canadian Car and Foundry Company in early 1939.

Hurricane specifications did not change appreciably through the entire series from the first Mark Is to the last Mark Vs. Wing span was 40 feet, length 31 feet 4 inches, height 13 feet 1½ inches, and wing area was 258 square feet with a wing loading of 24.1 pounds per square foot. Weight of the aircraft varied, by Mark, between 6,218 and 6,447 pounds loaded. Engine power, beginning with the Rolls-Royce Merlin C, increased from 900 hp to the 1,620 hp Merlin 24 and 27 engines over a period of four years, which, in turn, increased aircraft speed from 312 mph to 342 mph, climb rate to 30,000 feet in just over 17 minutes, service ceiling to 34,200 feet, and maximum range to 525 miles.

Armament was again based on the Mark series: the Mark I and IIA versions carried eight .303 caliber Browning machine guns capable of 14 seconds continuous fire; the Mark IIB was armed with twelve machine guns; the Mark IIC had four 20-mm Hispano cannons, and racks to carry two 250-pound or 500-pound bombs; the Mark IID had two wing machine guns, and two Vickers S 40-mm antitank cannons, with 17 rounds per cannon, were mounted under the wings; and the Mark IV was armed with eight wing machine guns, plus eight 60-pound high explosive rockets. (The Mark III version was never built, and only two Mark Vs were built but never ordered into production.) Canadian-built Hurricanes were allotted serial numbers Mark X, XI and XII; however, these were all similar versions of the British-built Mark IIBs.

A total of 14,233 Hurricanes were built, "The Last of the Many"— the wording painted on the fuselage of the last aircraft— was completed in September of 1944. During the years of the Second World War the Hawker Hurricane was flown in combat by pilots of every Allied air force and on every war front from Europe, Africa, the Middle

East, the Balkans, and Russia, to the Far East. Hurricanes even operated from the decks of several Royal Navy aircraft carriers. They also served with the British Merchant Service Fighter Unit where, as I've mentioned before in another chapter of this book, they were catapulted from the decks of CAM ships (Catapult Armed Merchant) to provide air defense against long-range German bombers searching for Allied shipping in the North Atlantic ocean.

On 3 September 1939, the day the Second World War began, a total of 497 Hurricane Mk Is had been placed in service with 18 Royal Air Force fighter squadrons, of which 14 were operational units. (Some 3,000 Hurricanes were still on order from the Hawker and Gloster factories.) Four Hurricane squadrons (Nos. 1, 73, 85, and 87) and two Gladiator squadrons (Nos. 607 and 615), formed the Advanced Air Striking Force (AASF), which supported the British Army's Expeditionary Force (BEF) in France.

The first few months of the war, because of a lack of action between allied and enemy land armies, was called the "phony war"; but this was not the case in the air war. Pilot Officer P.W.O. "Boy" Mould, of No. 1 Fighter Squadron, shot down a Dornier 17 bomber near Toul, France, on 30 October 1939—the first enemy aircraft of the war destroyed in air combat by an RAF pilot. In May of 1940 the honor of becoming the first RAF ace was attained by Flying Officer E. J. "Cobber" Kain of No. 73 Fighter Squadron. Records of No. 1 Fighter Squadron, during the period of the phony war (3 September 1939 to 9 May 1940), listed the destruction of 26 enemy aircraft in air combat and the loss of one RAF pilot. During this same period, the two Gladiator biplane squadrons of the AASF were being reequipped with Hurricanes.

On 10 May 1940 the real war began with the German surprise attack through the Low Countries of Holland and Belgium and then into France. For the next two weeks the Hurricane squadrons were almost continually engaged in providing fighter escort for the British Fairey Battle and Bristol Blenheim bombers to their targets, and in fighting off the superior number of German Luftwaffe Messerschmitt 109 and 110 fighters, Junkers 87 Stuka dive-bombers, and Heinkel 111, Dornier 17, and Junkers 88 bombers, which were attacking and destroying the allied armies. Six more fighter squadrons—Hurricanes, Defiants, and some Spitfires—were sent by the RAF Fighter Command to support the BEF and AASF, but the powerful tide of the German advance into

France could not be stopped. (The majority of the Spitfires were retained in England for home defense.)

On 21 May 1940 instructions were issued to begin the withdrawal of all British forces from France and the abandonment of AASF forward airfields and unserviceable aircraft, which, in another week, culminated in the miraculous evacuation of the BEF from the beaches of Dunkirk. By 3 June only 66 AASF Hurricanes and their battle-weary pilots had returned to the island fortress of England. The Advanced Air Striking Force had, however, destroyed over 250 enemy aircraft in air combat, with a loss of 22 Hurricanes. About 75 Hurricanes were destroyed on the ground by enemy aircraft stafing and bombing of RAF airfields, and some 120 unserviceable Hurricanes were burned by RAF ground crews to prevent their being captured by the German Army. In this three-week period of fighting No. 1 Fighter Squadron was credited with the destruction of 114 enemy aircraft for the loss of three RAF pilots.

The Battle of France was lost, but the Hawker Hurricane had proven itself to be an outstanding fighter. And the Battle of Britain was yet to come.

With the fall of France, Reichsmarshall Hermann Göring, the commander-in-chief of the Luftwaffe, began planning his great air assault against England—his "Adlerangriff"—the Attack of the Eagles. Two months later, on Thursday, 8 August 1940, on "Adler Tag"—Eagle Day—the Germans launched the first of their powerful air armadas and the Battle of Britain began.

During the brief breathing spell from 3 June to 8 August the RAF Fighter Command went flat out to reequip and reorganize its decimated fighter forces, which had lost an additional 198 Hurricanes and a few Gladiators in the unsuccessful defense of Norway against German invasion forces.

Air Chief Marshal Sir Hugh Dowding, AOC of Fighter Command, had organized his units into six groups, with each group responsible for the air defense of a designated geographical area of Great Britain. No. 10 Group, in the southwest area, had three Hurricane and four Spitfire squadrons assigned. No. 11 Group, defending the southeast area, was allocated thirteen Hurricane and six Spitfire squadrons. No. 12 Group, in the Midlands, had five Hurricane and six Spitfire squadrons. No. 13 Group, in the northern area, was assigned eight Hurricane and three Spitfire squadrons. No. 9 and No. 14 Groups were in the process of organization, but had no assigned squadrons. The total RAF air defense force then available included twenty-nine Hurricane and nineteen Spitfire squadrons, which, on 8 August, had a combined operational strength of 742 fighter aircraft. The Luftwaffe had, on that same day, an operational offensive force strength of 2,550 aircraft.

There was no doubt that the newer Vickers-Supermarine Spitfire Mk I was superior to the Hurricane in speed, climb, and altitude, but not in maneuverability and firepower. Based on these aircraft capabilities, tactics were developed in which the Spitfires were to engage the German fighter escorts while the Hurricanes attacked the enemy bombers. It should also be noted that No. 11 Group, commanded by Air Vice-Marshal Keith Park, and No. 12 Group, commanded by Air Vice-Marshal Tafford Leigh-Mallory, defending the areas within the radius of action of the German air forces launched across the Channel from French bases, would take the full brunt of the enemy's air assault. Their combined forces totalled 18 Hurricane and 12 Spitfire squadrons—some 540 fighters—which gave the enemy a five to one superiority.

The Battle of Britain was fought with a fury before unknown in the annals of air warfare until, on 15 September 1940, the Luftwaffe was defeated with terrible loss in aircraft and aircrews. Although the Hun bombers dropped 16,522 metric tons of incendiary bombs and 11,452 metric tons of high explosive bombs on British targets during the battle, they lost 1,733 aircraft destroyed and 643 aircraft damaged. Since the Germans were operating over British territory and the Channel waters, their aircrew losses were upwards of 3,500 men. Royal Air Force losses were 448 Hurricanes destroyed and 137 damaged, 248 Spitfires destroyed and 135 damaged, which totals to 696 aircraft destroyed and 272 aircraft damaged. RAF aircrew combat casualties totaled 313 killed in action or missing and 287 wounded. Nearly three enemy aircraft were shot down for the loss of each RAF aircraft, and the aircrew loss reached a ten to one ratio.

The first shot fired in the Battle of Britain was by a Hurricane pilot, Squadron Leader J.A. Peel. commander of No. 145 Fighter Squadron, on 8 August 1940. From this greatest of all air battles emerged the courageous and victorious RAF aces: Wing Commander R.R.S. "Bob"

Tuck, 29 victories; Squadron Leader Adolph G. "Sailor" Malan, 32 victories; Squadron Leader J.H. "Ginger" Lacey, 28 victories; Squadron Leader Douglas R.S. Bader, "the legless wonder," 22½ victories; Flight Lieutenant Frank H.R. Carey, 28 victories; Flight Lieutenant M.N. "Mike" Crossley, 22 victories; Flight Lieutenant Alan C. "Lucky" Deere, 22 victories (he was shot down nine times, hence the nickname), and many more of "the fabulous few" that I haven't the space to name here.

Flight Lieutenant J.B. Nicholson, a Hurricane pilot of No. 249 Fighter Squadron, deserves special mention, since his undefeatable courage typifies the valor displayed by many RAF fighter pilots. During a dogfight over Southampton with a formation of Me.110s, Nicholson, who was badly wounded twice and whose aircraft was shot up and in flames, continued to fight on and shoot down 110s until he was forced to bail out of his blazing Hurricane. For this heroic action, he was awarded the Victoria Cross, England's highest decoration for gallantry.

It was to honor Royal Air Force airmen such as these that Prime Minister Sir Winston S. Churchill expressed a grateful nation's tribute by his words, following the Battle of Britain: "All the great struggles of history have been won by superior will-power wresting victory in the teeth of odds or upon the narrowest of margins. Never in the field of human conflict was so much owed by so many to so few."

Pilot Officer William M.L. "Billy" Fiske of No. 601 Fighter Squadron, an American volunteer in the RAF and a gold medal winner in the prewar Olympic Games, fought in the Battle of Britain. He was the first American in the RAF to be killed in action. On 16 August 1940 Fiske's Hurricane was shot up by enemy fighters and set ablaze. He crash-landed his burning aircraft, was badly injured, and died the next day. Later, in St. Paul's Cathedral in London, a tablet was placed in memory of Billy Fiske. It reads: "An American citizen who died that England might live."

There were six other Americans in RAF service who fought in the Battle of Britain. Three of them I've mentioned in an earlier chapter—Red Tobin, Andy Mamedoff, and Shorty Keough—who also served later in No. 71 "Eagle" Squadron. During the battle these three were members of No. 609 Fighter Squadron. J.K. Haviland served with No. 151 Fighter Squadron, while P.H. Leckrone flew with No. 616 Fighter Squadron. A.G. "Art" Donahue was with No. 64 Fighter Squadron.

Tobin, Keough, and Donahue were all killed in action while in RAF service. Leckrone and Mamedoff were killed on active service in flying accidents. Only Haviland, of those "fabulous few," survived the war. He is now (1982) a professor of aeronautics at the University of Virginia.

Following the Battle of Britain, in October of 1940, Fighter Command's strength was 1,326 Hurricanes and 957 Spitfires. Although the Hurricane continued in its primary role as a fighter for another year or so, the more advanced Spitfire was gradually replacing it in first-line squadrons. However, the Hurricane's combat career was far from ended. It was adapted successfully to other equally important wartime missions: the "Hurribomber," the "Tank Buster," the CAM ship catapult version, and the night fighter. This last bit was a shaky do, to say the least. A DB-7, the British version of the American A-20 medium bomber, was equipped with a powerful searchlight in the nose (a Turbinlite, it was called) and would patrol the night skies with a Hurricane in formation on each wing. When a bandit was located by ground radar, the DB-7 would be vectored onto the enemy aircraft, turn on its bloody great searchlight, and the Hurricanes were supposed to go in and make the kill. In actual practice, everyone ended up nearly blinded by the bright light beam.

My introduction to the Hawker Hurricane came when I attended a "four-day damned short course" at the Debden OTU. Actually, the Hurricane was easy to fly, and like the Spitfire, had no bad habits. It was light and highly maneuverable; at 10,000 feet and with a true airspeed of about 300 mph it had a turning radius of 800 feet, which the Me.109s and FW.190s couldn't match. As a gun platform, it was steady as a rock. Stalling speed in level flight, with gear and flaps down, was about 70 mph IAS, and before it reached a high-speed stall it gave the pilot a long shuddering warning. Because of its low stalling speed and rugged, wide undercarriage, the Hurricane was ideally suited for small, unimproved advanced airfield operations. Normal landing approach speed was 85 mph with power, and about 90 mph in a glide.

Aerobatics with the Hurricane were a real delight to perform, and she could do them all with equal grace. Takeoff distances were extremely short—throttle open, tail up, and she was in the air. Landing rolls seldom required more than a couple of hundred yards. And she was rugged in construction, sometimes taking all the firepower the enemy had to offer and still making it safely back to home base. One guy whose Hurricane was all shot up belly-landed at about 200 mph, went through a stone fence and into a graveyard, knocking headstones in all directions, and then stepped out of the cockpit with only a black eye. Yes, it was a tough old kite, the Hawker Hurricane, a gallant war-bird and defender of the British Empire.

Some years after the war, in 1948, I was assigned as fighter advisor to the Imprial Iranian Air Force at Doshan Teppeh airfield, just outside of Teheran, to instruct on P-47 Thunderbolts. There I found the 1st Fighter Regiment, IIAF, equipped with Hurricanes. Much to my sur-prise and delight, since I had flown both the Hurricane and the Jug, I was directed to instruct Iranian pilots on both fighters. My last flight in the Hurricane—the first fighter I had ever flown and, consequently, my first love—was in September of 1949. The last Hurricane, as near as I can determine, remained on active service with the Portuguese Air Force until 1951. Since 1945 a single Hurricane (No. LF363) has tradi-tionally had the honor of leading the annual Royal Air Force fly-past over London each September 15th in commemoration of the Battle of Britain victory.

I can still hear in my memory of those bygone years the "Tally Ho" battle cry of my old wartime friend, Hurricane Squadron Leader Teddy Donaldson, who, upon sighting a gaggle of Huns, would shout gleefully over the R/T: "There are the sons-of-bitches! Let's go kill the bloody bastards!"

The Vickers-Supermarine "Spitfire" aircraft—the iron fist of the Royal Air Force's Fighter Command during the Second World War—has gained a well-deserved immortality in the annals of aerial warfare history. It was a nearly perfect fighting machine—fast, highly maneuver-able, with exceptional climb rate and deadly firepower, yet gentle and easy to fly with absolutely no bad flying characteristics. If you've ever flown a Spitfire you'll know exactly what I mean. If you haven't flown a "Spit," you'll never know the sensations and enjoyment of flight you've missed.

In its day, fighter versus fighter, the Spitfire was absolutely the very best combat aircraft. And I know something of what I speak, since I flew combat operations in the Hurricane, Spitfire, Thunderbolt, and Mustang. I have also had occasion to fly the Typhoon, P-38 Lightning, P-39 Airacobra, and P-40 Warhawk, but not in combat.

Of course, we must consider the entire evolution of the Spitfire production series—from the Mark Is of the 1938-1940 period to the last of the many, the Spitfire F21s and F22s, in 1946. (Some Spitfires remained on active service with the RAF until 1954.) Each version, in its day, was fully capable of roughly handling its adversary. The Spitfire Mk Is and IIs were a match and more for the German Me.109Es, Me.110s, and the bombers during the 1940-41 era, with the Battle of Britain terminating in complete defeat for the enemy's air forces to prove the point. The Spitfire Mk Vs could take care of the newer Me.109Fs and FW.190As from 1941 and beyond, and the Spitfire Mk IXs outclassed the Me.109Gs and FW.190Ds from 1942 until the European war was ended by the total defeat of Germany.

Fighter pilots of today seem to look back on our aircraft in those World War II days as sort of primitive, flimsy, slow flying machines. Of course they weren't primitive by the technological standards of that period. Nor were they flimsy. I knew a couple of guys who belly-landed through brick walls and came out the other side in one piece. I've seen Spits shot up and apart, with pieces of wings and tails blown off, yet they managed to recover safely at their home bases. Slow? Not bloody likely! One guy I knew hit 440 mph IAS at 27,000 feet, which figures out to be about 500 mph TAS! High altitude operations? 35,000 to 41,000 feet was not unusual. Yes, several versions of the Spit had pressurized cockpits and could operate at 45,000 feet or more. I have heard, but can't really confirm it, that a stripped-down Spitfire in the North African theater of war shot down a German photo reconnaissance aircraft at 56,000 feet in 1943.

Just for the record's sake, here are a few bits of background information concerning the Supermarine Spitfire and its several versions. The basic Spitfire, conceived by Reginald J. Mitchell, evolved from his 1925 to 1931 designs for high-speed aircraft to compete in the international Schneider Trophy Races—which his aircraft won several times. In 1933 Mitchell began work on his prototype Spitfire, but unfortunately he suffered a setback when it was found necessary that he be operated on for cancer. He continued his work, however, and on 5 March 1936 the first Spitfire was flown by Vickers Aircraft Company chief test pilot Captain J. "Mutt" Summers. The aircraft performed exactly as Mitchell had predicted it would, reaching a top speed of 342 mph at 17,000 feet.

At age 42, in 1937, Mitchell, his body worn out with work and ravaged by terminal cancer, died. The British Air Ministry placed an initial order for the production of 310 Spitfires on 3 June 1936. Production began in early 1937, and the first operational aircraft were delivered to No. 19 Fighter Squadron on 4 August 1938—the Supermarine Spitfire Mark I. By the outbreak of World War II, in September 1939, nine Royal Air Force fighter squadrons were equipped with Spitfires.

The Spitfire Mk I had a Rolls-Royce Merlin II 1,030 hp engine (later models had Merlin III engines), an armament of eight .303 caliber Browning machine guns, a maximum speed of 362 mph at 18,000 feet, a range of 575 miles, a climb rate of 2,530 feet per minute, and a ceiling of 31,900 feet. The aircraft was small: its weight loaded was 6,200 pounds, wing span 36 feet 10 inches, wing loading 26 pounds per square foot, and length of 29 feet 11 inches.

My first Spitfire, a Mark IIA, had a Rolls-Royce Merlin XII 1,150 hp engine, which made it about 10 mph faster than the Mark I, gave a better rate of climb by about 100 fpm, and increased the ceiling to 32,800 feet. The armament—eight machine guns with 350 rounds per gun (17 seconds of continuous firing time)—remained the same. Some later Mark IIB models had two 20-mm Hispano cannons installed, plus four machine guns, but we had a lot of trouble at first with the feed mechanism, which caused the cannons to jam after a few rounds were fired. I should add here, for the reader's information, that the letter following the Mark number of the aircraft indicated the type of wing armament and configuration. "A" indicated eight machine guns, "B" indicated two cannons and four machine guns, "C" indicated a universal wing which, with its guns, could also carry air/sea rescue flares, smoke bombs, food containers and dinghys, "D" indicated internal fuel tanks of 133 gallons fitted into the wing's leading edge, and "E" indicated two cannons and two .50-caliber machine guns.

The Spitfire Mk VB, a greatly improved version, had various Rolls-Royce Merlin engines installed, which ranged from 1,470 to 1,585 hp. Its weight was increased to 6,785 pounds. Range was extended to 1,000 miles, climb increased to 4,750 fpm, and the maximum ceiling was 35,500 feet. Speed reached 375 mph at 19,500 feet. Armament consisted of two 20-mm Hispano cannons (120 rounds per cannon), four .303 Browning machine guns (350 rounds per gun), and a bomb rack for one 500-pound or two 250-pound bombs.

The Spitfire Mk IX, the last model I flew, had a Rolls-Royce Merlin 66 engine rated at 1,720 hp. Maximum speed at 25,000 feet was 408 mph, climb was 4,100 fpm, and its ceiling was 43,000 feet. Armament included two 20-mm cannons (120 rounds per cannon), two .50-caliber machine guns (250 rounds per gun), and a rack for one 500-pound or two 250-pound bombs. The loaded weight of this aircraft was 7,500 pounds. With internal fuel its normal range was 435 miles; maximum range with a belly tank was 980 miles. The Mark IX had a four-bladed propeller which increased its overall high altitude and maneuvering efficiency.

The last of the Spitfire series were the F21 and F22 models. An F24 was built, only 81 aircraft, but it really was just a modifcation of the F22 version. Equipped with the Rolls-Royce Griffon 61 and 64 engine, rated at 2,050 hp, the top speed of these aircraft at 26,000 feet was 454 mph. They climbed at 4,900 fpm to 45,000 feet, had a range of about 900 miles with a belly tank, and were armed with four 20-mm 20-mm Hispano cannons (175 rounds inboard, 150 rounds outboard per cannon), and had the standard bomb racks. A number of F21s and F22s used the Griffon 85 engines and six-bladed counter-rotating propellers.

Of course there were a number of other models, or Marks as they were designated, in between the several versions I have noted here—the "clipped wing" Spit Mk V, the high-speed and high-flying Mark VIII, the Mark XIV with its five-bladed propeller and 2,035 hp Griffon engine, which was the first prop-driven fighter to catch and shoot down a German Me.262 jet fighter, the photo reconnaissance models, and the Fleet Air Arm's Seafire, Spiteful and Seafang versions.

It is my intent, however, to illustrate how the Spitfire progressed in development and capability during its service life—twice the engine power, 100 mph faster, nearly doubled climb rate, 13,000 feet more altitude, and fire power more than doubled. A total of 20,351 Spitfires were built and they served on every front, including the Russian front, during the Second World War. In addition, 2,408 Royal Navy versions, the Seafires, were produced. The Spitfire was the only Allied fighter air-craft in continuous production throughout the whole war.

The Spitfire was the most thoroughly honest aircraft I've ever flown, and I know that every Spit pilot would concur with my statement. For example, it would shudder and shake and do everything it could to tell you it was going to stall. When it finally did stall it would flick over, but not violently. Opposite rudder and neutralized control column, with power off, and you could pull her out in a single turn, or a turn and a half at the most. Normal level stalling speed was about 70 mph, and you could gently control its fall-through with ailerons. In a high-speed turn you could easily hold the aircraft just above a high-speed stall without falling off.

Takeoff speed was about 100 mph in a distance of 450 to 500 feet, and by the time you passed over the airfield perimeter the speed had increased to nearly 200 mph. In a stiff wind I've seen Spits get off the deck in 150 feet! Normal landing speed with the undercarriage and flaps down was 85 or 90 miles per hour, with touchdown about 75 mph. You could make a precautionary landing on a short field by dragging the Spit in nose high with the prop in full fine pitch, drop the gear and flaps, maintain a final approach speed of 75 mph, cut the power at the field's edge, and actually sink down and touch down at about 65 or 68 mph. The landing roll in this latter instance was usually less than 300 feet.

Some of us Spit pilots used to make an occasional landing designed to scare the bejesus out of everybody, especially yourself. It was done in this manner, and I don't recommend it for long life. Approach the airfield at about 1,000 to 1,200 feet altitude and cross over the field downwind. As you near the far edge of the field change the fuel mixture to rich, roll the aircraft over on its back and put the gear down—or rather, in this case, up—and slowly pump the Ki-gas knob to keep the inverted engine running smoothly. Now put the prop in full fine pitch, throttle back and let the nose of the aircraft drop to and through the vertical, and now dump the flaps. Then, with a few words of quiet prayer that you can pull the aircraft through a split-S before you run out of sky, complete a really spectacular flare-out and hair-raising landing.

This type of landing was certain to ruffle the generally even-tempered British squadron leader, who, after tearing a bloody great strip off you, would pass what was left on to the wing commander and group captain to chew on. The whole affair, however, had its own reward, since you were most probably grounded for a couple of days and could sneak off to London and that preplanned heavy date. We were young and gay in those days, and perhaps not too bright. Yes, sure, we lost a few guys at the flare-out point of the landing. It was sort of like Russian roulette, each guy wanting to make his inverted approach lower than anyone else, and it didn't always work out quite right. A thousand feet above the deck was finally determined to be just about the right altitude to start this foolishness in a Spitfire. The Hurricane guys could generally do it from 800 feet.

The Rolls-Royce Merlin, an exceedingly reliable hand-made engine, was the smoothest and most powerful engine available, and certainly, coupled with a beautifully designed airframe, made the Spitfire the outstanding fighter aircraft it proved to be. At takeoff you could pour the coal to it, the cockpit armor plate hit you in the back, the tail was in the air, and you were airborne in the length of time it takes to read the words in this one sentence. In just seconds you were passing through 200 mph, starting a climb of nearly 5,000 feet per minute, and in about six minutes or so you were at an altitude of 30,000 feet.

There was an emergency boost control in the cockpit which, if you got into trouble and needed a lot of extra engine power, you could engage with the throttle. Use of this small red painted lever, which permitted you to exceed normal boost, was called "pulling the teat." If you had occasion to use emergency boost, the engine gave a roar and a surge of power for about five minutes, and then you'd better throttle back before the engine blew up. This extra power was just what was sometimes needed in a dogfight to get out of a bad situation, or into a good position to squirt and bump off a bad guy. I've flown several fighters with the U.S. Packard-built Merlin engines (P-51s) and the Allison "time bomb" engines (P-51s and P-39s), all mass-produced, and there is absolutely no comparison with the dependable hand-made Rolls-Royce Merlin engine. (For you ground-pounders, the difference would be like getting out of a Ford and into a Cadillac.)

I've been asked numerous times if the Spit had ground-looping tendencies because of its narrow undercarriage. The answer is no, none at all. As noted before, the aircraft was very light in weight, had a low wing-loading factor, and was highly maneuverable. Aerobatics were easy to do—horizontal and vertical rolls, split-Ss, stall turns, low- and high-speed stalls, spins, loops, inverted flight, offered no problems at all to the pilot, unless he was a clumsy and heavy-handed clod. The aileron and elevator controls were light, needing only a gentle movement of the control column to respond. Yet you could, in combat, with the throttle fire-walled, grasp the spade-grip control column with both hands and really haul the aircraft around flat out. There were two sets of rudder pedals in the Spit—a lower set for normal flying comfort, and an upper set for dogfighting. This upper set bunched the pilot's body up more in the cockpit, and by doing so prevented a lot of high-speed, high-G blackouts.

The Spitfire was a thing of beauty to behold, in the air or on the ground, with the graceful lines of its slim fuselage, its elliptical wings and tail plane. It looked like a fighter aircraft and it certainly proved to be just that. It was an aircraft with a personality all its own—docile at times, swift and deadly at other times. One must really have known the Spitfire in flight to fully understand and appreciate its thorough-bred flying characteristics. Once you've flown a Spitfire it spoils you for all other fighters. Every other aircraft seems imperfect in one way or another and leaves something to be desired. Adolf Galland, the German ace and commander of the Luftwaffe Fighter Arm, when asked by Reichsmarschall Hermann Göring what he needed most to improve his fighter forces, replied, "Give me a squadron of Spitfires." I understand that "Fat Hermann" blew his stack, but Galland's reply certainly confirms the Spitfire's high performance rating, even with enemy fighter pilots.

As a note of interest, the highest scoring American Spitfire pilot in the Royal Air Force was Wing Commander Lance C. Wade, DSO, DFC and two bars, of San Augustine, Texas. Wade served in No. 33 and 145 Fighter Squadrons where he shot down twenty-five enemy aircraft. He was killed in a flying accident in Italy on 12 January 1944.

It has now been forty years since a Spit and I had a "go" at each other, yet somehow it doesn't really seem more than a couple of years ago. I still feel today, if I could fit my age-broadened posterior into the confines of its narrow cockpit, that we two old war birds together could again "slip the surly bonds of earth and dance the skies on laughter-silvered wings, where never lark or even eagle flew."

The Republic P-47 Thunderbolt has been affectionately called many different names by the fighter pilots who flew her—the Repulsive Scatterbolt, the Jug, Thunder Mug, Bucket of Bolts, T-Bolt, Big Ugly, and Cast Iron Beast. My own P-47D, when I was assigned to the 406th Fighter Group, "The Raiders," it may be remembered, was called "Posterius Ferrous" for a very valid reason. And the company that produced the Jug was generally referred to as the Republic Loco-motive Works and Iron Foundry. In more recent years, to maintain its dubious image as the manufacturer of the world's heaviest fighter air-craft, it was this same foundry that produced the F-105 Thunderchief—the "Thud," the "Lead Sled."

Be that as it may, the P-47 was a beautiful aircraft to fly in combat—tough, heavily armed, good range, reasonably maneuverable (when not loaded down with everything, including the kitchen sink), but most of all, reliable. It was said in the most elite fighter pilot circles that "she could fly through a brick outhouse and emerge smelling like a rose." She was indeed a beautiful beast.

The P-47 was a big aircraft when compared to other fighters of that day. The first time I ever saw a Jug was following my transfer from the Royal Air Force to the U.S. Army Air Corps in June of 1943, and my first thought was, "Where's the other engine?" The Thunderbolt was conceived and designed by Alexander Kartveli during the first months of World War II. Her lines were not exactly graceful, she sort of resembled a big, buxom, good-natured blonde, if you know what I mean. Wing span was 40 feet 9 inches, fuselage length was 36 feet 1 inch, and her height was 14 feet 2 inches. Wing area was 300 square feet. Aircraft weight with normal (clean) load was about 13,300 pounds. The P-47, however, had a maximum load weight of 15,000 pounds for the D-15 and D-20 models to 19,400 pounds for the D-25s. This maximum load consisted of 370 gallons of internal fuel, 267 rounds of .50-caliber ammunition for each of 8 Browning machine guns, ten 5-inch HVAR aerial rockets, two 500- or two 1,000-pound demolition bombs, and a 75-or 150-gallon belly tank. Later on, some of our guns carried 425 rounds per gun.

I suppose I'd better mention now that the P-47N model was even larger than the D models. It had two feet more wing span and had a maximum load weight of 20,700 pounds, which included 1,156 gallons of fuel! The 'N" was used primarily for long range bomber escort mis-sions in the Pacific theater of war, so it needed every drop of gas it could carry. I intend, however, to base my comments on the P-47Ds, which we used in Europe and in which I spent a considerable number of hours that were interspersed with moments of sheer terror.

The P-47 was powered by the rugged and dependable Pratt and Whitney R-2800-21 and -59 series engines. This engine, a radial double

Wasp with 18 cylinders, super-charged and air-cooled, was rated at 2,300 hp on takeoff. There was an emergency boost system as well, which injected a mixture of water and alcohol (methanol) into the engine. If the pilot got in a bind in air combat and needed some additional engine poop, he could "pour the water to it" and get a maximum of 2,535 hp for a period of about fifteen minutes. After that time limit the engine's cylinders began to come unglued.

Speed of the Jug, of course, depended on the aircraft's load configuration, but clean she could do 350 mph at about 5,000 feet and around 425 mph at 30,000 feet. Now, if you had occasion to give her the "water injection," she'd do about 440 mph at 30,000 feet. Rate of climb wasn't the greatest, even clean, about 3,000 fpm up to 5,000 feet, which then gradually decreased to 2,500 fpm at 20,000 feet. With a full war load, the rate of climb was sometimes as low as 400 to 600 fpm. Service ceiling for the D models, depending on the series, was between 40,000 and 42,000 feet. However, I once had my old favorite, a P-47D-15 Razorback, up to 42,800 (true) before we both fell out of the sky and came barreling down in a long compressability dive. That gets bloody exciting, as I'll explain later.

Fuel consumption was something else. The Jug drank gas like it was going out of style. It could carry 370 gallons internally, plus two external wing tanks of 75 gallons each, and a 75- or 150-gallon belly tank. Twenty-five or 30 gallons went down the tubes for warm-up, taxiing, and takeoff. Then she drank up between 90 and 110 gallons per hour at normal cruise speed (we used a rule of thumb—100 gallons per hour). In combat, in a good dogfight, her fuel consumption was about 275 gallons per hour. And, if you had to give her the water injection, she gulped gas at the rate of 315 gallons per hour. Normal range of the P-47D was 480 to 500 miles when carrying a full war load. Maximum ferry range was about 1,700 miles. The bigger "N" model, I'm told, had a war load range of 800 miles and a maximum ferry range of around 2,200 miles. I'll bet some boys got some damned sore seats riding in that thing all day.

The Thunderbolt's combat flying capabilities and limitations need some clarification before they can be realistically discussed. First, what's the mission? Is it to be fighter sweeps, bomber escorts, armed recce, dive bombing, strafing or rocketing? Second, what's the target? Will it be enemy aircraft, railway marshaling yards, tanks, artillery, troops, trains, trucks, airfields, radar and communication sites, canal barges, bridges, coastal shipping, or battlefield close support? Well, to be brief and to the point, the P-47 could successfully execute every one of those missions and clobber every one of those targets. The Jug's middle name was versatility. All that was needed was for the 8th and 9th Air Force staff weenies to come up with the mission. Then the Thunderbolt group operations guys would figure out how to do it right, the first time.

Clean, the Jug could take on a flock of Me.109s or FW.190s and hold its own, big as it was. It couldn't out-climb them, but it could stay with them in a tight turn, and it sure as hell could out-dive any of them. And the heavy firepower of its eight machine guns, using a combination of tracer, ball, and API (armor-piercing incendiary) ammunition, blew a goodly number of Kraut kites out of the sky. I've already noted the strength of the Thunderbolt's firepower when I shot down an Me.110; the fusillade of bullets literally shot the Hun aircraft to bits. Then again, several times we fought as many as 40 German fighters, shooting down a dozen or so without a single loss to ourselves.

Lt. Colonel Francis "Gabby" Gabreski, the famous ace of the P-47 equipped 56th Fighter Group, will certainly agree with the Jug's air fighting capabilities. He scrubbed 31 Hun kites, mostly enemy fighters. Colonel Herb Zemke, the group's commander, knocked down another 20 confirmed Krauts in air-to-air combat. Captain Bob Johnson shot down 28 German aircraft while flying the "Repulsive Scatterbolt." Colonel Dave Schilling toted up 22½ air victories. Colonel John C. Meyer, commander of the 352nd Fighter Group (later he became a four-star general), had 24 aerial kills. I've listed just five P-47 fighter pilots, and between them they shot down a combined total of 125½ enemy aircraft—that's the equivalent of ten German fighter squadrons!

The Jug was also the most practical fighter to be employed in air-to-ground strike operations and close air support during Army battlefield operations. She could survive in a heavy flak environment, where other fighter type aircraft with in-line engines were shot down, sometimes by only a single round through their coolant systems. Many Thunderbolt pilots were mightly happy, after being hit by flak, to have the rugged old girl tied to the seat of their pants and get them safely home.

The Thunderbolt was easy to fly, sort of like a big AT-6 (advanced trainer). Takeoff was fairly long, depending on the aircraft's load configuration. Landing on that wide-track gear was also simple. We usually put the gear down at about 180 mph, dumped the flaps on final turn at 150 mph, over the fence at 110, and touch down about 85 or 90 mph. She didn't float at all; just ease back on the stick and throttle and down she came, like a ton of bricks.

Her bad habits, as far as I was concerned, were her slow rate of climb, spin characteristics, and compressibility dive. The climb problem has already been mentioned. In a stall, at low or high speed, she'd fall out from under you with a snap that would shake your eye-teeth; down would go her big nose, and she could really wind up in a long spin. Spins weren't recommended for the Jug, according to the book. If you did an intentional spin, it should be started above 10,000 feet. If you hadn't gotten her out of the spin at 6,000 feet, you'd better start thinking about bailing out because she was probably going all the way in.

A compressibility dive was a shocking state of affairs, let me tell you. Entering compressibility at about 40,000 feet, her nose would gradually drop until it was just past the vertical, slightly on her back. There wasn't a thing the pilot could do to control the 600 mph plus dive, except sit there and watch the earth rushing up at him, scream a little, and pray a lot. At about 18,000 feet you began to recover some elevator control. Power on would begin to lift the P-47's nose, and by the time you reached 8,000 feet—pulling all the Gs you could stand— you'd come barreling out the compressibility dive, slightly sweaty and a little green around the gills. It was a tremendous experience to go through—once. Some new boys used to get in a panic and start rolling back elevator trim in the first part of the dive, which was a definite no-no. When they hit about 15,000 feet the trim would take hold and they'd zoom up, exceed the "G" limits, black out, and sometimes not recover. Luckily, my body could withstand very high "G" forces without blacking out. I have actually bent the wings on a Spitfire and a Thunderbolt when pulling out of high-speed dives.

The Second World War record of the Republic P-47 Thunderbolt was indeed impressive. In a total of 546,000 sorties P-47s destroyed 11,874 enemy aircraft, some 9,000 locomotives, and over 160,000 military vehicles (tanks, trucks, railway cars, etc.). And these figures do not include the great number of other fixed targets hit and destroyed, nor the temendous effort that went into providing battlefield close air support for our ground troops. Fifty-eight USAAF fighter groups were equipped with Jugs during those war years.

All in all, 15,660 P-47s were built. During the war years they were flown in combat by the U.S. Army Air Force, the British Royal Air Force, the Free French Air Force, and the Brazilian Air Force. After the war, Jugs were provided to the air forces of nineteen countries and to our Air National Guard. In 1948, when I was assigned to Iran as fighter advisor, I transferred 60 P-47D-20s and D-25s from the USAF to the Imperial Iranian Air Force. In 1954, while serving with the Joint Brazil-United States Military Commission at Rio de Janeiro, I met my old wartime Thunderbolt buddies again at Santa Cruz airfield, and assisted in the transfer of twenty-five more Jugs from the USAF to the FAB (Força Aeria Brasileira). Today, as far as I know, the last Jugs on "active service" are assigned to the Confederate Air Force's "Ghost Squadron," based at Harlingen, Texas.

Wise guys, years ago, used to try to needle us P-47 boys with such comments as, "Evasive action in the Jug is when the pilot gets up and runs around the cockpit." But the Thunderbolt's gallant record in war speaks for itself; she was an outstanding fighter. To us who flew and fought and survived in her, she was a very beautiful beast.

I flew the North American P-51 Mustang with four different fighter units during my service career—from the P-51A to the final P-51H model—and it was a good aircraft. But I never did feel quite comfortable in it. Some aircraft just seem right in every respect to the pilot, as the Spitfire and Thunderbolt did in my case, but the P-51 didn't feel quite right for me. Yet I realize that a lot of guys who flew the "Spam Can" will swear by her.

In 1938 James H. "Dutch" Kindelberger, the president of North American Aviation Company, visited British and German aircraft factories where he viewed the design and development of both nations' fighter aircraft. He was impressed by the capabilities and limitations of four particular aircraft: the British Hurricane and Spitfire, and the German Messerschmitt 109 and Heinkel 113. He sketched the design of a new fighter, incorporating the best qualities of the four aircraft he had seen. If the United States evantually entered the war that appeared imminent in Europe, he planned to build his own fighter for the U.S. Army Air Corps.

In the early spring of 1940 the British Air Purchasing Mission wanted to buy an increased number of Curtiss P-40 Tomahawk fighters for the Royal Air Force, but the Curtiss factory was unable to produce additional aircraft. North American was approached to produce the P-40s in their Inglewood, California, factory, but Dutch Kindelberger said "no." If the RAF wanted a fighter built, he would build his own design—a superior fighter—in 120 days. The British Air Ministry approved the design of the new fighter in April of 1940; prototype construction began soon thereafter, and 117 days later, in September 1940, the Model NA-73X "export pursuit" was born, the P-51 Mustang.

She had a sleek-looking airframe, this single-seat, low-wing, single-engine, all-metal-stressed-skin fighter. Her dimensions and specifications were: wing span, 37 feet ¼ inch; length, 32 feet 2½ inches; height, 12 feet 8 inches; wing area 235 square feet; weight empty, 6,300 pounds; weight loaded, 8,600 pounds; maximum speed at 8,000 feet was 382 mph; range was 1,050 miles. She had, however, one problem—the Allison in-line, liquid-cooled V-1710-39, 1,120 hp engine. The poor performance of this engine and its low-speed supercharger limited the P-51's altitude to about 18,000 feet. Armament consisted of four .50-caliber Browning machine guns mounted two in each wing.

The RAF was supplied with 800 Mustangs (600 Mark Is, 150 Mark IAs, and 50 Mark IIs), and the USAAC took two aircraft for testing at Wright-Patterson AAF, Dayton, Ohio. The first Mustangs entered RAF service with No. 2 Fighter Squadron at Sawbridgeworth, England, in April 1942, making their first wartime operational flights in July 1942. In the fall of 1942 the RAF decided to test the Mustang with the Rolls-Royce Merlin 65 engine installed. This engine change proved to be an outstanding success, with its 600 additional horsepower and two-stage supercharger. The Merlin-powered Mustang's speed increased to 433 mph, its climb rate to 3,400 fpm, and its service ceiling to 32,000 feet. With these improvements, the RAF Mustangs became the first Allied single-engine fighters to fly over Germany during a raid on the Dortmund-Ems Canal in October of 1942.

It's an odd thing, but the U.S. Army Air Corps showed very little interest in the Mustang in the beginning. Testing of the aircraft at Wright-Patterson, and its increased performance record with the Merlin engine installed by the RAF, however, soon changed all that. About 350 Allison "time bomb" powered P-51As were soon delivered to USAAC units, and one version of the Mustang, relegated to an army ground attack role, was designated an A-36. By December of 1943 the 8th Air force fighter groups in England began receiving the P-51B and P-51C models with the Packard-built Rolls-Royce Merlin engines installed.

Some of the things I didn't like about the P-51 were—in the A model—the Allison engine, the lousy visibility in all directions except straight up from the cockpit, the very rapid engine overheating during ground operation, the armament limited to just four machine guns, and the lack of high altitude performance. Also, it wasn't the greatest aircraft to fly on instruments in bad weather or at night. As I've already mentioned, the Packard-built Merlin V-1650-3 engine improved performance in the B and C models considerably. The RAF's installation of a Malcolm hood increased the pilot's visibility a bit, but still not enough. The addition of two more machine guns helped the firepower problem. Some early versions flown by the RAF had four 20-mm cannons installed, which was great. Two wing racks, for carrying two 500-pound bombs, or two 75- or two 150-gallon drop tanks, were added to strengthened wings. With internal fuel and two 150-gallon drop tanks, the P-51Bs and Cs could fly long-range missions of 1,300 miles.

The P-51D, the best of the lot, became operational in May 1944. The D model had a Packard-built Merlin V-1650-7 engine of 1,695 hp, which gave it a top speed of 440 mph at 25,000 feet, a rate of climb of 3,500 fpm, and a service ceiling of 41,900 feet. Range without external tanks was 950 miles, and increased to 2,080 miles with 175-gallon wing tanks. The pilot could now sit in the cramped cockpit of his P-51 for eight and a half hours of flying time before the kite went dry and his rear end went completely numb. Armament of the D consisted of six .50-caliber machine guns with 1,880 rounds, two 500-pound or two 1,000-pound bombs, or six 5-inch HVAR rockets. Of course, the aircraft's weight went up—empty 7,125 pounds; maximum 11,600 pounds. The back of the fuselage was also cut down and a 360°-vision bubble canopy installed. D models supplied to the RAF under the Lend-Lease Program were designated Mustang Mark IVs. As a note of interest, RAF Mustangs of No. 611 Fighter Squadron were the first to meet allied Russian aircraft over Berlin on 16 April 1945.

Although the Mustang was a fast aircraft straight and level, she was fast as hell in a dive, which Hun pilots of Me.109s and FW.190s soon found out to their disadvantage. A fast, steep dive had always been a good evasive action tactic for the Krauts, but now the P-51 could stay with them all the way down and shoot their rear ends off enroute. The Mustang could turn and maneuver easily with the enemy fighters, even out-zoom them, but their rate of climb was a bit better.

With the arrival on the air war scene of the German rocket-powered Messerschmitt 163 Komet and the twin jet-powered Messerschmitt 262 Schwalbe, a new era in fighter aircraft design began. The Komet—"the Devil's Sled," as the Hun pilots called it—had a top speed of 590 mph, and the Schwalbe (Swallow) had a high speed of 540 mph. In spite of the 163's high speed advantage, Mustang pilot Lt. Colonel John B. Murphy, 359th Fighter Group, USAAF, shot down an Me.163 near Leipzig on 16 August 1944. On 5 October 1944, a Spitfire XIV of No. 401 Fighter Squadron claimed the very first Me.262 jet fighter to be shot down by an Allied airman. Two days later Lieutenant Urban Drew, 351st Fighter Group, USAAF, shot down two Me.262s while flying a P-51D. Two leading German aces, flying Me.262s, were shot out of the sky by 8th Air Force Mustangs—Major Walter Nowotny was killed and General Leutnant Adolf Galland was wounded. Before I forget it, I should mention that many aviation historians credit the Germans with producing the first jet fighter of the war. Not so—they are very wrong! The British Gloster Meteor twin-jet aircraft went operational on 12 July 1944. The German Messerschmitt 262 went operational about three months later on 3 October 1944.

The Mustang had some undesirable flying characteristics and some very bad and dangerous habits. As an example, her low- and high-speed stalls were quick, with little if any warning, and she really snapped violently into a fast spin. Her spin was also violent and she fell a long way before you could recover. As a matter of fact, you had to be damned careful getting her out of a spin. Sometimes, just when you thought you'd recovered, she'd snap and spin in the other direction. If she was still spinning at 5,000 feet, get the hell out of her, fast! And that was another problem, bailing out. When you jettisoned the canopy, wind pressure pushed you so hard down into the seat it was most difficult to get out. The best way was to trim her nose heavy while holding back pressure on the stick, then release the stick and let the aircraft's down snap throw you out of the cockpit.

P-51s, all models, landed pretty hot—over the fence at 125 mph and touch down at about 100 to 110 mph. If you were too slow, she'd fall out from under you without warning; we lost a lot of good guys from landing crashes. Then there was the trim problem. Every time you changed speed, even a few miles per hour, the P-51 had to be retrimmed for both directional stability and level flight. When in the traffic pattern for landing you were constantly adjusting the trim, sometimes almost standing on a rudder pedal until you got the trim cranked in. There was another problem that usually occurred at the most inopportune times—the damned automatic air scoop door in the belly would malfunction, close, overheat the engine, and you'd lose most of your engine's power. If you couldn't manage to get the scoop opened quickly by manual procedures, the engine would blow all its coolant and promptly seize. This situation could get pretty exciting, especially if you were over enemy territory or large expanses of water.

When it was decided to extend the P-51s range to a maximum, an extra 85-gallon fuel tank was built into the fuselage, right behind the pilot's cockpit. The weight of this extra fuel load moved the aircraft's center of gravity toward the rear, causing more trim problems. Of course, the thing to do was use the fuel from this fuselage tank first so the center of gravity would move back forward. Another small problem was that at first these tanks had no internal baffles, so the fuel would slosh back and forth, giving you the feeling the P-51 was galloping through the air. But the worst thing they did to the Mustang was to stick a 400-pound tail-warning radar unit in the rear fuselage. This thing knocked the center of gravity all to hell, reducing the P-51's maneuvering capability considerably. Here you get a beautiful 360°-vision canopy on the kite so you can see an enemy aircraft getting on your tail, and then some idiot sticks a 400-pound radar in your tail to weigh you down so you can't fight and maneuver properly. It's things like that—hanging all sorts of trash on a good airframe—that ruin the performance of the aircraft.

The North American P-51 Mustang made its mark in the history of air warfare. There were, all told, 14,819 P-51s of various versions built. P-51 units in the European theater of war destroyed 9,081 enemy aircraft, 4,950 in air-to-air combat, including 120 Me.262 jet fighters. Dutch Kindelberger's hot little fighter, designed and produced in just 117 days, deserves a fair share of the credit for kicking the hell out of the Luftwaffe. After the war the Mustang served in dozens of air forces all over the world, with the U.S. Air Force, and with our Air National Guard units. She also fought gallantly in the Korean War, until replaced by more modern jet fighters.

The last P-51 I flew was the H model, when I was deputy wing commander of the 82nd Fighter Wing at Grenier AFB, Manchester, New Hampshire in 1947–48. The H model had a peculiarity that could prove to be disastrous if you didn't understand this problem. In other aircraft, when you shut down the engine, you gradually opened the throttle to burn out excess fuel. In the H, if you did that, a flutter valve would stick wide open so that the next time the H model was started up her engine roared into life full bore. She'd jump over the wheel chocks, flip her tail in the air, and most probably hit her prop on the ground.

L.C. Selden, my old buddy from the 406th Fighter Group in Europe, had an F-84 Thunderjet unit at Bangor, Maine. These were the straight-wing F-84s, nicknamed "Hogs." (The later swept-wing version F-84 Thunderstreaks were called "Super Hogs.") Occasionally L.C. and his mob would ride their "blow jobs" in our direction and buzz our airfield. We, in the 82nd, soon worked out a procedure to be notified when the F-84s took off. We'd scramble our P-51Hs, climb like mad to a good high altitude and, when the Hogs were approaching Grenier, come down on them in a screaming dive. Our high speed in a P-51H, straight and level, was 487 mph. This speed was exceeded considerably in our dives, so we would come "balls out" alongside of L.C.'s F-84s, fly right on past them, and salute them with our thumbs to our noses.

I, of course, never had the opportunity personally to fly a German fighter, so all I can write about their capabilities and limitations is what I know from fighting them and from what Hun pilots told me about them after the war.

Willy Messerschmitt's Me.109 fighter must be considered as a classic example of an outstanding military flying machine. Over a twenty-three-year period—from 1935 in Germany to 1958 in Spain—some 33,000 Me.109s of all versions were produced. Original designing of the 109 began at the Bayerische Flugzeugwerke, Augsburg, Germany in 1934 and the first aircraft flew in September of 1935. Oddly enough, the first Me.109 had a British-built Rolls-Royce Kestrel V, 695 hp engine installed because a Junkers Jumo 210A, 610 hp engine couldn't be obtained. Armament for the Me.109A, at first, consisted of two 7.9-mm machine guns which were positioned in the upper nose cowling above the engine. Later, a third machine gun, firing through the propeller spinner, was added.

The Messerschmitt 109 first saw action during the Spanish Civil War with Jagdgruppe 88 of the German-manned "Kondor Legion" in July 1937. These aircraft, Me.109Bs, had a 700 hp Jumo 210E or 210G engine, which gave a top speed of 280 mph at 13,000 feet, and a service ceiling of 31,200 feet. The aircraft was small: wing span 32 feet 4½ inches, wing area 174 square feet, length 28 feet 6½ inches, weight loaded 4,857 pounds. It was in the Spanish Civil War that two Hun fighter pilots—Adolf Galland and Werner Moelders—began their careers to acedom. Spain proved to be a good training ground for the Luftwaffe, where they learned and applied the newer lessons of air warfare.

When the Second World War broke out in September of 1939, Luftwaffe squadrons were equipped with the more advanced Me.109Es (Emil, as their pilots called it). This version had a Daimler-Benz DB 601A twelve-cylinder, inverted-Vee, liquid-cooled engine rated at 1,150 hp. Speed increased to 354 mph at 12,500 feet, and the service ceiling improved to 37,500 feet. Armament in the E model consisted of three 20-mm cannons and two 7.9-mm machine guns. Further modifications in the Me.109F (Franz) in 1941 and the Me.109G (Gustav) in 1942, included the more powerful DB 605D, 1,475 hp engine, which produced a top speed of 428 mph at 25,000 feet, a climb rate of six minutes to 20,000 feet, and a maximum ceiling of 41,400 feet. Armament changes in the latest G model included one 30-mm cannon plus two 13.1-mm machine guns. After the defeat of Germany in 1945, the Hispano Aviacion SA of Spain continued to produce Me.109s for its air force until 1958.

There were several serious deficiencies in the Me.109 that have been admitted by German pilots who flew them. They include very heavy controls at high speed, bad lateral control of the aircraft in a dive, short operating range, poor pilot visibility from the cockpit, and lack of stability in ground operation. In some models, a lack of sufficient firepower should be mentioned. At speeds of about 350 mph the 109's controls became very stiff; at 400 mph it was nearly impossible to move the control stick without brute force. We, in the RAF, soon discovered this flaw in the enemy fighter. When a 109 would come diving toward our formation to attack, we knew exactly what his attack pattern would be—fast dive down, try to line up a target and fire, roll and break away to the right. Therefore, we could split-S and engage the 109 as he rolled into his break-away, belly up, at a couple of hundred yards range. Invariably the Hun pilot executed this same maneuver. If, by chance, he broke to the opposite direction, he got away free without a shot fired at him. I'm certain the high engine torque and trim of his aircraft forced him to use this break-away pattern.

Short range of the Me.109 was another very serious problem. In mid-1940, during the Battle of Britain, the 109s escorting enemy bombers had about one hour and thirty minutes of fuel. It took thirty to forty minutes to assemble their formations over France and fly across the Channel, and about thirty minutes of fuel was needed to return to their home bases—so that left about twenty minutes of fuel to be used in the target area defending their bombers against RAF Hurricane and Spitfire attacks. This short range of escorting fighters, of course, hindered enemy bomber operations by reducing their radius of action. A fair number of 109 pilots, overstaying their fuel limits on bomber escort missions, splashed into the drink when they ran out of gas on the way home. Later on the use of an external belly tank improved the Me.109's range.

The pilot's visibility from the 109's cockpit was very poor. Besides being low on the aircraft, the "coffin lid" canopy provided a very restricted view over the aircraft's nose, and no rear view at all. This problem was never corrected, even on the last 1958 models. Ground operation of the aircraft was made somewhat difficult by a combination of poor cockpit visibility, the long nose (which had a rather high angle in the three-point position), and the narrow track of the under-carriage—all of which made taxiing the 109 a bit hazardous. The aircraft did have a tendency to ground-loop and drag a wing tip. Also, because of weak undercarriage legs, there were quite a number of landing gear collapses. Several ex-Luftwaffe pilots have told me that they "had to fly the Me.109 from the moment they stepped into the cockpit until the engine was shut off after flight."

Landings in the 109 were fast and hot, with a fairly steep approach angle, and generally a wheel landing. If the aircraft was landed in the three-point position, just as the pilot pulled back on the stick to round-out, the left wing would stall and drop. On takeoff, if the 109 was pulled off the ground the moment flying speed was attained, the left wing would not lift. Opposite aileron could correct this for a moment, and then the left wing would again drop until the wing's leading edge slots gained more lift by increased speed. There was no rudder trim control in the cockpit, which caused the pilot considerable difficulty in a fast dive. The untrimmed rudder became very heavy to move with the rudder pedals, and could suddenly reverse its trim. This, of course, was tiring for the pilot to operate in air combat. When the Me.109F first entered service it developed a violent vibration problem in the tail section, causing the pilot to lose all control and the aircraft to dive into the ground. Before this malfunction was corrected, several Me.109Fs had their tail sections break off in flight.

Well, I've mentioned about all of Willy Messerschmitt's Me.109 bumps and warts, but I must admit she was, without a doubt, a great fighter aircraft in those days of the Second World War. The fuel-injection system used in the Daimler-Benz engine was a great improvement over our carburetor system, permitting inverted flight and negative G maneuvers. The 109 was fast, reasonably maneuverable, had a good rate of climb, and could operate at very high altitude. She could out-dive everything in the air until the arrival of the Thunderbolt, Mustang, Typhoon, and Tempest in the last years of the war. She fought on every front—from Norway to France, Russia, the Balkans, Middle East, and North Africa—and under every climatic condition from the freezing northern regions to the heat of sandy deserts. A little tingling shiver used to run up and down my spine when someone in our formation would suddenly call out on the R/T: "Thirty bandits, six o'clock high. Snappers! Snappers diving to attack!" I have met Me.109s and their pilots quite a number of times in air battles. By my good fotune, I won most of those battles by shooting them out of the sky. They won a couple of times by shooting me down once and by punching me full of bullet holes on another occasion.

In the summer of 1938 the German Air Ministry directed the Focke-Wulf Flugzeugbau (aircraft factory) to produce a single-seat, single-engine fighter for the Luftwaffe. The result was the Focke-Wulf FW.190V1, called the "Würger" (butcher-bird). This aircraft was designed and produced through the combined efforts of Technical Director Kurt Tank and Design Engineer Blaser, and test flown by Hans Sander on 1 June 1939.

The 190 design was a departure from other German fighters, since it included for the first time a radial engine, a wide-track landing gear, was somewhat larger in size, and weighed nearly 3,000 pounds more. The V1 to V7 models were all experimental prototypes; the V1s and V2s had the BMW 139 engine of 1,500 hp installed, the V3 and V4 models were never completed, the V5 to V7 models used the BMW 801C, 1,560 hp engine. The V7 prototype became the first production model of the FW.190 and was designated Focke-Wulf 190A-1 by the Luftwaffe in June of 1941. General specifications of the 190A were: wing span 34 feet 5½ inches, wing area 197 square feet, length 29 feet 4½ inches, height 13 feet, weight empty 7,000 pounds, weight loaded 9,424 pounds, maximum weight 10,800 pounds. BMW engines varied through the various models of the FW.190A-1 to the A-10—from the 1,560 hp BMW 801C to the 2,000 hp BMW 801T. Armament also varied, but two 13-mm machine guns in the upper cowling, and two 20-mm cannons in each wing were generally standard.

Speed of the original FW.190V1 was 370 mph, but this was gradually increased to 408 mph at 20,000 feet by the FW.190A-10. Climb rate was 2,350 fpm to a service ceiling of 37,400 feet. Bomb racks were fitted on the A-4 to carry a bomb load of 1,100 pounds, the A-6 carried 1,650 pounds, and the A-10's bomb load was 3,860 pounds! To increase the FW.190's range of 560 miles, external fuel tanks of 66 gallons each were designed, with some aircraft carrying as many as three tanks.

There weren't too many flaws in the FW.190. Above 21,000 feet her performance began to fall off somewhat. Forward view from the cockpit for the pilot was poor. The worst problem was engine overheating in the first several variants; however, this was soon corrected by a large cooling fan fitted into the cowling in front of the engine. Two sets of wings were tested, the "kleine flache" or small wing and the "grosse flache" or large wing, with the latter wing becoming standard. The FW.190 was very fast in a dive and, unlike the Me.109, its controls remained light, permitting good aileron rolls and tight turns. The FW.190 series continued on up through the FW.190D model. At that time in the war we didn't know what the German designations for the various Focke-Wulfs were, so we simply called them FW "short nose" for those models up to the D, with the FW.190D called the "long nose."

Although the first recorded combat between FW.190s and Allied fighters occurred on 27 September 1941, their numbers were too few and they came too late. And, most important, the aircraft was employed in a piecemeal manner. Its excellent fighter capabilities were wasted by relegating a considerable number of the aircraft to the role of fighter-bombers. It was also wasted, a couple of years later, by assigning poorly trained pilots to FW.190 units. Some of these pilots were so badly trained that they had to be led by experienced pilots to their bombing targets. In many instances, when we attacked a 190 formation in 1944, the enemy pilots didn't know how to take evasive action in air-to-air combat. This lack of proper training reduced their life span on the battle fronts to a few days.

Besides the European war theater, the FW.190 was used on the Russian and North African fronts, but always, it seemed, in a "too little too late" capacity. During the latter part of the war, when RAF and USAAF heavy bombers were pounding the hell out of Germany and its war-making industrial complexes, the FW.190 was employed by Luftwaffe home defense units called "Sturmstaffel"—storm fighters. The purpose of these units was to make suicide attacks on our bombers by ramming them.

I've already mentioned that on 6 June 1944—D-Day of the invasion of Normandy—only two Hun aircraft attacked our forces on the beaches. They were two strafing FW.190As belonging to Jagdgeschwader 26. At dawn on New Year's Day, 1 January 1945, the Luftwaffe launched Operation Hermann Göring, an air attack planned to shoot up and destroy Allied aircraft on the ground. Some 650 FW.190s took part in this last-ditch strike, and they did achieve some success, but because of inexperienced pilots they lost more men and aircraft than they could afford. This operation was, for all intents and purposes, the last gasp of the defeated Luftwaffe.

Some 20,000 Focke-Wulf 190s of all variants were produced during the war. However, at the war's end, because of Allied bombing of aircraft factories and aviation fuel plants, hundreds of FW.190s were captured intact—with empty fuel tanks. And so the Würger, the "Butcher bird," died.

I guess I should make one last comment before closing out this account of our war birds. I have been asked, numerous times, which fighter aircraft I thought was the war's best. It's impossible to positively say which was the very best without taking into consideration the type of mission to be flown. If we are speaking of air-to-air combat, I say the Spitfire is my choice—it was fast, highly maneuverable, a good gun platform, and without any bad habits in flight. For dive-bombing and close air support operations, I'll take the P-47 Thunderbolt. She could carry a good load of mixed munitions for all sorts of targets, she could survive in a heavy flak environment, and she'd generally get you safely home if you were shot up. For long-range bomber escort missions, the P-51 Mustang would be my selection. She could fly for up to eight hours and fight off attacking enemy fighters in the distant target areas.

Each aircraft I've mentioned was perfectly suited for its primary mission. Now, if I had to make the choice of one fighter aircraft above all the others—one that I'd rather have tied to the seat of my pants in any tactical situation—it would be, without any doubt, the world's greatest propeller-driven flying machine—the magnificent and immortal Spitfire.

Index